THE WOLF
AT MY DOOR

Cancer in my Body
Cancer in my Mind

DOUG GOSLING

ISBN: 978-1-4251-6536-9 (Soft)
ISBN: 978-1-4251-6537-6 (e-book)

*Our mission is to efficiently provide the world's finest, most comprehensive
book publishing service, enabling every author to experience success.
To find out how to publish your book, your way, and have it available
worldwide, visit us online at www.trafford.com*

Trafford rev. 11/10/2009

 www.trafford.com

North America & international
toll-free: 1 888 232 4444 (USA & Canada)
phone: 250 383 6864 ♦ fax: 812 355 4082

PRAISE FOR *THE WOLF AT MY DOOR*

Doug Gosling tells it like it is. As a man with Cancer, he neatly and wittily tells the story of his diagnosis and the treatment, and of the emotional roller-coaster that seems to be almost universal when the disease has such a fearsome reputation.

Anyone navigating their way through the cancer treatment system will find a lot that they will recognize and which will help them in that activity that is sometimes called 'coping' but which is basically the same as 'living'.

Dr. Robert Buckman
Medical Oncologist, Princess Margaret Hospital
Speaker, professor and prolific author of such books as, *CANCER is a word, not a sentence* and *What You Really Need to Know About Cancer*
www.drbuckman.com

Doug Gosling has written a truly candid and thoughtful book about what it is like to be diagnosed and treated for Prostate Cancer. Several books have been written on the subject but few, if any, provide such a forthright description of the emotional roller-coaster patients experience during and after treatment. The sincerity of his writing makes you feel as though he is a close friend telling you about his experience with cancer and providing you with encouragement. At the core of this book is a passionate description of a realistic and hopeful experience of cancer. This book is one that will help patients and their loved ones "normalize" their experience and reduce feelings of isolation. This is not a Prostate Cancer book - it is a diary of an insightful man going through a difficult time - a physical and emotional journey that patients with cancer understand. A must-read.

Dr. Andrew Matthew, Ph.D., C.Psych
Assistant Professor, Department of Surgery, University of Toronto
Department of Surgical Oncology
University Health Network, Princess Margaret Hospital

What a gift to the world – not just to those of us punched by cancer (including our loved ones) – but to anyone who wants to live authentically; in other words, to truly live.

Doug had me nodding, shaking my head, laughing and crying (sometimes at the same time), and I was absorbed in his experience and consciousness. The Hopi Prayer, the story about the Mexican Fisherman, and mention of Don Juan added so much to and complemented the ultimate tale of Doug's own heart and psyche, which I and everyone else who reads this book will come to love. His life has meaning, indeed. And this book will help give others' lives more meaning as they see themselves in these pages. We should all jettison toxic friends! We should all go outside and rejoice in nature!

Thank you, Doug, for your powerful and novel insights, your wonderful imagery, your delightful wit, and your naked soul. Few men could be man enough to be so open and honest.

Lori Hope
Speaker, producer, blogger, cancer survivor and author of *Help Me Live: 20 things people with cancer want you to know.*
www.lorihope.com

DEDICATION

This book is dedicated to my love and soul mate Dianne, who has given me a wonderful life. To my daughter Caralia who continues to show a strength of character that fills me with pride each time I am with her. And to my restless son Sean, who has taught us all that joy can be found in a life lived simply.

TABLE OF CONTENTS

ACKNOWLEDGEMENTS

There are many people who I would like to thank for supporting me during the seven years I have spent writing this book and throughout my cancer journey. My dear wife, Dianne, gently pushed me to keep at it and to keep adding more and more of my experiences so the book would have its greatest impact. Dr. Rob Buckman, a kindred spirit and one of the most intelligent, caring and witty people I have ever met, who helped me to keep my focus and to "tell it like it is". Gayla Forer, counsellor, friend and confidant who provided insightful comments on several drafts and who has become family in the most meaningful sense of the word.

In particular, I would like to thank the many doctors and clinicians, who have my deepest respect and admiration, for all they have done for me and for countless other cancer patients. With few exceptions I have used aliases to protect their privacy. But in all other ways this book is meant to honour them and their commitment to saving our lives.

"….. I'LL HUFF AND I'LL PUFF TILL I BLOW YOUR HOUSE IN."

FORWARD

When Doug Gosling was diagnosed with Prostate Cancer at the relatively young age of forty-nine, it rocked his world and was the beginning of an incredible journey of profound discovery. As he says, "*I came to realize that cancer was really two diseases in one; a physical disease of the body and also an emotional disease – a cancer of the mind, if you will.*" In the deep and open discussion of these emotional characteristics, his story has relevance to people with any type of cancer and, equally, for those who love and care for them.

This book discusses in vivid detail the physical and emotional stages of diagnosis, treatment, recovery and recurrence and explores the deep emotional impact that cancer has on the person with the disease and on their loved ones. It is an intensely intimate story told with no holds barred, dealing openly with difficult subjects such as depression, spirituality, fears of recurrence and death, incontinence and sexual function.

Cancer can take so much from you, but it can also give you precious gifts in the form of a completely new and even healthier outlook on life, an ability to face other great challenges and a new appreciation for what is really important in your life, as so many cancer survivors have found. But it can kill you and, if you are not careful, it can destroy your soul. And because of this, it is as important to treat the cancer in the mind while you are vigorously fighting the physical destruction of your body.

Doug's heartfelt and deeply intimate story will inform and often entertain, offering tremendous insight to others who are faced with a cancer diagnosis or are learning to live with it. These insights will help you understand what to expect, how to cope, and perhaps even teach you how to find some of that precious commodity called hope.

INTRODUCTION

They say the world changed on September 11, 2001. And it did, for everyone in the civilized world, as something that always happened to "someone else, somewhere else" happened to "us". In a truly horrible way, we all lost some of our innocence that day. We came face-to-face with a brutal reality that we had largely ignored as we marched on through our day-to-day lives, utterly complacent and completely oblivious to the horrors that much of the world's population faces every single day.

My world changed forever on October 15, 2002 when I was diagnosed with Prostate Cancer. On that day, burned into my memory like nothing before, I lost my own innocence and came face-to-face with my incredibly naïve sense of immortality. I was wrenched out of an essentially unguided lifestyle and forced to directly confront my own survival. It scared the hell out of me!

The original working title of this book was "Lucky Man" because, early on, I felt very lucky to have found the cancer when I did, lucky to still be alive and lucky because the experience had helped me to discover who I really was and what my life was all about. But as you will see, things changed and, while those "lucky" aspects of my diagnosis are still valid, it has become a much more complicated journey. It has been an incredible journey of profound experience and learning that I will share with you openly, unabashedly and without reservation.

This is my story and, while it is also addresses the impact on those around me, it is still very much all about me. It's about my personal journey on a raging, storm-tossed sea called cancer. It's about how I

1

found it, how I fought it (and continue to do so), how I have survived it so far, and how my life has changed because of it. I wrote it partly for me as a kind of coping mechanism, but mostly because I believe my story has meaning to anyone who has to face this horrible disease and for their friends and loved ones who desperately want to understand. While everyone is different - and every cancer is different - we all share similar fears and feelings when faced with a cancer diagnosis (Mind you, if you are told you only have a few weeks or months to live, there's a whole other dimension to it!). But with the tremendous advances that have been made in cancer detection and treatment, the majority of cancer patients will live on for some time, potentially cured. So most of us have to deal with the disease itself, the symptoms, treatments and side effects, the possibility (or reality) of recurrence, and the tremendous impact it has on our lives and on the lives of those around us. I wasn't prepared for any of it. Nobody is. So I hope to give some advance warning to anyone who cares to listen. Whether you are the one diagnosed with cancer or whether you have a loved one who has been diagnosed, it sucks, and you need to know what you might be facing to steel yourself for the rough ride ahead.

On that day in October, the day after Canadian Thanksgiving, I was diagnosed with Prostate Cancer at the relatively young age of forty-nine. I say young (although my kids thought I was ancient when I hit thirty) because the average age for a Prostate Cancer diagnosis is around sixty-five. While every man in North America has a one-in-six chance of getting Prostate Cancer sometime in their life, very few men are diagnosed in their forties or early fifties. In fact, one source puts the odds at one-in-one hundred for men in their forties. For me, that made it a lot worse. In fact, I was mad as hell!

I am not afraid to die. I want to get that out in the open right away and then put it behind us because, while this book is about cancer, it's not about death. It's about life and living. It's interesting, though, that the very first time I tried to express how I felt about being diagnosed with cancer I prefaced it with those words. It was one of the first things I said to my wife, Dianne, when I told her the news. She told me that it was bullshit! Maybe she's right. She's a smart woman and I really do have to wonder if she knows me better than I know myself.

It's a very telling thing about cancer that we automatically equate it with death and dying, immediately followed by horrifying images of surgery, radiation, chemotherapy, severe weight loss and a bald head! It's what we have been brought up to believe from countless movies, television shows and, in some cases, from all-too-personal experiences. In spite of all of the advances made in the fight against cancer, and all of the statistics that prove otherwise, we first think about death. And while it is true that most cancers will kill you if left untreated, we all have treatment options available to us, and more than half of us will survive. Our first thought really should be, "Okay. How do I beat this thing?" While it wasn't my first thought, it arrived pretty fast and became the primary focus of my existence for some time. And when I finished my initial treatments, my thoughts then turned to the even larger challenge of getting on with my life.

I hope you will find my story interesting and that it will be of some help to you. I warn you now that I will be very frank and, at times, deeply intimate in describing all that I have been through. It's the only way I can be and the only way I can convey the true depths of the fears and emotions that I experienced throughout what became a very long and arduous journey. So as long as you don't mind reading about some very personal issues and the details of my male plumbing, turn the page and join me on this incredible journey!

MY LIFE BEFORE CANCER

VERY ABRIDGED

If we are going to get really intimate, it will help if you know a bit about the *"Life of Doug BC (Before Cancer)"*. I believe that much of what you feel, how you act, and how you eventually cope with a life-changing event like cancer, is conditioned by who you were before it happened. As I look back now, I can see how my evolving values and the goals that I set for myself along the way reflect the things that were important to me as I grew up.

I'll skip the part about the time I spent in my mother's womb, which I suppose has something to do with my makeup, and talk about being brought up in the bush. I'm not talking about Mowgli from The Jungle Book, or Tarzan of the Apes (although I once looked pretty good in a loin cloth!), but I did live a good part of my childhood in small, temporary communities that were carved out of the Ontario wilderness for hydroelectric construction projects. My father worked for Ontario Hydro (one of the largest electric utilities in the world at the time) and ran the fire department and safety programs on these projects, which were essentially small communities of about 2,000 people living in portable trailers or disposable tin-test houses surrounded by some of the densest forest in North America. While these communities had most of the amenities of any small village, once outside, you were in a wilderness wonderland of trees, streams, rivers and animals. For a young fellow, it was the biggest playground imaginable.

While "city kids" played in tiny parks and concrete wading pools, I was climbing giant trees, tracking small animals, snacking on wild berries, studying plants and learning to find my way in the deep woods (I find it quite ironic that I wouldn't even let my own kids go to the city park by themselves when they were the same age!). I developed a fierce independence during this time, a healthy respect for nature, and a high degree of confidence in my ability to look after myself. Even more important, I learned how to just sit - often for hours - and listen to the sounds of the forest while the wind and sun washed over me. There has been no greater time of peace and serenity in all my life except (strangely enough) the morning of my surgery, while I lay on a hospital gurney waiting to have the cancer cut out of my body. But I'm getting ahead of myself.

When I was about twelve, I moved out of the bush country and into the city where I learned to adapt to a new way of life and a new, scarier environment. I missed the wilderness terribly, but I accepted the fact that we all have to move on. But I have never lost the love of the great outdoors and I long for it all the time.

So just what kind of person was I? Well that's a complicated question and we are all, of course, very complicated people. I can tell you that I was reasonably smart, did okay in school and didn't get into serious trouble (although I came close a couple of times). I learned how to play guitar in a couple of rock and roll garage bands and grew my hair as long as my dad would allow. During my teenage years, I had a rough time when I moved from the city to a small town, leaving all my best friends behind, but I got over that and moved on with my life. I eventually moved out of my parents' home, went to University, got a job and married the most wonderful girl in the world. (Wow! I just covered half of my life in a couple of paragraphs!)

As I was growing up and, even when I started working, I had this conviction that I was essentially lazy. I'm not sure where that came from, except that I always grumbled about cutting the lawn or doing any other chores that required physical work. I carried this belief with me for the longest time in spite of the fact that I was always doing something. In fact, I always had to be doing something. As soon as I started working full time, I married Dianne and enrolled in night school for my MBA, working many hard hours while I studied in the evenings and on weekends. When I finished school, I filled the vacuum for about a year writing a fictional thriller that is currently buried in a box somewhere. Later on, I filled my time with volunteer work on a number of boards and committees while I continued writing short stories, magazine articles and screenplays with little commercial success (which was really okay because it was just a hobby). In 1995, I left the corporate world and entered the wonderful world of software sales, selling big computer software to big companies. That's when I *really* started working and when I finally realized that I wasn't lazy. In fact, I discovered that I was one of those classic Type "A" personalities that you hear so much about, usually in connection with big money and big heart attacks (neither of which applies to me, by the way). And that's the way I was and how I lived my life right up to the day that cancer came out of nowhere and smacked me down like a rogue tsunami.

For most of my life I have been pretty healthy and I fully expected that this would continue, although I never really gave it that much thought. My dad (Hank) lived until he was ninety-two and my mom (Doris) is in her late eighties. Both have had reasonably good health all their lives and my dad's mother actually lived to 99, so I figured I had the genes of Methuselah in me. I had the usual childhood diseases of my generation (measles, chicken pox) and was once hospitalized in *enteric isolation* with a pretty bad case of "Beaver Fever" that I got from swimming in a stagnant waterhole after a rousing paintball game. Other than that, I experienced the occasional back pain, stomach problems and the like for which my doctor sent me for numerous tests which always came back negative. I remember one in particular - a sigmoidoscopy, which involved sticking a long tube with a camera up my butt to look at my lower intestines. I was awake for the procedure and a little surprised when the doctor introduced me to one of the bystanders who turned out to be the salesman for the equipment he was using. He said we had a lot in common! (There really is no concept of modesty in medicine as I came to realize even more later.) Anyway, I didn't like that test one bit but, as usual, the results were negative. It was something I got used to hearing. I would have all of these tests and just naturally expect them to find nothing.

After being married for a couple of years and enjoying a healthy, monogamous sex life, my wife Dianne and I decided to start a family. Well, that didn't work out the way we expected. We never did find out why we couldn't get pregnant, but we went through test after test with nothing showing up (you can see a pattern developing). We used a calendar to align the hormones, the stars and everything else to maximize our chance. We even tried some early techniques designed to stimulate egg production, which required Dianne to wear an injection pump around her waist for months. Finally, we gave up on that and adopted two wonderful children (Sean and Caralia) from the Catholic Children's Aid Society.

Ironically, I had a vasectomy several years later because we didn't want to risk having children late in life by accident (we still didn't have an explanation for our infertility) when we weren't ready for them. When researching Prostate Cancer after my diagnosis I came across some interesting discussions speculating on a link between vasectomy and Prostate Cancer, but I believe that no one has been able to prove this link exists (and I'm certainly not interested in entertaining the idea that I caused this to happen.

Adoption is a pretty big life event itself. Nothing on the scale of cancer, but certainly something that dominates your life for a while. Dianne and I dived in head first, learning everything we possibly could and focusing a great deal of our attention on the subject. In fact, this is how we approach everything in our lives even to this day. We dig in and research so we can make educated decisions and never, ever have to second-guess ourselves. We even helped start an adoption support group where couples could share the trials and tribulations of the adoption process and give each other advice. Shortly thereafter, I was approached to join the Board of Directors of the Catholic Children's Aid Society and ended up doing volunteer work with them for close to nine years, filling up most of my spare time and satisfying my obsessive need to be doing something.

When I changed careers in 1995, moving into sales, I abandoned all of my volunteer activities to concentrate on work and family. To keep myself sane, I decided to pick up the guitar again. I felt that I needed something that I could do just for me and that, for a time, would take my mind off of anything remotely resembling responsibility. As with everything else, this turned into quite an obsession as I built a guitar and equipment collection that I would have killed for when I was younger. I write and play all of my own music and I don't really care whether anyone actually likes my stuff, because I do this for me.

My other great obsession was, and still is, sea kayaking. I was introduced to this wonderful sport when I was invited by a couple of old university friends to do a five-day kayaking/camping trip in the waters around Vancouver Island. This was for me! I fell in love immediately and now refuse to go out on the water in any other kind of craft. I feel so incredibly in touch with nature when I'm in my kayak. My butt sits comfortably below the water line and I can slice through the waves with the wind and spray blowing in my face - just me and the elements. At night, I can pitch my tiny tent just about anywhere and re-live the joys of being out in the wilderness, using only what I can carry with me in the flotation chambers of the boat. I bought my own boat and equipment so I can head out at a moment's notice, by myself or with a friend. Even my choice of automobiles is dictated by their ability to carry a couple of kayaks. Some of my best, more recent memories are the seven or eight day kayaking trips around Georgian Bay where I have been able to escape the stress and worries of everyday life in the big city.

Now let's look at the reality of my life just before cancer - probably not a lot different from many people, but relevant to this story. The things that occupied my mind night and day were thoughts of work, money and obligation, which were all very important to me before my cancer diagnosis. I worried about making money, spending too much money, upcoming expenditures and generally being able to fulfill my obligation to support my family as they were growing up and for Dianne and I after the kids left. This was all made much worse by an overbearing sense of duty that I have come to realize is a fundamental flaw in my mental make-up. Not that a sense of duty is bad. It's just that I felt it far too much and, since no one can ever live up completely to their lofty ideals, it gave rise to a lot of guilt. Whenever my kids or Dianne were unhappy, I felt like I had failed in some way and would feel tremendously guilty. This was not good (nor healthy), but that was the way I was. Ironically (there's a lot of irony in life when you really think about it), my biggest worry at that time was that I might live *too* long and run out of money to support Dianne and I!

Other than that, I really didn't think much about mortality and death. I've been very lucky to have had both of my parents as long as I did, yet I always knew their death was inevitable, as it is for all of us. But that was an abstract concept to me. I just knew that some day they wouldn't be around anymore and that I would miss them terribly. The closest I came to really understanding this was a year before my diagnosis when my Dad was in the hospital with pneumonia. It was the first time that I actually saw him think about death and talk about the effects of getting old. He was very depressed about it and talked about how he couldn't play golf anymore (he was a huge golfer!) and I truly believed he thought he was going to die. I told him that most men would think they had already gone to heaven if they could retire and continue to golf for over twenty years, as he had! I thought that would make him feel better but I don't really know whether it did. Sadly, my father passed away in early 2007, having lived a good and full life.

As I said, my side of the family had absolutely no experience with major disease. While people died all around us, our bloodline seemed to be pretty clear. In fact, every few years, my parents would lose another whole group of friends their age and have to start over again! But this was not the case on Dianne's side of the family, which had numerous bouts of cancer over the last couple of generations. In the fall of 1996, cancer hit close to home when Dianne's sister Judy was diagnosed with cancer. At first, we thought it was Lung Cancer but, when the doctors removed one of her lungs and did the pathology, it turned out to be Melanoma. Generally, Melanoma can be cured if it is caught early but, once it metastasizes, there is no cure. The year before, Judy had found a strange mole that she had shown to her family doctor who, in turn, referred her to a dermatologist. But some time in the period between the two appointments, the mole fell off, and Judy just never went to the second appointment.

Over the course of the year following her lung surgery, Judy grew sicker and sicker as the cancer spread to her liver and eventually to her brain. She had tried one course of chemotherapy but decided not to continue because it made her too sick. At that time, most of the family (including me) didn't understand enough about cancer to realize that she really was going to die. There was, in fact, an air of innocent, blind optimism that we all shared even while we were faced with the clear evidence of her physical deterioration. Perhaps it was denial or just an inability to absorb that fact that this wonderful woman, who we all loved dearly, could actually die! But, sadly, she did in September, 1997. And we were all changed because of it. It was a loss that we felt deeply.

Judy's cancer had a significant impact on Dianne. Judy was her best friend as well as her sister and she took it exceptionally hard. At the time, we were living several hours away in Ottawa and Dianne was travelling more and more often to Toronto to be with her. After several months of this, Dianne asked if there was any way we could move back to Toronto, so I asked my boss Eleanor (who subsequently became a close friend), if this would be possible. Not only did she get the company to support my move back, they also paid for the movers! So back we went, renting the house next door to Judy, and Dianne became one of Judy's primary caregivers. It amazed me to see her spend so much time with her sister, never hesitating to do whatever was necessary as Judy became more and more helpless. While I always knew that Dianne was a very special, selfless woman, it was wonderful to see her in action, and I don't think anyone else in the family ever knew the full extent of her caring. Unfortunately, it wasn't long before she would be called on again.

About a year after Judy died, Dianne's sister-in-law, Ruth, was diagnosed with Breast Cancer. In the same way that we had naively assumed that Judy would be okay, we naively assumed that Ruth was going to die. There is such a tremendous lack of understanding of cancer that, unless it hits you directly, you don't spend the time to really understand it and you tend to make uneducated assumptions. If someone you know had a particular type of cancer and died, you assume that everyone with that type of cancer will also die. If you know someone who survived it, then you assume that everyone will. There are over two hundred different cancers and each case is unique, which complicates things greatly.

Ruth had it bad. Within twelve days of her diagnosis, she went under the knife to have one breast removed along with about seventeen lymph nodes. She was then immediately put on chemotherapy followed by radiation treatments (this is called the "slash, poison and burn" approach). The chemotherapy just about killed her and it was horrible for us to watch this happen. Her veins were collapsing from all of the chemo injections, her hair fell out, and her blood count was so low she was literally on the verge of death during most of her treatment.

In the same way that Dianne jumped in to help take care of her sister, she was right there to help Ruth through the worst of it. While Dianne couldn't be with her all the time, she was always there to drive her to the hospital and to stay with her during her treatments. She became her guardian angel and, once more, endeared herself to me. Actually, Ruth drove Dianne's car to and from the hospital because Dianne didn't like to drive on the highway and Ruth was always raring to go. You would think that she would be too sick after her treatments to do anything, but they would give her a dose of Dexamethasone (a steroid) to help with the nausea, which gave her this boundless energy such that she wanted to go shopping afterwards! It was later that she would collapse when exhaustion would hit her like a crushing wave.

After almost a year of treatments, Ruth was "cancer-free" and has been for over seven years. But this doesn't necessarily mean it's gone forever. While a cure is possible for some people, depending on the type of cancer, there is always some chance of recurrence. With Ruth, the probability is quite high and she continues to worry about it (although the probability decreases with time for Breast Cancer). Because there are no markers (blood tests, etc.) for Breast Cancer, the only way she will know if the cancer has returned is if she starts experiencing symptoms. So, while she is now healthy, happy and well into a new life, she worries every time she gets the flu or a pain somewhere. She probably always will.

Shortly after Ruth finished her treatment regime, I had the opportunity to participate in a fund raising event for Breast Cancer research that suited me to a "T". It was called "Paddle to a Cure", a multi-leg, summer long kayaking trip through the Great Lakes. I signed on for a one-week leg on Lake Huron, the final stage of the trip and one designated for relatives and friends of Breast Cancer victims. I managed to raise several thousand dollars myself and had the opportunity to meet some absolutely wonderful people with whom I shared a very special time and some very personal stories. It is another great irony that I have now become a cancer victim myself. And who will paddle for me? I will, dammit!

Time heals all things and, over the years, Judy's death and Ruth's cancer became past events that we recall often with great sadness as we moved on with our own lives. Life was pretty good actually. In 2002 (a month before I was diagnosed), I started a new job with a great company and, in July, Dianne and I celebrated our 25th wedding anniversary. Quite an accomplishment these days, and we celebrated with a big party at our house. All of our closest friends and family were there and we had a wonderful time. There were no concerns about anyone's health and, if anything, we felt that we were beginning a new, more exciting phase of our lives. Our main challenge was to try to achieve some degree of balance in our lives, particularly between work and the rest of life. This is always a challenge for a Type "A" personality, particularly given that I had just started a new job and needed to prove myself, as well as make some money! I was working most evenings and a least one day on the weekend, so we didn't seem to find the time to socialize much or to go anywhere. But we were pretty happy. We were even looking at houses in the Beaches area of Toronto that would have required a substantial financial commitment, but this was indicative of people still looking ahead with little to worry about.

On October 14, 2002 - Thanksgiving Day – we visited an open house in the Beaches on the street where my niece (Meghan) and her husband (Andrew) lived. Dianne loved it and wanted to buy it. I might have even gone along with the idea except that, the following morning, my life changed forever.

THE DIAGNOSIS

For most of my life I have been very careful with my health although, to be honest, I pretty much took it for granted. Every year, religiously, I had a full physical with my family doctor. Once in a while, he would send me for some additional tests, but they would always come back negative. And why wouldn't they? There was no family history of any major health issues and the only thing that I had wrong with me was a skin condition called Vitiligo, which caused me to gradually lose pigmentation in my skin. This is what Michael Jackson claims he has but, it my case, it just means that there are areas on my body that won't tan. But it's mainly a cosmetic condition and I just have to be careful to keep out of the sun. If anything, I worried about getting Skin Cancer from overexposure to the sun, but I was very careful and didn't really give it much credence. So when my doctor informed me that he could feel something on my prostate, I really didn't think I had anything to worry about.

I went for my annual physical with Dr. Gates (I've changed all of the doctor's names in the book to honour their privacy) on August 28, 2002. He did the usual procedures including the old "finger-up-the-ass" (otherwise known as a DRE – digital rectal exam) which he did while I lay on my side on his examination table. To be honest, I never knew why doctors did this. In fact, I didn't even know what a prostate was and I realize now that most men probably don't! We've all certainly heard about Prostate Cancer and we know that it is something that only men get but, beyond that, I don't think most men give it any thought at all. I just assumed the doctor was feeling for swollen glands of some sort. So when he said that he could feel something on my prostate, I was sure it was just a cyst or some other kind of growth that I needn't worry about. I never, ever thought it was anything else. I remember my sister having cysts removed from her ovaries and it being nothing to worry about. Even Dr. Gates said he thought it was nothing, but suggested I see a urologist just to be on the safe side. I should have thought to ask, "The safe side of what?"

It took a while to get an appointment with the urologist but, finally, on September 27, 2002, I went to see Dr. Bones at the local hospital. He did a DRE himself (same technique as Dr. Gates) and told me that it felt "pebbly" and that he didn't think it was cancer. I remember thinking, "Of course it isn't cancer! What the hell are you talking about?" He then asked me what my PSA was but I didn't have a clue. I knew that Dr. Gates had done a PSA test (I had been having them done for a couple of years) but I didn't know the results. Dr. Bones booked me for a biopsy, which I dutifully entered into my organizer, and thought nothing more about it. At the time, I also asked him to do a testosterone test because I had noticed that my erections were not as hard as they were before. After a little more intensely personal physical examination, he pointed out that my left testicle was shrinking but that this was likely a normal sign of aging.

I told Dianne about all of this and promptly forgot about it, not giving a moment's thought to the idea that the biopsy was to check for cancer. I thought he was doing a biopsy to see what the bump was (a cyst?), not to eliminate *cancer*. Based on my history of test results, I knew with absolute certainty that it would be negative. But Dianne wasn't so sure!

I went for the biopsy on October 3, 2002 at the local hospital where Dr. Bones works. I followed the usual procedure of getting undressed, putting my stuff in a locker, and walking around in a too-short hospital gown, something I had done several times before for other tests. It was a little different walking into an actual operating room, but Dr. Bones was there, preparing his equipment and acting very casual and friendly, which reinforced my optimism. I climbed up on the table and joked with the doctor about using the stirrups that were attached to the table, but he assured me that I didn't have to do that. He had me lie on my side (just like for the DRE) and proceeded to gently insert something one hell of a lot bigger than his finger up my ass. I investigated this later and learned that he had used a biopsy "gun", guided by ultrasound, which fires a hollow needle deep into the prostate where it takes a core sample and then retracts. Because the needle penetrates the wall of the rectum, I had to do a preparatory enema to clean me out (always a pleasurable experience) and take antibiotics before and after to prevent infection. Dr. Bones took about three samples from the side with the lump and two from the other side. Most of the books on the subject suggest that you need at least a half-dozen from each side to be sure you don't miss anything, but he was the doctor and, at the time, I knew nothing about it. Besides, it hurt and I wasn't at all interested in prolonging the experience. He told me that it "moved around on him", but I had no idea what the significance of this was. He also warned me that I would find blood in my ejaculate for a little while (which proved true) but this was more of a freaky by-product than anything to worry about.

I thought nothing more about the biopsy until I went for my results on the morning of October 15, 2002. Dianne told me later that she had worried all night about it, but I had slept like a baby without a care in the world. I hadn't even asked Dianne to come to any of these appointments with me because I was so sure there was nothing to worry about. I knew the results would be negative! The doctor would tell me that the lumps were just fatty tissue, one more symptom of "getting older". I couldn't have been more wrong!

I was Dr. Bones' first appointment of the day after a long weekend. I had my suit on because I had customer meetings later that day and was quite relaxed as I followed him into his rather smallish office and took a seat opposite his desk. He looked at the file in front of him and announced, "The biopsy results came back and they're not good." My heart stopped. "They indicate that you have Prostate Cancer." I was stunned! At that moment my mind locked into some kind of automatic state that allowed no room for emotion, focused simply on information processing. "What does this mean?" I asked.

Dr. Bones went through the facts and figures of my case. He told me that it was unusual for someone of my age, but not unheard of.

The grade of the cancer was something called Gleason 7, which was neither highly aggressive nor slow growing but could go either way. He thought it was Stage T2a, which meant that he could feel it, that it probably involved only half of one lobe, and that it likely hadn't spread. Interestingly, he pointed out that my PSA was only 1.26 ug/L, well below the threshold level of 4 ug/L that would have made them suspicious. This too, he said was unusual, but PSA was not accurate for one out of four men and I fell into that 25% range. He pulled out a card from his desk drawer and started reading off some more statistics (I learned later that these were the famous Partin Tables – more on this later). According to his interpretation of the tables, I had a 70% chance of a cure. There was a 30% chance that the cancer had penetrated the prostate capsule, a 7% chance that it had spread to the seminal vesicles, and a 3% chance that it had spread to the lymph nodes. This was my first introduction to the world of Prostate Cancer "numbers" which we will talk much more about later.

The doctor then outlined the treatment options that I had - mainly surgery or radiation - and strongly recommended surgery. This was the "gold standard" for Prostate Cancer treatment, particularly for someone my age as it had the best chance of curing the cancer if it hadn't spread. There was another option called brachytherapy, which had to do with implanting radioactive "seeds" into my prostate, but it was not recommended, nor was it allowed (i.e. funded) for anyone with Gleason 7 or higher. He told me that with surgery, something he could do in the local hospital, I would have a 70% risk of impotence and a 5% risk of "significant" incontinence. Talk about kicking a man when he's down! Not only did I have cancer, but I might never have another erection and might even have to wear diapers for the rest of my life! I pushed away a mental image of what it would be like to wear a diaper under my suit – not a pretty sight. I was getting the first glimpse of how life was never going to be the same.

I struggled to take all of this in even as I asked for more information on the options. I felt like I should be bawling like a baby or showing my anger, but I was treating it all like a business meeting. I don't know whether this was some form of denial or some kind of coping mechanism that I didn't know even existed that had kicked in when my brain registered the shock of what I had just been told. I asked questions and listened calmly and attentively.

The surgery would take somewhere around three hours and I would be in the hospital for three or four days, leaving with a catheter that I would have to keep in for a couple of weeks. Depending on what he found during the surgery, I may then have to go for radiation. Radiation treatments would consist of short five minute bursts every day for a couple of weeks. He offered to get me an appointment with a radiation oncologist at Princess Margaret Hospital (PMH) if I would like to learn more. In the meantime, he would book me for a bone scan and a CT scan to see if there was any evidence of spread, but he felt confident that these would be clear. As I was leaving, his administrative assistant gave me dates for these and also told me that it could take anywhere up to a couple of months to see anyone at PMH. I told her to go ahead and put in the request and then I left, carrying a couple of pamphlets on Prostate Cancer that Dr. Bones had fished out of one of his drawers.

Later that day, Dianne talked to Dr. Bones' assistant who told her that even the doctor was shocked at the biopsy findings. He had considered calling me to suggest I bring Dianne, but didn't because he thought that it would only alarm me. While he handled the whole affair very calmly and factual, I realize now that it must have been very uncomfortable for him. It was a heck of a way to start the day after a nice long weekend – for both of us. Definitely more for me though!

I was shocked and still numb as I got into my Jeep and started to drive home. I had planned to go right to the office, but I felt an incredible need to see Dianne and I knew she needed to hear this horrible news. On the way home, it slowly started to sink in. I think I was more shocked by the "hugeness" of it rather than the fact of it. Cancer has such an overwhelming connotation to it that most people, I suspect, can't really put it into any kind of proper perspective when they first hear their diagnosis. As I drove, I thought about how to tell Dianne and whether or not I should even tell my kids. Dianne had to know, of course, but maybe it was better if the kids didn't. In fact, why did anyone else have to know?

My cell phone rang when I was about two minutes from home. It was Dianne, but there was no way I was going to answer because she would insist on knowing what happened and I really didn't want to do it over the phone. As I pulled in the driveway, she met me at the door with a concerned look on her face. She knew something was wrong, particularly when I hadn't answered her call. She knows me so well. I stood in the doorway and told her that I had Prostate Cancer. She said, "Okay. What does this mean (the same thing I had asked Dr. Bones)?" I sat down on the arm of a chair in the living room and told her everything Dr. Bones had said, including all of the numbers and what they meant. Dianne says that I cried a bit that morning but I don't remember if I did. I just wanted to get it all out and then go do something else, as if I could somehow put it all behind me. I just didn't want to deal with it at that time. I couldn't. I think that the mind has some kind of protective mechanism that tries to soften the blow of bad news. I suppose it's a form of shock that numbs your brain and your emotions to give you time to mentally prepare yourself to deal with it. Whatever it was, it kicked in and I left for work immediately. I didn't want to talk about it anymore. Unfortunately, I left Dianne at home alone to deal with all of this by her self. I didn't think about it at time but I now realize just how thoughtless that was. I was running away.

I remember the rest of that day vividly. I met one of my co-workers, Adele, and went to a meeting with a customer who had been ignoring our calls until we had sent a note to his boss. What a prick! Adele and I sat on a couch in this guy's office while the pompous ass gave us shit for going over his head. In sales, you don't get anywhere if you start arguing with your customers, but I remember thinking that I wanted to tell this guy to just *fuck off*. I had cancer and what did I care about this guy's bruised ego! It kept popping into my head even as I did my thing, acting very polite and suitably conciliatory. I don't know how I was able to carry it off that day and, later, Adele told me that she had no clue that anything was wrong. For me, however, it marked my first awakening to the fact that work was not and should not be the most important thing in my life.

Later that day, Dianne and I told the kids. While I had entertained the idea of not telling them, they clearly had to know. Dianne had told my daughter Caralia that afternoon. She had called Dianne from school and somehow sensed that something was wrong, so she came home at her lunch break. There was no hiding it because Dianne's eyes were red from crying. When I came home, Caralia asked me, "Are you going to die?" I was honest and said that I didn't think so, but that there was always a chance if it had already spread. When my son Sean came home, I told him too, but I don't think he really understood. In fact, he told his friends that I had Testicular Cancer. And after that first talk, he never asked about it again.

Strangely, I did very little on the cancer front for the rest of that week. This was very unusual for me, as I normally dove headfirst into anything new to ferret out every possible bit of information. As hard as it was on her, Dianne tried to leave me alone to let me digest everything. That night I did my expense account for work, generally a very boring and time-consuming exercise, and for the rest of the week I attended various meetings. I even flew down to Chicago to visit some customers for a day. The only cancer-related thing I did do was to call Dr. Bones' office on Friday to see if they had a surgery date for me and was surprised to find that they hadn't booked one! It seems they were waiting for me to see the radiation oncologist at PMH (as yet unscheduled) to get a "second opinion". While this may have seemed like a clear-cut either/ or choice to them, I assumed that cancer meant surgery, radiation *and* chemotherapy. I also thought that Dr. Bones understood that I wanted to go ahead with the surgery. When I asked his assistant to please book the surgery, she pushed back a bit because she didn't want to tie up a surgery spot if there was a chance I might cancel. Talk about not being on the same page! I assured her that I would do the surgery and we booked for December 3, 2002, the earliest date they had, and just in time to recuperate over the Christmas holidays.

I experienced a mixture of feelings that first week as my mind struggled to come to grips with the fact that I had cancer. The first night I fell right to sleep but awoke at 4:00 in the morning with my mind spinning. After an early morning meeting, I met up with my buddy Greg for a coffee and told him. He was absolutely stunned and insisted I stay downtown and have lunch with he and his wife Nancy. In one of those strange life ironies, Nancy, a gynaecologist, had been downtown that day being interviewed about cancer on a local television show. She too was shocked to hear the news. It was a wonderful thing for me to be able to talk to both of them that day. They were great friends and had some great advice. In particular, they encouraged me to get a second opinion and said that I should immediately find out who the top doctors were in the field and Nancy offered to check them out for me. This made a great deal of sense to me. Why would I not want to be looked after by one of the best doctors in the field?

I was distracted for the rest of that day and found it very difficult to concentrate on work, although it was a blessing to have something else to do. That evening, Dianne and I had dinner with our good friends, Russ and Randy, to celebrate their anniversary. Dianne had already told Randy and they were very supportive but we tried not to let it dominate the dinner conversation. Dianne had also been busy that day talking to a fellow from the local Man To Man Prostate Cancer support group. He had also suggested getting a second opinion and gave her a list of the top Prostate Cancer doctors in Toronto. I promptly passed these on to Nancy to check out through her colleagues. By the time I went to bed that evening, I was absolutely exhausted, but I still found it hard to sleep because my brain was working in overdrive, so much so that I was afraid I was having a panic attack! I thought about how I didn't really know if the cancer had spread yet and started to worry about every little twinge that I felt in my body. My mind wrestled with the idea of getting a second opinion, which was a good idea, but I really didn't want to risk delaying surgery. It was the beginning of an escalating trend of self-doubt and second-guessing that would become almost an obsession with me.

Very quickly, I came to understand why they call it "the Big C". I always thought that this just referred to the fact that cancer was a bad thing - a big, bad thing – but now that I had it, it seemed so all-pervasive and, yes, BIG! It was always *there*, even when I was concentrating on something else. On the plane to Chicago three days after my diagnosis, I wondered if the people around me could tell that I had cancer. I even wondered if people with cancer could recognize each other the same way I've heard that alcoholics can. Everywhere I went there were reminders. My eyes homed in like lasers on every ad for cancer awareness and on every coloured ribbon on anyone's lapel. My ears tuned immediately into every television and radio mention of cancer. It seemed to be everywhere!

On the Friday night, we went for dinner with Greg and Nancy. Nancy had researched all of the doctors on the list I had given here and had called Dr. Tracks, one of the top guns at PMH, to see if I could get in to see him. To our surprise, I was able to get an appointment for the following Wednesday! It was going to be a rush though because Nancy, as the "referring physician" (I was to take a lot of ribbing about being referred by a gynaecologist!) had to get my PSA and biopsy results to Dr. Tracks on Monday. This meant that I had to get them from Dr. Bones first thing that morning. Dianne stepped up to the plate and insisted that she would park herself in Dr. Bones' office until they were sent, even if it took all day. As it turned out, she had them sent from Dr. Bones to Dr. Gates who then faxed them to Nancy. It's amazing how understanding and accommodating people can be when you have a cancer diagnosis. I told Nancy that she was now my new best friend.

By that time we had told a lot of people and calls were coming in from all over. Dianne handled most of them, which was fine by me, and I think that it helped for her to be doing something. We both felt a need (especially Dianne) to reach out to our friends and family for support. One evening, my niece Meghan came by the house with a big bag of some weird-looking tree-bark tea in a bag. I didn't know whether to drink it, eat it, or smoke it! It was so sweet of her to do this but I started to feel bad about imposing this "thing" on so many people. I worried about telling my parents and about telling people at work, and I started to get emotional whenever I talked about it. I felt it was time for me to get off my ass and start finding out more about Prostate Cancer, what my chances were and the pros and cons of the few options I had available to me. I started online. There is so much information out there on the Internet that it can quickly become overwhelming, but I dove right in and immediately scared the shit out of myself. In researching the Partin Tables, I discovered that everything was expressed in ranges and found that I had up to a 53% chance that the cancer had spread (the other end of the range was only 7%, but that's not what captures your attention). But the more I found out, the worse I felt! On Saturday morning, Dianne and I visited the local Chapters bookstore and pulled out every book we could find on Prostate Cancer. Dianne had already picked up three books for me, holding one back because it was so negative. We discovered a whole new world. While every writer's style is different, most of the books covered the same material. There were numerous, incredibly vivid drawings of male genitalia and cross-sections that showed how everything fit together. It was the first time that I had ever seen a prostate! There were sections on prevention, diet and diagnosis, followed by detailed discussions of the treatment options that were available. There were lovely descriptions of incontinence and a veritable encyclopaedia of aids for erectile dysfunction. I read about drugs like Viagra, vacuum pumps, penis injections (ouch!) and rigid or inflatable rods that could be surgically installed in your penis. The inflatable kind could be brought into action by squeezing a bulb that would be hidden in your scrotum and the rigid ones just had to be bent up to the proper angle. Gee, I had nothing to worry about! By far the scariest sections were the ones that talked about recurrence and how there was little that could be done beyond trying to slow down the progression with hormone therapy (I could grow breasts!) and making you "comfortable". The only light note was one of the books that recommended no housework for five years following surgery, but Dianne wouldn't let me purchase that one! We ignored books that described how to use your mind to cure yourself and went home with three or four that looked promising.

Saturday evening, Ruth and her friend Greg came over and made Dianne and I a gourmet meal. With the newfound knowledge that we had gathered during the day and Ruth's personal experience we talked a lot about cancer and what it can mean. Ruth was such a pillar of strength. She shared with us how she felt when she was diagnosed with Breast Cancer and how it affected her then and how it continues to affect her. It was that night that Ruth became my "cancer buddy". She was, in fact, the only one I knew who had actually gone through the cancer experience and the only person close to me who could truly understand what I was going through. This was to become very important to me in the coming months. But for all of that, it didn't stop the worrying. That night, lying in bed, I worried about how Dr. Bones described that lump as "pebbly" and how he had to "chase it" with the biopsy needle. It made me think that the cancer had already penetrated the prostate capsule and had likely spread. That, in turn, could explain the low back pain that I was experiencing at the time. Maybe it had already metastasized to my spine! But even these worries were overshadowed by the thought that I was going to tell my parents the next day. I was definitely not looking forward to that.

On Saturday, I had called my parents and cheerfully told them that we would be dropping by for a friendly visit. They were very pleased, but I felt like I was lying to them by being so cheerful. So on Sunday, we headed out with a great sense of trepidation and I drove in an emotional fog, on a kind of mental autopilot. We kept up the cheery front when we arrived and throughout the afternoon. I didn't want to just walk in the door and hit them between the eyes with this. I wanted to wait until after dinner when we could sit around the table and have a good old fashioned family chat. It was reminiscent of a similar trip that Dianne and I took over 25 years earlier to tell my parents we were getting married, after only knowing each other for a few months and dating only a few weeks (when you know it, you know it!). That one hadn't gone over very well. While they liked Dianne, they had only met her once before. My father developed an instant migraine and my mother asked for a double rum-and-coke! I didn't think this would be any better.

After we ate, I told my mother to stop clearing the table and to sit down. A look of dread come into their eyes as I took a deep breath and told them that I had been diagnosed with Prostate Cancer. It was one of the hardest things I have ever done. I quickly filled in everything I knew to that point, emphasizing the very low probability that it had spread. It is times like this when you talk about the other end of the range – the 7% rather than the 53% – whether you believe it yourself or not. To say they were shocked was an understatement. They didn't know what to say at first. My mom pointed out that this was the first serious health issue that our family had ever experienced. We had been pretty lucky so far. If anything, we would have expected one of my parents to get sick before any of us kids, given their age, but at the time they were still going strong. We talked with them for quiet a while. I found out that my dad had some prostate problems a while back and had a procedure to open up the urethra and I think he initially thought that my surgery would be essentially the same, but I corrected that.

This was not going to be a simple procedure! It was good to get it out in the open and talk to them about it. They were clearly afraid for me as I was, after all, still their little boy. Later, I called my brother Art, who is four years older than me, to tell him and to warn him that his chances of getting Prostate Cancer were now doubled to one-in-three. He said, "Thanks a lot," but he promised to get checked regularly. We commiserated, but it was a short conversation. My brother is a great guy but a man of few words.

The next night, at home, my sister Colleen called from out west. My parents must have called her because I hadn't yet, so she called to tell me she loved me and that I "would be fine." She said it so many times that I began to think that she was saying it more for herself than for me. It was a way of convincing herself that my cancer was not that serious so she didn't have to worry about it. I think many people do that. After about five minutes, she seemed to be satisfied with talking about me and then proceeded to talk about what was going on in her life. We had a similar conversation a couple of nights later. She wanted to tell my parents some bad news about something but I told her they had enough to deal with. I don't think she really understood the full significance of what had happened to me. I kept telling her that I was exhausted and that I wanted to go to bed, but she kept talking. In the following weeks, she called several more times but I didn't pick up the phone. I didn't want to talk about her. I was having trouble dealing with my own problems. Don't get me wrong, I appreciated her calls and I understood that she might have felt uncomfortable talking about my cancer yet still wanted to reach out to me. I've learned that this is not uncommon. All I really wanted was for my friends and family to say, "This sucks. I'm sorry it happened to you. Is there anything I can do? Do you want to talk about it? I'm here if you do." But who really knows what to say?

On Monday, I had a chance to drop in on Dr. Gates to thank him for finding the lump. He told me that he was as shocked as everyone else because of my age and, in fact, had never had a patient as young as me diagnosed with Prostate Cancer. He was very perceptive. He asked if I was having trouble sleeping, which I was, and prescribed sleeping pills for me. I thanked him profusely. I definitely needed to get some sleep!

It's exponentially more difficult to deal with something like this when your mind is not rested.

That evening, my buddy Russ took me out for a beer and to offer me his support. He was very interested in the whys and wherefores of Prostate Cancer and we had a great, long chat. Talking about it, I felt that I was starting to get a grip on this thing; that I might be able to handle it if I took it one step at a time. I stopped the research binge I was on and concentrated on getting on with things. Like work. Like cutting the grass. Anything that would take my mind off the horror that was growing inside of me.

My fortuitous appointment with Dr. Tracks was confirmed for Wednesday at 1:45. (Ironically, I got the appointment because an anaesthetist's work-to-rule had resulted in cancellation of several Prostate Cancer surgeries, so the doctor ran an unscheduled clinic!) Ruth and Dianne encouraged me to prepare a list of questions before I went in to make sure I didn't forget anything. Normally, I would rely on my memory for this sort of thing, but this was different than anything I had experienced previously and I just didn't trust my own faculties. I wrote the following questions in my journal.

- Why me at such a young age?
- How can my PSA level be so low?
- When can he do the surgery?
- Can they do it laproscopically (like my hernia operation)?
- Where should I have my bone scan and CT scan done - PMH or locally?
- How long is the surgery?
- How long will I be in the hospital?
- How long will I have the catheter?
- How long before I can go back to work?
- What are the chances of recurrence? Incontinence? Impotence?
- Should I have radiation?

Armed with this list, and with Dianne at my side (as she would be from then on), I entered the world of Princess Margaret Hospital, the premier cancer treatment facility in Canada and one of the best in the world. PMH was built on the site of an old Ontario Hydro office, where I had worked a good part of my career (and where I had met Dianne), so it felt very strange entering the building. While they had kept the external façade of the century-old building, the inside had been converted to a sparkling, airy and very modern décor that contrasted sharply with the fact that the place was full of people with cancer. We took the glass elevators up to the fourth floor and followed the signs to The Prostate Centre. I was impressed. It was a large room with many comfortable chairs and racks of literature. Two large counters dominated the north and south ends of the room where several women sat working on computers. I checked in, received my blue hospital card and sat down. Looking around, I couldn't help noticing that I was the youngest man in the room.

After a relatively short wait, my name was called and I was asked to follow a young man who said he was Dr. Tracks' assistant. This was the form-filling part of the process, where I gave them permission to get all of my medical information and signed papers absolving them of any liability should I die on the operating table. While this assumed I would go the distance with Dr. Tracks (which I hadn't yet decided), I knew I could always change my mind. After about a half-hour, I was ushered into an examination room to meet the doctor, Dianne at my side.

Dr. Tracks is one of the top Prostate Cancer specialists in the world, so I expected someone who was larger-than-life with a good dose of arrogance. To my surprise, he was neither of these. In fact he was friendly, compassionate and more than willing to answer my questions. For example, rather than ask my wife to leave so he could do a DRE, he took me into another room. He used a little different technique than what I was used to, asking me to drop my pants and lean over the table (what some guys call *Deer Hunter* style). It was only a couple of minutes before we were back with Dianne.

The great thing about going to someone as experienced as Dr. Tracks, who deals exclusively with Prostate Cancer, is that he can tell a lot from a simple DRE. He told me right up front that he would have to take one of the two cavernous nerves that cause erections so that he could take a wide enough margin to ensure he got all of the cancer. While this would increase the probability of long-term or even permanent impotence, he told me not to worry as they had been having a lot of success in treating that of late. He mentioned a new technique that he was just starting to do which involved taking a section of nerve from your leg and splicing it in to replace the lost cavernous nerve. But just from feeling my prostate, he knew that this wasn't possible; that there would be no place to attach the repaired nerve. I was definitely not happy about this new development, but I was so impressed that I immediately trusted him.

He answered all of my questions with facts and figures and the voice of experience. Clearly, surgery was the best option – the "gold standard" – particularly for someone as young as I was. The surgery would take about two-and-a-half hours and I would be in the hospital three or four days (I had heard him tell an older guy in the hall that he would be in the hospital for four or five days, so I assumed there was an age factor at play here as well). They didn't do laparoscopic surgeries because these took twice as long and didn't improve the results (except for recovery time) while eating up scarce operating room resources. The big problem (and this was really big!) was that he could not give me a date for the surgery. The anaesthetists were cutting back on surgeries to protest the fee structure which paid them the same for a long surgery as for a shorter one, and which was causing a mass exodus to the cosmetic surgery industry where they could do four or five operations a day. As a result, all of Dr. Tracks' limited spots were booked for the balance of the year and he didn't have any dates yet for the new year. This was not good, but I trusted him so much that I agreed to go with him and my name was put on his waiting list. It was yet another irony that the anaesthetist's job action had helped me get an appointment quickly but was preventing me from getting an early surgery date! In the meantime, he told me to continue doing what I was doing and not try to change my lifestyle overnight. I had enough to deal with. His only suggestion was to lose about ten pounds to make the surgery easier and my recovery faster.

Following my session with Dr. Tracks, Dianne and I met with Dr. Andrew Matthews, a psychologist working at the Prostate Centre to help patients and their families deal with the emotional impact of being diagnosed with cancer. Little did I realize at the time just how much I would need him in the months and years ahead. Andrew reviewed with us the extensive resources available at The Prostate Centre, including an impressive library and access to specialists in every aspect of the disease. He talked to both of us, explaining that, while I had the physical disease, both of us had the cancer and we had to work together to effectively deal with it. He invited us to join a research study on Joint Decision-Making in Prostate Cancer that he and a colleague were conducting. We agreed to join the study, assuring him that we were about as close as two people could get.

Dianne and I talked about everything at great length. For the first couple of weeks, she wouldn't leave my side and kept touching me as if I could disappear any moment in a puff of smoke. She said it was much, much different from Judy or Ruth; that having a spouse with cancer hit so much closer to home. She said it was always in the forefront of her mind, every minute of every day and even while she slept. Normally, I would tell her not to worry until after the surgery when we would know more, but that was an old defence mechanism of mine that didn't seem to hold up in the face of this horrible new situation. It was clear that we were both going to have to do a lot of adjusting. We were facing a new world order.

In those early weeks, I kept vacillating between, "Oh my God! I've got cancer! I could die!" and the feeling that it was *only* Prostate Cancer, not *real* cancer like Judy and Ruth had. I'm not sure whether this was some form of denial or a feeling of guilt that I was making too much of it. Dianne told me I was crazy to even consider not taking it seriously and even Andrew had a good chuckle over that. I now realize that it doesn't matter what kind of cancer you have or how bad it is, it is a horribly terrifying disease that can kill you as surely as stepping out in front of a freight train. And there is *nothing* about having cancer that can minimize the emotional impact that it has on everyone it touches. It's just too big. Yes, there was a good chance that I could beat it, but I couldn't ignore the unalterable fact that my own body was trying to kill me! And for all of those well-meaning people who kept telling me, "You'll be fine." What the hell did they know?

A PRIMER ON PROSTATE CANCER

This book is a about my cancer experience and the impact it had on me and on those around me. My intention is to describe everything that happened to me, and everything that went through my mind, to give you some insight into the immense emotional and psychological trauma that comes hard on the heels of a cancer diagnosis. In keeping true to this noble purpose, I don't want to turn this book into a comprehensive text on Prostate Cancer. There are many great books available, written by doctors, that will tell you everything you need to know about the physical aspects of the disease and details of the options available to you (Dr. Patrick Walsh's "Guide to Surviving Prostate Cancer" is one of my favourites). I would be remiss, however, if I didn't include some of the basic facts and opinions relating to Prostate Cancer to provide some context for my story. But don't rely too much on this. Purchase at least one book written by a doctor, do your research on the Internet (carefully), and talk to your own doctor. Be informed!

Prostate Cancer is the most common form of cancer for men and the number two killer cancer, second only to lung cancer (the incidence of lung cancer is lower, but the mortality rate is much higher). In North America, one in six men will be diagnosed with Prostate Cancer sometime in their life. It is often considered an "older man's disease" because the average age at diagnosis is around 65. This is changing with early detection, but the rates of incidence drop quite significantly for men in their forties or fifties. There is also a racial element to this disease that no one has a definitive explanation for. Black men have a significantly higher rate of incidence while Asian men have a much lower rate (until they move to North America where their incidence rate increases!). The important point in all of this is that all men need to be aware of what Prostate Cancer is and what their risks are.

The rates of incidence of Prostate Cancer for men are actually greater than for Breast Cancer in women. I doubt if there is a women alive who doesn't know all about Breast Cancer and what to look out for. Men, on the other hand, are embarrassingly (and dangerously) ignorant, unaware, naïve, or just plain stupid about Prostate Cancer. Why? Because we're men! And men are indestructible! We are such macho beasts that we never think that something can kill us, let alone our own body turning on us. Only wimps get sick, right!? This lack of awareness is the biggest issue with Prostate Cancer because the evidence is overwhelming that early detection increases the probability of a cure! If you're not getting checked regularly, you're essentially playing Russian roulette with your health. One-in-six odds are the same whether you're talking about bullets or cancer cells, but you can't cure a bullet to the head. Think about it. Get checked regularly.

The primary tests for Prostate Cancer are the Digital Rectal Exam (DRE) and the PSA test, but there is some controversy as to when men should start having these tests. It is generally recommended that men start being tested when they reach the age of fifty, or by forty if there is a family history of Prostate Cancer. With more and more men being diagnosed in their forties, and with the steadily improving treatment results from early detection, most Prostate Cancer survivors and their loved ones believe that testing should be done routinely from the age of forty. There appears to be two main reasons for the controversy. One is that the PSA test is not completely accurate (false indications in one-out-of-four cases) so most health agencies feel that it is not something that should be mandated. The other reason is that inaccurate, borderline or fluctuating results lead to many "unnecessary" biopsies, which are a costly drain on the health system. Having been diagnosed at forty-nine, understanding that the cancer had probably been growing in me for a good ten years, I recommend to everyone I meet to get tested starting at forty or even earlier. Why not? It's your body and if there's something growing inside you that can kill you, you should know about it!

I talked earlier about the joys of the DRE, but what is the doctor looking for? The prostate is about the size and shape of a walnut and rests up against the wall of the rectum. When the doctor sticks his finger up your rectum, he can feel the prostate through the wall. He is feeling for any change in the size or firmness of the prostate, which can be an indication of Prostate Cancer or other prostate problems like unusual enlargement, Benign Prostatic Hyperplasia (BHP), or Prostatitis (an infection). An increase in the firmness of the prostate or evidence of lumps can be a strong indication that cancer is present (as it was in my case). Even though the doctor can feel only 60% of the prostate surface, this area has the highest incidence of cancer, so it's a very good indicator. The down side is that, by the time the cancer tumour is palpable, it can be quite far advanced. Prior to PSA testing, this was the main diagnostic tool, so you can see how many younger men may have been missed.

PSA stands for Prostate Specific Antigen, which is a hormone produced by the prostate gland and released into the blood stream. The PSA test measures the level of PSA in the blood and is used as an indicator that cancer might be present. Most men have a relatively steady PSA level that increases slowly with age but generally stays below a threshold level of 4 or 5 ug/L. If the level rises above this threshold, or starts to rise rapidly, doctors will then order a biopsy to see if cancer cells are present, because Prostate Cancer cells (which are screwed-up prostate cells) produce ten times as much PSA as regular cells. There are other causes of rising PSA levels, such as the other prostate illnesses above and, as I mentioned earlier, the PSA test gives false results one-out-of-four times (as in my case). Nonetheless, the combination of a DRE and a PSA test (followed by a biopsy) gives you the best chance for early detection of Prostate Cancer. In fact, some recent studies have suggested that the PSA threshold level be lowered to increase the chances of catching earlier cancers. The debate on this continues.

PSA is also used to monitor men who have been treated for Prostate Cancer to see if there has been any recurrence. In fact, recurrence is often defined as "biochemical failure" which simply means that PSA levels are rising, even though the prostate may be gone. For men treated with radiation or other non-surgical techniques (where the prostate is left intact), some level of PSA may remain and it is an increase that you look for. This is usually a very reliable test as it measures PSA created by Prostate Cancer cells that have started to grow in the prostate bed or in some other site and is, therefore, a good sign that the cancer has returned and is possibly metastasizing. Men with Prostate Cancer must generally look forward to regular PSA tests (starting at three months, increasing to six and eventually to twelve), hoping always to hear that it is "undetectable". For people like me, where the PSA levels did not indicate cancer, there is some uncertainty that recurring cancer will show up on a PSA test. In fact there is a dearth of information on this whole anomaly, which is unfortunate for me.

If Prostate Cancer recurs, it can take several years to show up because it is a relatively slow-growing cancer. If it comes back quickly, within the first couple of years, that usually means it is very aggressive and will spread rapidly. If it takes longer to come back, there is a chance that is has begun to take root in the prostate bed (the area where the prostate used to be before it was removed by surgery) and "salvage" radiation treatment may successfully treat it. Unfortunately, in many cases the cancer has spread to the bones or to other organs such as the lungs or the brain. This is really not good, because it is then incurable and treatment shifts to slowing it down to buy you more time.

Prostate Cancer victims tend to get very familiar reciting their "numbers" as this is the basis of communicating the extent and aggressiveness of their cancer to others. PSA levels (before and after treatment) are key numbers. The other key indicators are the Gleason Score and Stage.

The Gleason Score is determined by visually inspecting prostate cells that have been obtained through biopsy or by doing a full pathology on a surgically removed prostate. Cells are looked at under a microscope (by a trained pathologist) and are graded on a scale from 1 to 5 depending on their degree of "differentiation" or irregularity. Grade 1 is essentially normal and grade 5 is very bad (highly differentiated). For some reason, the predicative value of the Gleason Score is better if readings are combined from two different sites, which leads to scores like 3+3=6 or 4+3=7, where the first number is the primary site. Looking at the combined number, Gleason Scores of 6 or under are considered less aggressive, 8 and higher are considered very aggressive, and 7 can go either way (a 4+3 is considered somewhat more aggressive than a 3+4). Combined with the PSA level, these two numbers can dictate treatment options. Often, the post-surgical Gleason Score is different than the biopsy results because the pathologist has more tissue to work with.

Staging is another form of measuring aggressiveness and the extent of spread of the cancer. The following table describes the current staging method for Prostate Cancer (Stage T1a and b are found incidentally through other procedures).

- Stage T1a – Tumour not palpable on DRE; 5% or less of removed tissue is cancerous
- Stage T1b – Tumour not palpable; greater than 5% of removed tissue is cancerous
- Stage T1c – Tumour not palpable, cancer found through biopsy
- Stage T2a – Tumour palpable on DRE; confined to less than half of a single lobe
- Stage T2b – Tumour palpable; more than half of one lobe but not both
- Stage T2c – Tumour palpable; both lobes involved
- Stage T3 – Capsular penetration
- Stage T4 – Capsular penetration with seminal vesicles involved
- Stage TN – Lymph nodes involved
- Stage TM – Cancer has metastasized to other parts of the body

As with the Gleason Score, it is much more accurate after surgery than before when it must be surmised from biopsy and DRE results.

So it is very much a numbers game. My original diagnosis was PSA of 1.26, Gleason 7, Stage T2a. Later, when my biopsy results were reviewed by pathologists at PMH, my Gleason Score was changed to 6. While the difference in the Gleason Score could have impacted my choices, I really don't think I would have made any other decision.

These key numbers start to become very meaningful when used as input to the Partin Tables. These tables, based on thousands of historical cases of Prostate Cancer, allow you to input your numbers and derive the probability of capsular penetration, of spread to the seminal vesicles, and spread to the lymph nodes. Recent updates to the tables also allow you to estimate the probability of recurrence after treatment. Depending on your numbers, this can make you feel good or bad. As a rule of thumb, capsular penetration is not too bad unless it has spread (because it takes awhile for the newly-released cancer cells to learn to survive outside of the prostate), seminal vesicle involvement is not good, and lymph node involvement is pretty bad. Regardless of what odds the tables give you, there are no guarantees and most doctors will point out that each case is unique. There is a lot of talk about probabilities when dealing with cancer but, the way I looked at it back then, it was either going to come back or not. That's a fifty-fifty chance in my book.

So now that you have been diagnosed and your numbers have been tattooed on your forehead for all to see, what do you do about it? There are several options that vary in applicability and desirability depending on your personal situation. Again let me caution you not to take my word for any of this. Talk to your doctor, get a second opinion, research the hell out of it, and then make an informed decision. Take your time and don't be rushed into one treatment or another by anyone. It's your body, your life and your choice, and you don't ever want to have regrets. Now that I've covered my ass, let's look at the options.

If you are younger and the cancer is detected early, the "gold standard" for treatment is surgery, specifically the radical prostatectomy (referred to as an RP). An RP can be done from either the front (retro-pubic – the most common technique) or the back (perineal) and involves complete removal of the prostate and the seminal vesicles and, if necessary, the lymph nodes. This is major surgery! Don't let anyone tell you differently (just read the rest of this book). You are sliced open from the navel to the pubic bone and, since the prostate rests against the rectum wall, the doctors cut pretty much right through your body. As an integral part of the surgery, the urethra (which drains from your bladder to your penis, travelling through the centre of the prostate) and the lower part of your bladder are cut out and have to be reconnected. As a result, you wake up with a catheter that must remain in for a couple of weeks. Dr. Walsh's landmark book "Guide to Surviving Prostate Cancer" has some great drawings that describe the procedure in vivid detail (Dianne did not want to see these). Many doctors are now doing this laproscopically and even robotically (and new techniques are being developed all the time). These methods can take twice as long but have a faster recovery time and the evidence is suggesting that they have the same outcomes as traditional surgery.

As of the time of writing, effective chemotherapy treatments are not generally available for Prostate Cancer so radiation is the next most popular choice, particularly for men who hate the thought of major surgery. The radiation is targeted at the prostate and focused as much as possible on tumour sites that can be determined using a CT scan or MRI. Essentially, radiation burns both the cancerous cells and the surrounding healthy cells and generally turns the prostate into a blob of scar tissue. Because of this, surgery after radiation is not an option, while the reverse is. After radiation treatment, it takes awhile for the PSA level to drop and may never reach undetectable levels as some prostate tissue remains. A recent variation on radiation treatment, called Brachytherapy, involves the placement of tiny radioactive "seeds" directly into the tumours (there tends to be more than one) through precisely guided needles. This is thought to be somewhat less invasive and destructive and is a good option for some men, except those with more aggressive cancers (in some jurisdictions, Brachytherapy is not available if your Gleason Score is 7 or higher).

More recently, a technique known as High Intensity Focused Ultrasound (HIFU) is being offered in several major cities. HIFU uses ultrasound to heat and destroy the prostate cells with the claim of fewer side effects.

The only other option is something called "watchful waiting" which essentially means do nothing and monitor the situation. This may not sound that attractive to a man just diagnosed with cancer but, for older men with less aggressive cancers, it may be preferable as they are more likely to die of other causes long before the cancer gets them. Another consideration is that some older men may not be able to take the strain of major surgery or radiation treatments. This is a good example of how your personal situation can significantly impact your options and ultimate decision.

Hormone therapy is also used to treat Prostate Cancer but is not considered to be a cure. By reducing testosterone levels that can promote the growth of Prostate Cancer cells, it can be effective in slowing things down. I have heard of some doctors who put newly diagnosed men on hormone therapy to slow down or even shrink tumours prior to surgery but, more often, it is used to extend the life span of men with Advanced Prostate Cancer. Hormone therapy essentially puts you into male menopause, so men can experience hot flashes, mood swings, a significant decrease in their libido, possibly impotence, and even breast enlargement. Yikes! None of that sounds very attractive, but I guess the alternative is much worse. A related therapy, which has the same aim of blocking testosterone from the body, is to surgically remove the testicles, but I don't even like to think about that!

All of the treatment options available for Prostate Cancer share two critical side effects – incontinence and impotence. Either of these, alone, can strike terror into the hearts of men. Together, they represent the main reason why men don't like to even think about Prostate Cancer, let alone talk about it.

Incontinence results from damage to the urinary tract caused by surgery or radiation. As we discussed earlier, during a radical prostatectomy, the doctor removes a portion of the bladder and the urethra along with the prostate and then reconnects the urethra to the new bladder opening. In a healthy male, both the bladder neck and the prostate act as sphincters, along with the main pelvic floor muscles for a total of three points for controlling the flow of urine. After surgery (or prolonged radiation treatment), men are left with only one operating sphincter, which takes some getting used to. Once the urethra/bladder connection is healed enough for the catheter to be removed, doctors recommend special exercises (called "kegels") to strengthen the pelvic floor sufficiently to regain control. It is not unusual for younger men to regain control immediately; however older men can retain varying degrees of incontinence for some time. This means wearing diapers, pads or special underwear to guard against those little accidents that can be so humiliating. Not a very macho image! Even after continence has returned, men will watch their liquid intake carefully and will make a point to always know where the nearest washroom is.

And then there is impotence - the big ED (Erectile Dysfunction). Whatever treatment regimen you choose, you will be faced with the possibility of not being able to "get it up". No more Mr. Stud. No more "Me Tarzan, you Jane". No more, "Come and get it baby!" Sex is such an incredibly important part of a man's life – in fact of his entire self-image – that the thought of not being able to get an erection is almost worse than death and some men will literally risk death to avoid it! Ironically, this is the very choice that men face immediately upon getting a Prostate Cancer diagnosis. In many cases, potency will gradually return but may never be quite the same and may require the use of "sexual aids" such as Viagra-type drugs, penile injections, vacuum pumps or other. Impotence is a virtually unavoidable by-product of Prostate Cancer treatment because the two nerves that control erections (that send messages to the brain to pump your peter full of blood) pass over the sides of the prostate and, in the case of surgery, must be "peeled" away very carefully to avoid damage. Even with the best surgeons doing this, there is still significant trauma to the nerves, which takes a long time to recover. While I have heard of some men who are lucky enough to have their erections return in as little as a month or so, it can take up to two years or longer (if at all)!

In surgeries conducted years ago, there was too much blood around the prostate during the surgery and it was impossible to see the nerves well enough to save them so they were routinely "sacrificed". Dr. Patrick Walsh found a way to tie off the proper blood vessels to provide a bloodless field to work in and thereby pioneered what is now routine "nerve sparing" surgery. In some cases (such as mine), one of the nerves is sacrificed because of the location of the cancer tumours, which increases the odds of permanent impotence and, at a minimum, delays the return of erections. In the case of radiation therapy, impotence is also caused by nerve damage from the treatment, coming on more gradually and also returning more gradually.

What more can I say on this topic? It is one of the biggest considerations in decision-making around Prostate Cancer treatments. I have heard that radiation treatment can offer better odds for regaining potency and continence than surgery, but ultimately, the choice depends on your own particular situation and the relative priorities you place on life, sex and dry underwear.

Can you prevent Prostate Cancer? The jury is still out on this. Genetics and race play a significant role in whether you get cancer and there is not much you can do about who you are and where you came from. Most Prostate Cancer sources provide guidelines for a healthy diet that is high in anti-oxidants and other cancer fighting foods, bolstered by supplements such as Vitamin E, Selenium and Saw Palmetto (although recent studies have questioned the efficacy of some of these supplements). These are generally good healthy diets that also reduce the risk of heart disease so they are not a bad idea, but there are no guarantees that they will prevent you from getting Prostate Cancer (or heart disease for that matter). Apparently, there is a school of thought that suggests masturbation is a good preventative measure because it "washes out" the prostate more frequently and perhaps prevents cancer cells from building up. Again, there does not appear to be any hard proof of this, but it's a pretty good story if your wife or your mother catches you at it!

If you are unlucky enough to join "the club that no one wants to join", you can be assured that you are in good company. Recently, many famous people have come forward to talk about their experiences with the disease. General Norman Schwarzkopf was diagnosed after Desert Storm (like me, with a very low PSA level). Rudolf Giuliani, Bob Dole, John Kerry, Robert DeNiro and Harry Belafonte all have been treated for Prostate Cancer along with many more. Bill Bixby (one of my favourite actors when I was a kid) was diagnosed too late and eventually died. Others who have died include Don Ameche, the Ayatollah Khomeini, Timothy Leary, Dick Sargent, Telly Savalas and Frank Zappa. A while back, Jerry Orbach, the tough *Law & Order* cop and a Broadway icon died of Prostate Cancer, working right up to the end. I was a big fan and it tore me up inside. More recently, the music icon Dan Fogelberg died of advanced Prostate Cancer at the age of 56.

So you can see that you are not alone and, if you do join the club, give some thought to how these men faced up to it and draw a bit of inspiration from it. I did and, boy, did I need some inspiration!

SPREADING THE NEWS

A cancer diagnosis is the beginning of a long, complex and emotionally challenging journey that immediately overshadows everything else in your life. At first, it is a very personal thing; a close-kept secret that shrouds you and your spouse in an oppressive blanket of despair. Slowly, you begin to tell other family members and then your closest friends, partly because you feel they need to know and partly out of a need to share the immense burden. Very shortly after my diagnosis, I had told my children, my parents, my siblings, other close relatives and a few of my good friends. After about a week or so, I started thinking about who else to tell and how to tell them.

How do you tell people that you have cancer? Will they understand? Will they look at me differently? Will they treat me differently? Do I need to tell them? Do they really need to know? Will they really care? Ruth, Dianne and I talked a lot about this. I had no idea how people would react, particularly in light of the naïve reactions I myself had experienced when I learned about other people who had cancer. Ruth shared her own experiences, which I found very illuminating. She said that people react in many different ways. Some are very supportive while some go overboard with concern and treat you like a fragile piece of china. Others are so terrified by the whole idea of cancer that they don't say anything. Still others would like to be supportive but have absolutely no idea what to say, much like I was in the past.

I called my long-time friend, university roommate, best man and painless dentist, Steve. We have known each other for over thirty years and have always been able to talk about anything. He was noticeably upset at the news and very supportive, offering to help in any way he could and, as my journey continued, he played a central role at some key times. Steve told another old school friend, Dave, who I hadn't talked to in a long time. He called and we had a long chat, which meant a lot at the time even though we have not had much contact since.

As I started to open up more, I was anxious to tell my good friend Eleanor. As my first boss in the software business, she had become both a friend and a mentor and I placed a high value on her advice and her perspectives. She knew me professionally as well as anyone and we had shared enough personal stories and emotions that she could see through any false bravado and knew when I was bullshitting myself. We sat in the lobby of a downtown office building with a take-out coffee and talked a lot about how stressful it was working in sales and how detrimental it could be to your health. At the time, I still didn't know what I was facing and was particularly worried about whether the cancer had spread. My plan, I told her, was to try to make as much money as I could over the next few years so that I could either retire early to a lower stress lifestyle or be able to leave Dianne and the kids in a comfortable lifestyle if I should die earlier than my time. She looked at me in shock and then zeroed in on the essential flaw in my thinking. She said, "So you've just been diagnosed with cancer and your solution is to work even harder and add more stress to your life! Are you nuts?" She was right. It was nuts. But it highlighted one of most difficult challenges I continue to struggle with.

Methodically, I began to call other friends and acquaintances, not so much because I felt everyone should know, but that I felt it would be more personal if I told them myself rather than having them hear about it from others. They reacted in various ways, showing concern, commiserating with me and asking questions. Some continued to check up on me from time-to-time while others never mentioned it again, although I didn't hold it against them because I realized how difficult a thing it was to talk about. My daughter, Caralia, told her church group and her high school that I had cancer and had the entire community praying for me on a regular basis. In fact, some of our old neighbours and friends called after hearing my name mentioned in church. I was in good hands from a religious perspective, as my Aunt Molly made sure her entire Presbyterian congregation was praying for me also. My mother told me I couldn't go wrong when the Presbyterian's were on my side!

I was starting to feel a bit better as I spread the news and received such a warm outpouring of support but, aside from Ruth, I had not had a chance to really talk about what I was feeling with anyone who had a similar experience. I knew that this was necessary and very important so I decided it was time to attend a meeting of the local Man To Man support group.

Man To Man is a wonderful support organization with chapters across North America. The local chapter has a strong affiliation with PMH and, along with its companion organization for spouses called Side By Side, meets twice a month in a central location. Dianne had spoken to one of the members the day I was diagnosed but I was not personally ready to take that step until November 5, several weeks later. I showed up at the meeting and was warmly welcomed by a number of the regulars. The most notable thing for me was the age of the attendees. I had to be at least ten to fifteen years younger than just about every man there. It brought to mind a newspaper article that Dianne had clipped out for me about an incontinence device called the "Geezer Squeezer". I honestly felt like I was at a meeting of my father's friends! I was quickly bombarded with questions about my numbers, who my doctor was and whether I had decided on a course of treatment yet. I found this latter question strange because I couldn't see how anyone could leave such an important decision for so long (I found out later that many men take months to make up their minds).

The meeting started with a statement of their principles and rules. They were there for support but not medical advice and there would be no doctor-bashing. Then each of the new guys was given an opportunity to tell their story and ask any questions they might have. It was a strange feeling to open up to men I didn't know but I surprised myself with how open I was and how much emotion I felt as I spoke. I had to pause a couple of times to avoid breaking into tears, which I saw several men do during their turns. One of the other new guys shocked the hell out of me by saying that he would have killed himself after his diagnosis had it not been for the support of his wife. Wow! There was a great sharing of advice, encouragement and recommended reading that I really appreciated. I became a little worried about all of the talk of incontinence and the liberal sharing of stories of dribbling, leaking, diapers and absorbent underwear. One guy wondered about taking a long flight only six weeks after surgery and received what I considered the best piece of advice of the night – "Just don't wear khakis!" It reminded me of some advice my friend Steve heard from an older fellow on the subject of aging – "Never pass a washroom. Never take an erection for granted. And be very, very careful when you fart!" Boy, did I come to learn the truth of this.

It was interesting that there wasn't as much talk about impotence, although I had thought it would be a bigger issue. It seems that, even amongst a group of men experiencing the same problems, it is a difficult thing to talk about. There were a few jokes about how your penis could disappear up inside your body after surgery, which was explained to me as being the result of shortening the urethra. I worried about this for quiet a while, particularly when I read about it in a book and found it to be a much talked about topic on the Internet.

Overall, I found the group to be very supportive and would highly recommend it to anyone. In one way, however, it scared me to see just how prevalent Prostate Cancer was and how significant it was to be able to attract twenty-some-odd guys two times a month. I don't attend very often now, which probably has more to do with the age difference than anything else, but I can honestly say that I got something new out of every meeting I have attended.

One remaining challenge loomed larger and caused me more worry than anything else. How was I to tell my work? What should I say to my boss? Who else should I tell? I was less than six months into my new job with the company and was technically still on probation. While I didn't think they would (or could) let me go due to a cancer diagnosis, I couldn't help but worry. I had responsibilities, bills, a mortgage... One saving grace was that I had closed a large software deal the month before and had thereby demonstrated my abilities and value to the company, but I wondered how much currency that held for me. The management team consisted of some great people, and I trusted that they would do the right thing, but I wondered how my co-workers, who were all young, energetic and health-conscious, would view me. Would they think I was weak or somehow "damaged" and therefore less capable of doing my job? Would I be the old guy with cancer? Would I not be given the really good opportunities because management thought they would be too stressful for me? Some of this was just the way my brain worked, but there was a core of legitimate concern based on stories I had heard and read. But I had to tell them something because I was going in for major surgery and would be away for some time.

The first major challenge was when and how to tell my boss. John was a much younger man – the nicest guy you could meet – who was relying on me to deliver a lot of new business. I felt that if I told him I had cancer and had to go in for major surgery he could (reluctantly perhaps) restrict my territory or feel that he would have to "back me up" somehow. I decided to wait until my six-month probation period was up (more for my own piece of mind) and then to play it down a bit. I sat down in his office and said, almost matter-of-factly, "I have to have my prostate removed because there is a little bit of cancer in it. I'll probably be off for a couple of weeks." He was very concerned and very supportive and assured me that I didn't need to worry about anything. We then talked about telling his boss, Andy, and how to tell the rest of our team. I told Andy myself, with much the same reaction. Andy felt it was good for people to know I was going through something like this, because I would benefit from their support. The reactions from both of them were a pleasant surprise.

John and I agreed to tell the rest of his team at our Monday morning meeting. These meetings usually covered sales forecasts, training, upcoming events and other administrative things so it took all of them by surprise when I announced, out of the blue, that I had cancer. I told them that I wanted them to know because they were my friends and that I would need their support personally and professionally over the coming months. I also wanted to encourage the guys to get tested and the girls to make sure the men in their lives were also tested. They were shocked and, while little was said at the meeting, they each talked to me afterwards expressing their concern and support. With this, of course, the word spread and many more people approached me. I started to experience some of the different reactions that Ruth had warned me about. Kerry, who worked with me, was very interested and asked many questions, showing genuine concern and compassion. Others seemed not to know what to say and even later rarely broached the subject. The guys who approached me were very interested in it from a personal perspective because it was a guy thing. I encouraged them to get tested and to learn as much as they could about the disease. I was a clear example of how it could strike any guy, any time.

I couldn't be more pleased at the degree of support that John gave me. He would often leave me a voice mail to tell me he was thinking about me. He told me he was amazed at how I was able to concentrate on closing a complex sales deal while I was undergoing testing for cancer. A week after I told him about my cancer, he received an invitation to the Bay Street Breakfast, a fund-raiser in support of the Prostate Cancer Research Foundation to be held in the heart of the Toronto financial district on November 22. He showed me the invitation and said, "Let's go!"

Interestingly, the event was sponsored by Ed Clark, the CEO of Toronto-Dominion Bank Financial Group, who was a Prostate Cancer survivor himself. I had heard about his story from a friend who worked at the bank. Apparently, he had sent an email to everyone in the bank to tell them about his cancer diagnosis and that he would be back shortly after treatment. To his credit, he barely missed a beat in jumping back into his high-powered job. After hearing him speak, I wrote him a personal email to thank him for his inspiration and for his support of "the cause". For me, it was the first clear indication that there could be life after cancer.

The breakfast itself was very interesting. John and I sat at a table with about eight other people. I saw Dr. Tracks and Lee-Ann (the head urology nurse) and I believe many of the other top Prostate Cancer specialists were there as well. Sitting beside me was a young researcher from PMH who started talking about her research on drugs that fluoresced in cancer cells, thus aiding treatment. Inevitably, she asked why I was there and I soon found myself telling my story in public for the first time. It felt very comfortable, and surprisingly liberating. As we listened to the speakers throughout the morning, John and I were amazed at the prevalence of the disease and clearly got the message that lack of awareness was the biggest issue facing the Prostate Cancer community. I came away thinking that I wanted to do whatever I could to spread the word and become a strong advocate for early testing. John wanted to send an email to everyone in the company to tell them about me and to share the information we received. I asked him to hold off until later because I didn't yet feel comfortable enough to have such a "big deal" made out of it. He finally did send it out the day after my surgery. I've reproduced it below.

> *As some of you know, Doug Gosling was recently diagnosed with Prostate Cancer. Obviously this has been a trying time for him and his family. The good news is he had surgery yesterday to remove his prostate and the Doctors believe the surgery was a success and that the cancer has not spread. Please join me in wishing Doug a speedy recovery.*
>
> *In typical Doug fashion, he is taking this adversity in stride and is now on a personal campaign to develop greater awareness about Prostate Cancer. Make sure you or your spouse gets checked annually. FACT: This is not just a cancer for men over 50 anymore. While men over 50 are the most likely to contract this form of cancer, cases have appeared with men in their 40's (Doug is an example) and as early as their late 30's. Here are some other facts to consider:*
>
> - *1 in 6 men will contract Prostate Cancer in their lifetime.*
> - *It is now the leading form of cancer, with slightly higher death rates than Breast Cancer. The good news is the death rates have been coming down due to early detection (GET CHECKED!!!), awareness, and research.*
> - *Poor diet is the major cause - Asian men have substantially less chance of contracting Prostate*

Cancer, unless they move to North America. Lack of vegetables combined with fatty, deep fried foods are the main causes.

Here are some health tips to consider:
- *Antioxidants are the key to fighting Prostate Cancer - These antioxidants neutralize the damaging molecules that can lead to Prostate Cancer.*
- *Vitamin E - found in nuts, sunflower seeds, olive oil, green leafy vegetables and whole grains.*
- *Minerals - Selenium - most commonly found in garlic, leeks, shallots and chives.*
- *Zinc - found mostly in meat, poultry, eggs and seafood, particularly oysters and crab meat, black-eyed peas, tofu and wheat germ.*
- *Lycopenes - found in tomatoes, papaya, watermelon and pink grapefruit. Processed tomatoes such as tomato paste or chilli sauce are higher in Lycopenes.*
- *Vegetables - like broccoli, cabbage, cauliflower and brussels sprouts.*
- *Omega 3 fatty acids - mostly in fatty fish like salmon, trout, anchovies, sardines, bluefish and white albacore tuna. Also found in leafy green vegetables, tofu, walnuts and canola oil.*
Green Tea - powerful antioxidant (I started drinking this every day now thanks to Doug).
- *Red Wine - yahoo!! Skins of purple or red grapes, berries, cranberries are good antioxidants as well.*
- *Soy.*

Please share this email with your family, friends and colleagues and wish me in joining Doug a speedy recovery.

John

What a prince! Not only did he want to get the whole company behind me, he wanted to use the opportunity to drive home an important health message to all the people we worked with. I can't thank him enough.

Soon, I began receiving emails from many of the people in the office offering their condolences and support. Several of the guys told me that they were going to get tested and that they were starting to drink green tea and red wine. One fellow asked me whether it was eight-to-ten cups of green tea a day or eight-to-ten glasses of wine. I suggested he do both to be sure! While I was touched by those who reached out to me this way, there were many others who have never acknowledged it. I understand their discomfort and hope only that they heed John's message.

As I began to tell more people at work, I also felt an obligation to tell some of my customers. On the one hand, I wanted them to know that I was going to disappear for a while, but I also wanted to deliver the message about early testing and generally about taking good care of oneself. In my business, I see a lot of the same people frequently and, while only a few ever become close friends, I do care about them. Overall, I received a great deal of support from those I told before and after my surgery and was amazed at how open they were about their own health experiences. While I sell my company's products and they spend their company's money, we are all just people with DNA that can turn against us.

I found it the same everywhere. The more people I told about my situation, the more they told me about their stories. It's incredible how many people have had their lives touched by cancer. One fellow told me about his Testicular Cancer scare. Another told me that he was regularly having cancerous skin lesions removed. One of the ladies I worked with told me about the huge Liver Cancer tumour that her husband had removed. Everyone has an aunt, mother, grandmother or friend of the family who has had or is fighting Breast Cancer, and many knew men (typically older) who had Prostate Cancer. I had a long chat with one woman whose husband had died of Brain Cancer many years ago and who almost lost her son in a horrible accident. And the stories were not all about cancer. I heard about one spouse who was fighting severe depression, about another fellow who was diabetic and yet another who suffered from chronic asthma. I shared a few serious moments with one of my customers whose father was dying of Brain Cancer and spent an hour with another executive going through the results of his annual physical in amazingly open detail.

This was a catharsis for me because it put my situation in much clearer perspective. There are so many stories in this world and everyone has a life full of joys and tribulations outside of the context in which we all interact on a daily basis. We're all human after all! And while I knew that I needed to focus on *me* in order to fight this disease, it was oddly comforting to know that there were so many other people focusing on their own "me". And, on the other hand, it was just plain nice to talk to business associates about personal things. It puts all of your relationships into perspective.

It was equally gratifying to have so many people come up to me and tell me that they were getting tested or that they were marching their spouses to the doctor to get tested. My boss John became much more health conscious and our team's number one objective became "good health". I started to see how important it was to get the word out. If, out of all the people I told, even one of them detected Prostate Cancer early and had it successfully treated, I would have done some good. So I decided to become an advocate for healthy living and early detection. I realized I didn't need to be out waving a placard on the street corner, and I certainly didn't have the profile to do the talk show circuit, but I knew I could help in other ways.

Ironically, shortly after my surgery, I was asked by the PMH Foundation if they could use my story as part of their fundraising efforts. Every year, they send a letter to prior donors with a personal appeal from a cancer survivor/patient. Women get a letter from a woman and men get a letter from someone like me. My letter read as follows (below a lovely picture of my smiling "I beat cancer" face):

> *Dear Mr. Smith*
> *I'm sending you this letter because you were kind enough*
> *to send a charitable gift to Princess Margaret Hospital in*
> *January, 2002.*

*Your gift of $xx was put to good use (cancer research)
and it put <u>you</u> in the good company of a long line of
Canadians that have supported the Hospital's life-saving
work for nearly 50 years.*

*I hope you'll take just a moment to read my story. It
contains valuable information for you (about your
health), but it's objective is also to ask you to once again
help people living with cancer by renewing your support
of the Princess Margaret Hospital.*

*Let me begin by telling you what I was. I was a "Type
A" personality. You know the type. Workaholic. High-
pressure sales job. Long hours. Commute. Mortgage.
Bills. Go, go, go. Faster, faster, faster.*

*Now I'm none of that. In seconds, it all changed. Now,
I'm a husband. A father. And I'm a cancer survivor.
That's all I am. Those three things. Everything else is a
distant second.*

I mentioned I work in sales?

*Relax. I don't want to sell you something. On the
contrary: I want to give you something.*

*On behalf of the wonderful caregivers at Princess
Margaret Hospital, I want to give you some advice.
"Man-to-man," as the saying goes. That's because the
advice concerns Prostate Cancer, a disease that all men
should be knowledgeable about.*

*I'd also like to give you an opportunity to help – not only
yourself – but others, too. In return, all I ask is that you
make a gift today to help the thousands of Canadians
(and their families) who, on this very day, are struggling
with cancer.*

You could match your last gift. Or give whatever you

feel you can afford. I know your gift would be accepted most graciously by the group of people I'm about to tell you about. They work hard every day to save lives. And when you support this work, you help save lives too. A life like mine. Or maybe the life of someone you love.

Now, as I was telling you…

In an unusual turn of events, I found that one of the symptoms of my Prostate Cancer diagnosis was a major case of verbosity. That's right. I just couldn't stop talking about it.

And because Prostate Cancer is "a guy thing," I found that I wanted to tell the men I know – friends of mine, colleagues, relatives – to please have a check up. I'm only 49, after all. That's young; especially when you consider that the average age for Prostate Cancer is 65.

So when I returned to work, I told my colleagues about my experience – and sure enough, everyone had questions. Even the younger guys I work with. Guys in their 20s and 30s who are into fitness, taking care of themselves… they all had questions and concerns.

Any my advice is always the same, and it's three-fold. So this is the advice I mentioned I'd give you:

First, take care of yourself. Early detection (of any cancer) is still the best medicine. So… get a check-up! Do it this week. Do it soon.

Second, educate yourself. You can start right now, by checking the Send Me Information box on the enclosed invitation form. The team at Princess Margaret Hospital will send you a free brochure on prostate health.

And believe me, you'll be amazed at the simple preventative measures you can take. In terms of diet, for example, did you know that tomato juice has been found to shrink – and even prevent – cancerous tumours? Same with broccoli. Before, I didn't know any of this stuff. Now, I know it all. (You should know it all, too.)

Third--- make a donation to cancer research. Send your gift today, before you put my letter aside. (Perhaps you'll even make your gift a monthly contribution.) Here's why I feel your gift today is so important, and will be so very helpful:

While Princess Margaret Hospital is a Canadian hospital, it is recognized as one of the top cancer research centres in the world.

Of course, I wondered how this was possible. How does Canada (with such a small population) compete with the best hospitals in the U.S., Europe, and around the world?

Soon enough, I learned it was because of donations. For fifty years, people have been sending donations to Princess Margaret Hospital. And I can tell you, I was a direct beneficiary of that long tradition of support and generosity.

Because of those generous people, my cancer experience was as positive as it could have been. I sometimes can't believe I say that, especially given the fact that I was such a wreck when I was first diagnosed.

But, it's true. Just being there, surrounded by these caring people – all experts in their field – really helped to strengthen my mental state at that time. Translation? I was scared – scared out of my wits – but somehow, the Princess Margaret team managed to instil a calm in me.

And sure enough, I soon found myself going from, "My God, I have cancer!" to "I can beat this. I know I can beat this."

That's why I volunteered to share my story. The Princess Margaret team helped me so much, and I'm so grateful, that I needed to give something back, to help people who were in a situation like mine.

And in recalling my cancer experience for the purpose of this letter, I realized it was the people on staff that made all the difference to me.

There was Andrew Matthew, a counsellor in Patient and Family Support Services. When I was introduced to Andrew, I was still in shock from my diagnosis. Somehow, Andrew (and his vast array of resources) brought me around, almost full circle, so that I could deal with my cancer, understand it, and prepare to fight it.

Andrew had advice on those things we just don't think about…like whom should you tell about your cancer? Which, if any, of your co-workers should know? And what about family? What about friends? Andrew was helpful on all of these fronts. (Andrew even advised me on how to help my 20-year old son, who took the news especially hard.)

You see? These are the things I remember. The people.

There was Lee-Ann, too, the nursing coordinator with the iron fist and heart of gold. Lee-Ann's was a friendly face I always looked forward to seeing. Lee-Ann (like everyone there) just seemed to have some innate knowledge of what I was going through. I could sense it. And it meant a lot to me.

And there was Dr. Tracks, generally regarded as one of the top five oncologists in the world. Yet when he talked with me about my cancer, and how he intended to treat it, it was like we were neighbours chatting over the backyard fence. He put me that at ease.

*These seem like small things, I know – but if you ever
have an experience like mine, you'll quickly find that
these are, in fact, the biggest things of all. The people.
The people that help you through the most trying and
frightening experience of your life.*

*After my diagnosis, I might have curled up in a ball,
and shut things out. But instead, I'm talking about it;
I'm getting involved in projects that will ultimately help
people – projects like this letter. Let's just say I didn't
make it to this point on my own!*

*I made it here because of the wonderful group of people
who are completely dedicated to finding a cure for cancer.*

*And I made it here because people like you decided one
day to join in and help. You helped simply by sending
a donation. I hope you'll continue with that generous
support. You don't realize just how much you helped me.
So please, take my word for it – you helped me more than
you'll every know. And I thank you for it. Thank you for
giving.*

*Yours sincerely,
Doug Gosling
Cancer survivor*

It still brings a tear to my eye when I read it, and it's about me!

Apparently the letter was quite successful and the Foundation sent me a personal note that one of their contributors addressed to me. It felt damn good! I felt that I had done something very worthwhile and it reinforced my commitment to helping out wherever I could. I wanted to give back something to the caring folks at PMH who took such good care of me as well as raise awareness of Prostate Cancer.

Through all of this – as emotional as it was – I developed a degree of openness that I never knew I was capable of. I had never talked to so many people about something so personal ever in my life. I took a risk (because I didn't know how people would react) and it paid off enormously for me. Now I talk to anyone who will listen and even some who don't seem to want to. I never let an opportunity go by to tell someone to look after themselves and I'm right there with all the facts and figures to try to scare the hell out of them. Dianne says I act like a reformed smoker and, in many ways, I guess that's true. She often has to take me aside to tell me to stop talking about incisions, erections and pissing my pants!

In spite of this openness and outreach to literally hundreds of people, I learned one other very important lesson. I think it was Ruth who first told me about "toxic personalities" and I came to quickly understand what she meant. There are people – friends, acquaintances, co-workers and even family members – who are "toxic" to your health and well-being. These are people who raise your stress level every time you talk to them or who find some way to make life difficult. In the past, I would try to appreciate that everyone had their quirks and that I should just ignore them. Or worse, I would put up with toxic behaviour out of some twisted sense of duty or because I didn't want to offend anyone. Well, screw them! When you are faced with a life-threatening disease, and dealing with your own mortality, you quickly realize that you don't have time enough on this earth to waste on people like that. Concentrate on the people who care about you and who make you feel good. Don't waste one precious minute on people who make your life miserable. What possible reason is there for you to accept a higher level of stress that will push you more quickly into the grave? So I say get rid of the stress. Get rid of the toxic people in your life. I choose to concentrate on my own life, on those who love me, and on getting better.

THE DARK DAYS
WAITING FOR SURGERY

What am I gonna do when the morning comes?
What am I gonna do when the night is gone?
What am I gonna do when the sun shines in
And I'm still lying here,
Drowning in a mystery?

What am I gonna say to all my friends who call?
What am I gonna do when they ask me why?
How am I gonna tell them all I want to do
Is just keep lying here,
Wandering through a mystery?

> *Nobody really knows the price that I have paid.*
> *Nobody really knows the sacrifice I've made.*
> *Nobody really knows just why I'm so afraid,*
> *Afraid to face the world this way.*

What is it gonna take for you to understand?
What is it gonna take for me to turn around?
How am I gonna find the strength to take your hand
To carry me away,
Away from all the mystery?

I don't know what you've gotta do to make me smile?
I don't know what you've gotta do to make me laugh?
I really wish that even for a little while
That I could find my way,
My way out of this mystery?

Nobody really knows the price that I have paid.
Nobody really knows the sacrifice I've made.
I wish that for just one time, I weren't so damned afraid
And that I could finally find my way.

Doug Gosling 2003

Waiting, waiting, waiting.

I had made my treatment decision very quickly - more or less on the day of my diagnosis, and now I had to wait for surgery. While some people take a lot longer to make up their mind, I had no interest in stretching this out any longer than necessary. I was angry and scared and I needed to do something, to be in control. One fellow I met took ten months to make up his mind, but he was a Gleason 6, no palpable lumps, and was taking hormones to slow the growth of the cancer until he did make up his mind. He also had more choices in that he qualified for Brachytherapy, something that I was not eligible for. Personally, I doubt if I could have waited that long. I'm the kind of person who collects the facts quickly and makes a decision. But that's just me. It's very important that you take whatever time you feel comfortable with to make the decision that's right for you. Going through all of this is bad enough without second-guessing your decision when it is far too late to turn back!

I had little choice but to wait. I had given up my original surgery date of December 3 without a second thought when I switched from Dr. Bones to Dr. Tracks. While even the original date meant a long wait, at least it was a firm date and now I had nothing. At the time, the average wait for cancer surgery in Toronto was sixty days and all indications were that it was going to get a lot worse as the anaesthetists continued their job action. They still hadn't allocated the surgical resources to the doctors for the new year and there were rumours in the local news that more hospital cutbacks were coming in January. The only hope I had was that someone would cancel out before Christmas. I was on the top of the waiting list mainly because of my age and also because I wasn't on blood thinners like many of the older men were. That meant I could go under the knife immediately without risk of bleeding out, while other guys would have to wean off their medication. I quietly and selfishly prayed that someone would chicken out. In the meantime, I could only wait, with a gnawing fear in my gut.

While I waited, I used the time to read more and research extensively on the Internet. I wasn't trying to second-guess my decision, but I wanted to know everything I possibly could about what had happened to me, what was going to happen to me, and what could happen to me. I wanted to see pictures and tables and statistics and I wanted to know what the probability was for successful treatment and what the chance of recurrence was. I searched high and low for anecdotal stories from other Prostate Cancer victims to get a feel for what I might have to go through, physically and psychologically. One night, Dianne and I attended a Prostate Cancer Awareness Night hosted by Man To Man. This was, of course, attended primarily by older men and their spouses and both of us felt somewhat out of place. I was already feeling like I had crossed a line into some other dimension and, while I was now a member of the club that no one wants to join, I felt distant even from the other members of the club. Some of the fellows that I had met at the previous meeting tried to make us feel at home but I kept thinking that I was somehow in the wrong place, and certainly at the wrong time of my life. We chatted for a long time with the fellow who had the Gleason 6 score and was taking his time deciding. Dianne told me later that, at the time, she was thinking, "Why can't Doug be a 6?"

In spite of our mild discomfort, we found the information session very informative. A well-know oncologist was the first speaker and he did a great presentation on nerve-sparing radical prostatectomies with extensive facts and figures on the risks and probabilities of impotence. It was truly an eye-opener for me. While I knew that the odds of regaining potency were much lower when one nerve is sacrificed, I was shocked at how bad they were. It seemed that all I had going for me were my age and the skill of my doctor. It was the first time I had really confronted this issue and it scared me almost as much as the cancer itself. As for Dianne, she was hearing some of the facts for the first time and I think it really hit home with her.

The second speaker of the evening was Lee-Ann, Dr. Tracks' nurse-coordinator. She gave a very practical and humorous talk on Kegel exercises and how important they were to regaining continence. There wasn't a guy in the room who wasn't squeezing his cheeks together as she talked! I was less concerned about incontinence than I was about impotence and the fact was my odds of regaining full continence were one heck of a lot better. Again, my age was a big plus in this. We left the session holding each other tightly and with both our heads spinning.

As my mind processed a steadily growing river of information, and as I became increasingly obsessed with anything relating to Prostate Cancer, I began to notice interesting little things such as just how often I had to urinate. And when I started thinking about it, I realized that I had not noticed any symptoms like that at all prior to my diagnosis. While frequent urination is often associated with getting old, it shouldn't happen to someone of my tender young age. Then Dianne reminded me of the many times that I called from my car on the way home from work to make sure the front door was unlocked, the bathroom was empty and the way clear because I had to rush in and "pee like a racehorse". And I started to notice how difficult it was to get rid of those last few dribbles. Looking back now, I believe these were symptoms of the cancerous tumours constricting my urethra where it passed through the prostate, but I guess they weren't bad enough for me to really take notice. I had also noticed that my erections where no longer of the raging variety and I believe this too was related to the cancer.

I felt like I had to do something while I was waiting. I was a control freak, remember, and here I was with nothing to do but wait, hope and worry. And did I worry! I needed to take control of something - anything - so I decided to focus on changing my eating habits. Frankly, they hadn't been that great. I was a snacker and I loved big meals with lots of meat and gravy. I could down a couple of large boxes of New York Fries, smothered in salt, without blinking an eye. It showed in my weight but I also began to realize that this kind of eating wasn't good for my health. Dr. Tracks had told me not to go overboard until after surgery, but he did suggest that losing ten pounds would help with the surgery and my subsequent recovery. Certainly, my appetite wasn't what it used to be (I wasn't in the mood to eat very much at all) but I knew I could do better. I had some guidelines that I picked up at the Bay Street Breakfast and the Prostate Centre at PMH had a great cookbook that was designed to help in the prevention of Prostate Cancer. It was a little late to try to prevent it, but I reasoned that the same diet might slow down the cancer while I was waiting. So I started to cut out red meats, dairy products, desserts and generally anything that was fatty, greasy or overly sweet. This was quite a change from my usual diet but having cancer proved to be a powerful incentive. I also started taking a variety of supplements that were marketed to supposedly, possibly, maybe reduce the chance of getting Prostate Cancer (such as Selenium, Vitamin D, Vitamin A and Saw Palmetto) with the hope of slowing it down while I waited for surgery. Nancy managed to get me some samples of a supplement made from red clover, which was showing some early success, but I couldn't take them for long since they thinned my blood and would prevent me from having surgery. For the same reason, I kept away from Vitamin E, which is another recommended supplement. There's a lesson here - make sure you know the effects of what you are taking. I have no idea whether any of this helped to slow the growth of my cancer tumours prior to surgery, but I did lose about ten pounds and, even more importantly, I felt like I was doing something.

But whatever I did, it wasn't enough. There is nothing that can make you feel so utterly out of control as cancer. It wasn't my fault! I didn't deserve it! And I was too damn young to get Prostate Cancer! All of these things went through my mind minute-by-minute, hour-by-hour and day-by-day. I plunged into the deepest depression I had ever experienced. I felt as lost as if I had fallen off the back of a cruise ship in the middle of the Atlantic. My family doctor, Dr. Gates, saw this coming and had prescribed some sleeping pills. While I don't like to be drugged up, I found I couldn't sleep without them. I would simply lay in bed thinking about cancer. My mind would go over and over the testing, the diagnosis, the material I had read, the odds of cure, the odds of recurrence …. around and around. And when I finally fell asleep, I dreamed about it.

Just having cancer is enough to turn your whole world upside down, but the fact that I didn't have a surgery date made it hundreds of times worse. It was rapidly becoming a huge problem for me and the weight of it was almost palpable. I bugged the hell out of Andrew and Dr. Tracks but there was nothing they could do about it. I had to wait, knowing that this horrible, poisoned thing was growing inside me. If my mind was running in high gear when I was trying to sleep, it was in overdrive during the day. I wondered (sometimes aloud) why this had happened and, especially, why it had happened to me. Was I meant to die? Was it something programmed into my DNA that dictated I wasn't going to live a full lifetime? Was it fate? Karma? Just plain bad luck? I had always thought of myself as one of the good guys. Why didn't this happen to the bad people? It just didn't seem fair! There are some people who get a great thrill out of risking their lives, of staring death in the face, and I admire their courage. Perhaps they have a much better understanding of life and death by pushing themselves to the edge. But I'm not one of them. Death has always been an abstract concept and not one to keep me awake at night.

As the days went by it became an incessant part of my waking thoughts. I could talk to Dianne about it, and sometimes Ruth, but otherwise the questions just ricocheted around my head with no answers. There were many times when I wished there were some other guys around my age with Prostate Cancer that I could talk to, but everyone seemed to be a lot older and already retired. Just thinking about that emphasized how unfairly young I was to get this disease.

I thought about it every time I urinated. I imagined the stream of urine passing through my cancer-riddled prostate. Each time I had an erection, I wondered whether I would ever have one again. I began to look at my penis like it was some kind of foreign object, even though the cancer didn't have anything to do with it directly. It was just a poor victim. Ruth told me once that she had thought of her cancer as an alien creature growing inside her that she wanted to get out right away. She had her surgery within days of her diagnosis and couldn't imagine how awful it must be for me to be carrying it around for as long as I did, growing insidiously deep inside me, cell after cell mutating into something that wanted to kill me. I soon realized what she meant and, yes, it was awful.

My emotions were going crazy. On the rare occasions that I forgot about it for a few minutes - when I inadvertently allowed myself a moment of peace - I would catch myself and wonder what the hell I was doing. I felt like I shouldn't be laughing about anything. Watching television or movies became an ordeal because I would get overly emotional at the silliest thing. I felt like crying even over happy endings. I swear that I even got choked up watching one of Dianne's decorating shows! And it wasn't any better for her. In spite of the brave front she put up, she would burst into tears at a moment's notice and it broke my heart because I knew that I was the cause of it. Meanwhile, Caralia was dealing with it in her own way. Although we didn't talk about it, I knew it was on her mind and that she was talking about it with her friends.

Day by day it seemed to get worse. I was falling uncontrollably into a deep pit of cloying darkness that felt almost physical. Nothing else seemed very important to me any more. The cancer had become my number one priority and my biggest obsession. I lost all interest in news and current events and didn't care if I missed the latest episode of my favourite television shows. Sadly, Dianne and I decided that we would just skip Christmas that year because we felt like there was just nothing to celebrate. The only thing I wanted for Christmas (that we all wanted) was a surgery date.

I also found that I couldn't work with the same intensity that I had before. Work became an exercise in coping. In some ways it was good to work because it gave me something else to think about, but I found myself sitting in meetings with one half of my mind concentrating on the matter at hand and the other thinking about my cancer. Sometimes I would manage to push it away for a while but it always came rushing back with a vengeance. It was pulling me down both mentally and physically. Looking back, I wonder how I could even work at all.

While I was somehow able to hide my emotional fragility at work (at least I think I did), there was no way I could hide it from my family and friends. I was losing weight and developing dark bags under my eyes. Looking in the mirror, I could see for myself how drawn and sad I looked. I couldn't even manage to smile convincingly. I was honest about it. I told them all that I was just not handling it very well and, frankly, I didn't care that I might appear weak to them. For the most part, everyone was very considerate and I appreciated it more than they could know. Poor Dianne was horribly worried about me and felt completely helpless, all while she was dealing with her own feelings of depression over my illness. My Mom and Dad called me every single day to ask how I was and to let me know that they were thinking about me, which meant so very much to me. Meanwhile, I had two teenagers in the house who, in spite of everything, continued to act like teenagers. They bitched and complained about everything and nothing and constantly fought amongst themselves. On more than one occasion, Dianne and I had to sit them down and tell them point-blank that we did not have the emotional capacity to deal with their petty arguments and that they needed to contribute to lessening the level of stress in the house. Caralia seemed to get it but Sean never did. It's hard for kids.

As I struggled through each day (drugging myself to sleep at night), I realized that something else had profoundly changed. I had gone to the doctor for what I thought was a routine test, expecting it to come back negative like always, and got hit right between the eyes. It couldn't have been more unexpected. My confidence had been shattered into a million pieces, gone now and forever more. I realized for the first time that I was not invincible and I started to think that anything bad was now possible, that where there was smoke, there likely was a raging fire waiting to fry my ass. I began thinking that every ache or pain anywhere in my body was somehow related to the cancer, and I'm quite sure that I even imagined some of them. At one point, I started to experience pain in my lower back and, while I had dealt with similar pain in the past, this time it seemed different. Drugs didn't seem to help and neither did my Chiropractor. My extensive research on Prostate Cancer told me that this could be a sign of metastasis to my spine and I became more and more convinced that this was what was happening to me. The pain was new and different. It didn't go away when I lay down and it was steadily getting worse, all signs of a spreading cancer. Finally, I couldn't live with the uncertainty anymore, and I went to see

Dr. Tracks. He listened patiently to my paranoid ramblings and told me that he didn't think it was the cancer spreading but that he would arrange for a CT scan if it would make me feel better. I didn't know how to react to that. He seemed so sure of himself and I began to feel a little foolish, but I couldn't let it go. I had to be doing something.

I went for a pelvic CT scan on November 18, about a month after I was diagnosed. Strangely, it was this experience more than anything else that made me feel like a cancer patient. With my blue PMH hospital card in hand, I entered the building and located the area where they did the scans. Dianne was with me, as always, and I think she was feeling the same sense of strangeness. At the time, we had no way of knowing whether this was a one-time thing or whether it was just the first of many visits to PMH for tests and treatment. We talked about how nothing would ever be the same anymore. This feeling of entering a new phase in our lives was reinforced when I was asked to fill out a routine information and consent form that had a section on medical history. You know the kind. Most people just tick off NO to everything (at least I always had) but this time I had to write in *Prostate Cancer*. Since they had given me a fat marker to use, the words appeared overly large, bold and colourful on the paper, emphasizing their significance. The technician read it over without raising an eyebrow and I realized that, for him, this was just a normal day-in-the-life. While I waited, I remember looking around and reflecting on the reality that everything around me existed just for cancer patients - that everyone who went into that room and lay on the table had cancer. It was the first time I felt that I had joined a community of people who, like me, had their lives changed forever.

The CT scan turned out to be no big deal. I had worried about being stuck in one of those long, narrow tubes and freaking out with claustrophobia, but I guess I had the wrong machine in mind because this one was more like a giant donut with a table that passed through the middle. The technician gave me an injection, telling me that I would feel some heat and that I may feel like I had to urinate. While I didn't feel the need to pee, I did feel a rather pleasant warmth flowing through my body, except that my feet were freezing (an inevitable side effect of being in a hospital). Before I knew it, it was all over. My next visit with Dr. Tracks confirmed that the scan showed nothing, which was a tremendous relief. We also learned that day my Gleason score was a 6 rather than a 7 (based on the PMH pathologist's review of the biopsy slides from Dr. Bones). Dianne and I could hardly believe it. Finally, a ray of hope. And my back pain? It just went away. Go figure!

As I plodded through these darkest of days, still waiting for a surgery date and still worrying about every little twinge, I was extremely fortunate to have a safety net, thanks to PMH. Of course, Dianne was always there for me, but she was having as much difficulty coping as I was. She wrestled with her own feelings of despair while trying to shore me up every minute of every day. We talked a lot about what we were both going through, which brought us much closer together, but we were like two people cast adrift in the middle of the ocean with only each other to hang on to for comfort and safety. And while I knew Caralia was having her own difficulties with it, we tried to protect her as much as possible from the perpetual darkness that surrounded us. If anything, she was a bright light to both of us. But we desperately needed help and we got it through The Prostate Centre at PMH in the form of Dr. Andrew Matthews and Jeanette McGrath.

We had already met Andrew during my initial visit to Dr. Tracks. He was part of the psychosocial therapy program at PHM and was there to help anyone who was a patient of The Prostate Centre. He was someone I could contact at any time. As a psychologist, he would sit and listen patiently to whatever was on my mind and provide advice and counselling to help me deal with the fact that I had cancer. He was a godsend for me. Someone I could reach out to when I felt like I couldn't take it anymore. But I quickly learned that he could help in other ways.

On October 28, I called Dr. Bones' office to ask for the results of the testosterone test I had requested on my first visit. I had totally forgotten about it, overshadowed as it was by my cancer diagnosis, so I left a message asking his office to call with the results and talk to Dianne if I wasn't available. Dianne called me at work the next day in panic. My testosterone level was fine but there was evidence of the "beginning of primary testicular failure"! What the hell did that mean? Was it related to the cancer? Was my body starting to break down? It scared me. I had visions of my balls falling off! I immediately called Andrew and left him a message, which he returned within an hour. A half-hour later he called back and told me that he had walked into Dr. Tracks' office and asked him what this meant. According to Dr. Tracks it was a normal thing and I need not worry about it. It just meant that my testicles were beginning to shut down sperm production, which happens normally as you get older. I breathed a huge sigh of relief and called Dianne right away. But think about this. You have a health concern and need to find out more about it. Normally, you call the doctor's office and then wait a week or so for an appointment. You never get to talk to the doctor directly. Yet, in this case, I had an answer from the best doctor I knew in less than two hours. Amazing!

I would come to rely extensively on Andrew's guidance in one-on-one sessions, but there was more help available for both Dianne and I. At our first meeting with Andrew, we had agreed to join a research study that he was doing jointly with Jeannette entitled, *Couples Decision-making and Adaptation in Prostate Cancer Treatment*. This required each of us to answer an endless number of questions during several interview sessions but also gave us access to several free-form counselling sessions. We used every minute we could to talk about how we felt and, in particular, to explore how to deal with my depression. They recognized what I was going through and assured me that it was normal to feel the way I did. I asked constantly, "Is it just me?", but they insisted that many cancer patients experienced the same fears, doubts and feelings of helplessness that I struggled with every day. I was not alone. We were not alone. And it felt so good to have understanding and caring people to talk to. One of the many things we talked about was my fear that I was not working up to par and my concerns that I was only six months with a new company. Andrew dissected these feelings with the skill of a surgeon and helped me realize that I didn't have to be the number one sales rep right now. That working at 80% instead of 120% was good enough while I was facing a life-threatening disease. He asked me if I would fire a good employee if I found out they had cancer and if I would expect them to keep working as hard as before. Putting it that way finally gave me some needed perspective.

During one of these sessions, Jeanette suggested that I see my doctor to get a prescription for anti-anxiety medication, as many other men in my situation had done. Since it generally takes several days to get into my family doctor, I dropped in to a local walk-in clinic the next day. Dr. Goodman was just setting up a new practice in the neighbourhood and he sat and talked with me for a good hour, trying to understand what I was feeling and ultimately recommended that I try an anti-depressant rather than anti-anxiety medication. I liked him immediately and felt very comfortable talking to him. While I started on the anti-depressants, we made arrangements to meet for an hour every Friday just to talk, and as the weeks went by this became a very important part of my treatment. I felt a little more in control. Now I had Dianne, Ruth, Andrew, Jeanette and Mory to talk to and I used every minute I had with each of them. While I don't think the anti-depressants helped much (there really wasn't enough time for them to work), my cadre of counsellors and confidants got me through the worst of the days. I don't know what it would have been like if things had dragged on any longer than they did but, for the time being, I was okay. Not great - just okay.

My life had changed tremendously in a few short weeks and I began to adapt to life as a cancer patient. Thankfully, I wasn't sitting through radiation or chemotherapy, and while I waited impatiently for a surgery date, I was thinking, researching, medicating and getting counselled on a regular basis. I started to incorporate all of this into my day-to-day life. My organizer started to fill up with appointments, phone numbers and addresses related to the new world in which I now lived. I bought a new wallet with an extra flip-up section to hold my PMH hospital card, my provincial health card and my health insurance card. Dianne found me a large wicker basket that I began to fill up with all of the papers, books, pamphlets, test results and other paraphernalia related to Prostate Cancer. This was always close at hand, by my bed or in the living room, and a day didn't go by that I wasn't poking around in it or adding something new. I felt like my life was slowly being poured into that box.

As I waited and worried, I started to think beyond the immediate medical aspects of my diagnosis and started to think about how my life was going to change. To be honest, I had never worried too much about things like insurance and was content with the knowledge that my mortgage would be paid off eventually and that I had many years left to make enough money for Dianne and I to have a comfortable retirement. Now I was faced with a couple of other scenarios. Perhaps I didn't want to continue working in a high-stress job until I was sixty-five. I knew that I needed to reduce the amount of stress in my life so I could fight off the cancer, so maybe I should be thinking about moving somewhere less costly and taking a job that had a lot less stress. What's wrong with selling plumbing supplies at Home Depot? What about my dream of retiring to a little bait shop on a lake somewhere? But then there was the other scenario where I didn't live long enough to even worry about retirement. What about Dianne and the kids? I had initially thought that I needed to start working even harder to earn more to provide for any eventuality, but Eleanor had made me realize how self-defeating that could be. I convinced myself that it wasn't necessarily bad to continue carrying my mortgage because it was life insured and, if I died, Dianne would have the house free and clear. I worried just as much about the short term because I knew that my emotional condition and the surgery would cause me to lose some of the momentum I had developed in my sales territory at work. But someone was looking out for us and, in November, I received a hefty commission cheque for the business I had closed in September. I took Dianne out for dinner and casually showed her my commission statement. We were going to be okay (at least financially)! We could make it through this. It was a huge weight off my shoulders. We decided then and there that we were going to celebrate Christmas after all. Caralia had wanted to all along and this finally freed us up enough emotionally to do it.

I had appointments with Dr. Tracks and Andrew on Tuesday, November 26 and by the time I got home, Dr. Tracks' assistant called to tell me I had a tentative surgery date of December 4! We were ecstatic and I barely listened to Mariko emphasizing that it was only tentative. But that was okay. It was something to hold on to. And, surprisingly, it was only one day later than my original surgery date with Dr. Bones! Apparently, another fellow had his surgery cancelled because his pre-admission x-ray showed a spot on his lung that could indicate that his cancer had metastasized, effectively eliminating surgery as an option for him. I really felt sorry for the poor guy, but that was life. It could easily have been the other way around. Mariko called back the next day with an appointment for pre-admission testing at the hospital on Friday, November 28, warning me once again that the surgery was tentative and that I may have to repeat pre-admission later. I brushed off the warnings and Dianne and I celebrated.

I arrived at the hospital a little early for my pre-admission appointment feeling more relaxed than I had for weeks. It was just the preliminaries, and it wasn't a sure thing yet, but it was something. Things were moving and I had steps to follow, which appealed to my usually ordered way of thinking. The surgery was getting close and I could feel the potential of it. At the hospital, I had to register at the pre-op desk where I made arrangements to get a private room, which cost me a bit over what my medical insurance would cover but I didn't want to have to share a room with anyone else. They sent me for a routine blood test and chest x-ray and, following that, I met with Lee-Ann, the nurse coordinator for The Prostate Centre at PMH. It was starting to feel very real. Lee-Ann asked me a bunch of questions, including some facts for the before-and-after assessment. While some of the questions concerned my current levels of continence and potency, I felt no discomfort sharing this with her as I had been talking openly about it for a couple of months. She went through what would happen the day of the surgery and afterwards and really made an effort to ensure that I was comfortable with everything. She confirmed to me that the other fellow's surgery had definitely been postponed which was something I really wanted to hear. She also told me that she had seen several men come in for Prostate Cancer surgery who were my age and even younger. One fellow was only thirty-eight years old. Another ran the Boston Marathon a year or so after his surgery and sent her his participation pin which she wears proudly on her uniform. I didn't see myself doing anything like that, but it definitely gave me hope. As I left, Lee-Ann gave me a shopping bag with a huge jug of bowel preparation powder and an apparatus to exercise my lungs after surgery. She wished me luck and told me not to worry. I left the hospital, bag in hand, feeling like I was finally getting somewhere. It was so close I could taste it.

But things were still not confirmed. I left a message with Mariko that Lee-Ann had confirmed the other fellow's postponement, but she called back to say there were other things going on that might prevent it from happening and that I would just have to wait. Since I had no insights into the mysterious world of medicine and surgical scheduling, I just let it be and tried to think positively. The depression that was my constant companion was held somewhat at bay, but it was still there and had the potential to come back and slap me in the face at a moment's notice. Dianne worried terribly about how I would handle a postponement. I tried not to think too much about it.

Then, on Sunday, Sean left home. During the weeks following my diagnosis, he had become increasingly difficult to deal with. In retrospect, I can't honestly say whether it was because he couldn't handle the fact that I had cancer, or that he was just tired of being parented and our new family crisis sped up a decision that was inevitable. Whatever it was, he just walked out the door and moved in with a friend, three days before my surgery. I felt a terrible loss, but I had to concentrate on my health and couldn't let this bring me down any farther than I had already been. While I kept reminding myself about this, it wasn't easy. He was my son. I loved him but I felt he had deserted me.

As I turned my attention to my upcoming surgery, I concentrated on getting things out of the way. I cleared up the bills and updated all our finances. I did a few household chores that I wouldn't physically be able to do for a while after surgery, I got my hair cut and I spent time with Dianne. While I was the one going in for the surgery, it was just as important to her as it was to me. We talked about what it meant and about our hopes for successful treatment. We prepared a list of questions for her to ask the doctor when he came out of my surgery and made plans to get her back and forth to the hospital. Two days before surgery we tried making love one last time, not knowing when or if we would ever be able to do it again. But I just couldn't get it up. Whether it was the depression, anxiety over the surgery, or the anti-depressants that I had been taking, I was unable to perform. We lay and held each other tightly and Dianne told me not to worry about it. She would rather have me alive.

That night I dreamed I had mixed up the dates and had missed my surgery.

SURGERY

The fact that I didn't have a surgery date for over a month had weighed heavily on me. It was like a cancer itself, eating away at my mind! I had no control. I had this horrible disease growing in my body and I wasn't able to do anything about it. I wanted it out. I wanted it over and done with. I wanted my life back. Everyone knew this, and Dianne was particularly concerned with what it was doing to me and to our whole family. She has told me many times how horrible it was to watch me fall deeper and deeper into depression, isolating myself, and how helpless she had felt at the time. When I finally got a date, however tentative, both of us had breathed a sigh of relief.

Mariko kept emphasizing to us that the date wasn't firm and that it might not be firmed up until as late as the day before the surgery. Other forces were at play here and I didn't understand why they couldn't just lock in the date. Perhaps it had to do with the politics around operating room allocations or something else that was out of Dr. Tracks' hands. I had no choice but to cling to the belief that it was going to happen, like a drowning man holding tightly to a lifeline tossed from a distant shore.

If the surgery was to go ahead, I had to prepare myself the day before. I had to use that huge jug of bowel preparation stuff to clean out my entire gastro-intestinal tract. Surely they could confirm the surgery before I went through that. At least I thought so. That morning I had to go downtown and meet with a fellow from my company who flew in to Toronto for some important meetings with a number of my customers on that day and the next. With the surgery going ahead, I was going to miss the meetings myself so I had to brief him as well as my boss,

John, who had readily agreed to substitute for me. We were sitting in a restaurant going over the details for the meetings when Dianne called to tell me that the surgery had been confirmed. Everything was a go. I could finish my meeting and be home by noon to start the bowel prep process. It was an incredible relief! I could feel the tension and uncertainty lifting from my shoulders. I was back in control. It was later that I found out she hadn't quite told me the truth.

Dianne and I have always been completely open and honest with each other, particularly about the important things. It was not easy for her to tell me that my surgery was confirmed when, in reality, it wouldn't be until the very morning of the surgery. But she knew how the uncertainty was killing me and, bless her, she didn't want me going through all of the preparation with the threat of cancellation hanging over my head. How she held it all together for those last twenty hours or so, I don't know. She was absolutely doing the right thing and had, in fact, talked to Andrew at PMH about it. It was a mini-conspiracy designed to get me through those last few hours. And if the surgery had been cancelled ... well, we would all just have to deal with it. It was worth the risk. Dianne insists that it wasn't a lie, it was an *omission*! As it turned out, my surgery went ahead, but the day after, all other surgeries were cancelled for an emergency lung transplant. It could just as easily have been my day. The situation was that fluid.

As soon as I arrived home and walked in the door, I changed into track pants and a t-shirt so I would be ready for the footrace to the toilet. I wanted to be able to sail into the bathroom ass-first while whipping down my pants so I could land squarely on the toilet. I was ready. The bowel prep was a powder in the bottom of a huge jug, which I had previously mixed with water and placed in the refrigerator (it was supposedly much easier to take if it was chilled). I had to drink a tall glass of this stuff every hour for what turned out to be about eight hours. It didn't taste as bad as I had thought, but it was explosively effective. By the time I was through, my anus felt like I had been wiping it with sandpaper and I felt weak in the knees. But was I ever clean!

Throughout the day, I thought constantly about the poor guy whose surgery time I was taking. I was sure he would much rather be having an enema than sitting around waiting to see if his cancer had metastasized, but my own incredible sense of relief overshadowed my compassion.

The day turned into the proverbial "night before" and I spent it getting ready by packing a few clothes and getting my survival package ready – toothbrush and toothpaste, a book, eye-glasses, wallet, etc. Dianne puttered around getting the house clean and ready for Caralia who would be left alone at least overnight as Dianne had planned on staying at the hospital with me that first night. My Dad called when I was upstairs alone in my room later that evening to wish me luck for the next day. Both of my parents had been great, calling me just about every day since my diagnosis, and I felt closer to them than I had ever felt before. As I sat on the bed, my stuff laid out neatly around me, Dad wished me luck and then choked up completely as he told me he loved me, for probably the first time ever. He couldn't finish talking and I could sense the tears welling up in his eyes. As I said goodbye, I promptly broke into tears myself. There is something so out-of-the-ordinary, yet incredibly touching, about your father crying over you. Sitting alone in my room, I came completely unhinged for the first time since my diagnosis. Why I had never really cried up to that point, I couldn't tell you. All of my emotions had seemingly been channelled into some kind of black hole and they finally bubbled up to the surface, triggered by the fears and sadness of my father as he faced the fact that one of his sons was being treated for cancer. Dianne came upstairs and found me sitting on the floor by the bed, in tears. She sat down beside me and held me in her arms as I cried, and told me that everything would be all right. Later, in bed, she hugged me so tightly I almost broke down again. As I drifted off to sleep, I wondered how I'd be that time tomorrow, cancer-free and carved up like a Thanksgiving turkey.

We awoke the next morning in plenty of time. There was just no way we were going to be late. At that moment, nothing else was as important to us as having that surgery. I got up, cleaned my teeth, shaved and had a hot shower, knowing it would be a couple of days before I could do that again. Standing under the hot water, I looked down at my penis and wondered whether the poor little fellow would ever be the same. Were my erections a thing of the past? Did it really matter to Dianne or I when my life was at stake?

As I was getting dressed, I thought about Caralia and Dianne and how they were feeling. Up to that point, it had truly been all about me and, to be honest, I was a glutton for all that attention. But Caralia was very, very sick (she is a high-risk asthma patient). For weeks, she had been suffering with a bad case of whooping cough (which I thought had gone the way of the Nehru jacket) that wiped her out completely and kept her out of school. A couple of nights before, Dianne had called the ambulance in the middle of the night when Caralia complained of a terrible headache, stiff neck and a high fever. The paramedics thought that she might have meningitis, which is a very rare, highly contagious and potentially dangerous illness, so they rushed her to the hospital (with Dianne at her side) and took them in through the back door of the emergency department. While I snoozed soundly, thanks to my wonderful sleeping pills, Caralia was put through a battery of tests including a very painful lumbar puncture (the worst pain she has ever felt). Thankfully, it wasn't meningitis but she was really not well. In spite of that, she told Dianne and I that she was fine and not to worry about leaving her alone. It was her turn to tell a lie. She was a very brave girl and I loved her dearly for it. Poor Dianne had no sleep that night.

So here we were. I was going into the hospital for major surgery and Caralia was going to suffer in silence at home. Just to keep it interesting, Dianne was feeling worse by the hour. I'm sure it was the stress of the previous couple of months, far too little sleep, and the strain of taking care of me as I held on to her for dear life. She had serious pain from acid reflux, a very sore throat and a worsening sinus infection. She was feeling miserable, but she too suffered in silence so she could concentrate on looking after me. In spite of what was happening to me, I thought about how lucky I was?

As previously arranged, Ruth arrived early in the morning - cheerful and loving -to take Dianne and I to the hospital. She had brought me a care package with a book, a teddy bear and a box of chocolates. The book and teddy bear were for me but the box of chocolates was for the nurses. This was a great idea and I highly recommend it. While you lay helpless in your bed following surgery, you are totally at the mercy of the nurses for your comfort and for just about everything else. They are all hard-working, dedicated and caring people who love to be appreciated and a box of chocolates (and donuts another night) at the nursing station is worth its weight in gold. Just remember to make sure they know it's from you. The teddy bear was perhaps the sweetest thing in the care package. Ruth told me how comforting it was to wake up and have something other than stiff hospital sheets and plastic tubes to touch and feel. She was so right.

But Ruth was not there just for me. She was there primarily for Dianne. She was there to hold her purse, get her coffee, check on things, remind her of all the questions she wanted to ask the doctor, and to provide a shoulder to cry on. She was there for Dianne (as Dianne had been there for her) so that Dianne would be there for me.

We arrived at the hospital and were directed to a comfortable waiting room. There was another family huddled together in the room and, while we wondered what their story was, we kept quietly to ourselves. I gave Dianne my wallet, which felt strangely like I was taking an irrevocable step. She told me I was lucky she wasn't going shopping! She ran around, gathering as much information as she could and ordered me a television for my room. She was all business and I felt like I was in the very best of hands. They could carve me up like a turkey and leave me helpless as a baby full of tubes and intravenous needles, but I knew that Dianne would be there to look out for me. It was a wonderfully comforting feeling.

I was expecting to be taken away and given a bag for my things but, to my surprise, a nurse showed me to the private room that would be my home for the next few days. Dianne and Ruth were sent down to the surgery waiting area while I changed into the standard, ugly, too-short hospital gown (I'm six foot two) and sat down to wait. As I sat there, I was thinking, "This is it. It's really happening. I'm going to get this out of me!" It wasn't long before this little guy showed up with a kit to shave my crotch. I don't know why, but I was expecting some ancient old nurse (at least a female) with a stern look and a straight razor. While I wondered how a guy got into a job like that, the magnitude of what I was doing overshadowed any sense of embarrassment or discomfort I would normally have felt. Besides, before this was all over, my genitals were going to be displayed in all their glory to a heck of a lot more men and women.

I didn't have to wait very long before a nurse came to take me to the pre-op room. Walking by the nurse's station, I noticed on the schedule board that I was Dr. Tracks' second patient of the day. Was that good or bad? Was it better to be first or second? Not that I could do anything about it, but these things do go through your mind when you're going under the knife. It's like the old adage about not buying a car built on a Monday. Maybe the doctor needs to warm up with the first one. Or maybe he'll be tired out and not as sharp for the second. Hmmmm.

The nurse led me though a set of swinging doors into a bustling area full of doctors and nurses. I felt out of place as I walked through in my gown and paper slippers, like a grade school student walking into the teachers' staff room. She took me into a long room lined with beds and set me up on a short gurney, covering me with a warm blanket. And I do mean warm. They put them in some kind of oven to heat them up and with all the cool air circulating up under my gown and around my privates, I really appreciated it. An older lady occupied a bed further down and I wondered whether she was there for cancer surgery as well. She could have been there for anything but, by this time, my whole world was cancer, cancer, cancer.

I lay there for about ten minutes alone, letting my mind wander back over all that had happened since October 15. For the first time, I felt very relaxed and unconcerned and, after a couple of minutes, my mind centered on just the space around me, the cool air, the warm blanket and the texture of the sheets. The depression and anxiety that had been my constant companions for so long had somehow disappeared and I experienced an incredible feeling of peace. I think the proper expression for it is that I was feeling "in the moment". It was most likely a combination of being committed to a course of action that had seemed so elusive for some time coupled with the realization that, in a couple of hours, the cancer would be gone, hopefully forever. I can't remember any other time in my life that I felt quite like that. The only images that come close are childhood memories of laying on my back on the cool grass looking up at the millions of stars in the sky, or more recent times when I floated alone in my kayak on a surface so perfectly smooth that I dare not disturb it with my paddle. At those times, I was intimately connected to nature but, this time, I was one with myself. Almost on cue, Dianne arrived to share the moment with me, having asked one of the hospital volunteers to track me down and lead her to me. It felt even more complete. Meanwhile, Ruth stayed in the waiting area to hold all of Dianne's stuff and to fetch food and coffee for the two of them. I found out later that my brother-in-law Bing had dropped by to sit with them for a while, which was very thoughtful (Dianne's sister Judy was married to Bing until she passed away from Melanoma).

The time grew closer and activity picked up around me. Several people came by to check the name on my hospital bracelet to confirm that I was the right person, including a young anaesthetist. He asked me several questions and told me it would not be long. I told him how sick I had gotten before from anaesthetic (puking for six hours after a double hernia operation still fresh in my mind) and begged him to do anything he could do avoid this. For me, nausea is worse than any kind of pain that can be inflicted and I hoped he had some special medication he could give me to avoid having to wake up to that. While he was there, an older doctor arrived who turned out to be one of my nephew Mike's clients and, coincidently, the chief anaesthetist at the hospital (my nephew had asked him to drop by). What luck! It was the young guy's boss and I hoped he would be sufficiently impressed to give me whatever magical, outrageously expensive drug they had to help me out.

After they left, I asked if I could have one last pee before they took me down, thinking that it would be a lot better for everyone when they cut into my bladder (I'm a very considerate guy and didn't want to piss anyone off – pardon the pun). Back in bed, I was given an injection to relax me even though I was feeling pretty relaxed already. Shortly after, Dianne and I said our goodbyes and I was wheeled off to the OR, wishing that she could have come with me.

My trek took me down several long corridors and a quick ride in an elevator before arriving in the operating room. Several gowned doctors and nurses scurried around getting things ready and a couple of them transferred me gently onto the operating table and strapped me down.

I was amazed at how narrow it was. I was six-foot-two and over two hundred pounds and I felt like I was strapped to a two-by-four. I realized that it would be easier for the doctor to get in close and personal. Both of my arms were strapped onto boards at the side of the table, which gave me a fleeting image of Christ on the cross. My gown came off and my arms were punctured with IV needles and wrapped with a blood pressure cuff. I remembered one old fellow at a support group meeting telling me how the surgery team had applauded when he walked into the operating room, telling him he was the star of the show. That was something I didn't need and I was thankful for the professional way it was all handled. I did ask someone how many people there were and was told that there would be two surgeons, the anaesthetist, and several nurses and that they were all there just for me. I felt so special.

Keeping in mind that it was December, it wasn't too surprising to hear Christmas music playing in the background, although I couldn't imagine that it would be very inspiring for a surgery. I asked if they switched it to something raunchy after I was out, but I never heard the answer. It was the last thing I remembered before the lights went out.

And then I woke up! It felt like I had been asleep for only a couple of minutes rather than several hours, but I knew immediately where I was and that the surgery was over. I felt drugged and was more or less unable to move (or maybe just unwilling). My first thought was to wonder if I could breathe, again remembering back to when I woke up after my hernia surgery in a panic because I couldn't catch my breath. But I was okay and, wonderfully, I had no nausea! What a relief that was.

Gradually, I slipped more fully into the world and tried a few tentative movements. There was definitely some pain, which I knew would get worse when the anaesthetic wore off, and I seemed to have a lot of tubes in me. Otherwise, I felt pretty good. Much sooner than I had expected, they wheeled me carefully back to my room and finessed me into my bed. Now that hurt! A lot! Everything was starting to hurt by then. Dianne must have been hanging out by the door with Ruth because, only a few minutes later, she tiptoed in and kissed me tenderly. Nothing could have felt better, except I didn't yet know the verdict.

Dr. Tracks had come out to see Dianne after the surgery was over to give her the results. Ruth knew that she would be too flustered to remember all the questions she wanted to ask so she wrote them all down for her. As it turned out, she was right. Dianne was in a blur, terrified about what she might find out. But Ruth sat right beside her and made sure she got all the details.

We knew what we didn't want to hear. If they had opened me up and found that the cancer had spread, they would have closed me right up without removing my prostate. But thankfully, that wasn't the case. Dr. Tracks told Dianne that everything had gone perfectly; it was a textbook operation. For some reason, they had booked a double session so they had lots of time to do the procedure. There was no visual evidence of spread and my lymph nodes looked and "felt" okay. So out came the prostate but not the lymph nodes. This was all good news. Great news, in fact. He said, "You'll be fine. Just fine!"

But was I cured? Intellectually, I knew that the immediate threat was over but that there was always a chance (small, I hoped) that the cancer could return sometime down the road. For the moment, though, that didn't matter. The tumour was out. After all of the waiting and agonizing and worrying, I had finally had the surgery. I reminded myself that the doctors referred to the surgery as the "gold standard" and that I had the best possible chance of a complete cure. Overnight, I went from the deepest, darkest time of my life to complete elation. I felt like I was on a tremendous high that nothing could dampen, not even the battered condition of my body.

Every muscle in my body felt incredibly weak and even the slightest movement triggered a sharp jab of pain somewhere. I inventoried my body. There were no compression stockings on my legs (which I had read about many times) and an oxygen tube was clipped to my nose. Intravenous tubes were taped to the back of my left hand, feeding me glucose from a bag that hung on the pole beside me as well as morphine from the metered pain pump that I had expected. A long catheter tube tugged at my penis and snaked out from under the sheet and down to some hidden spot at the side of the bed. Dianne told me later that she was shocked at the amount of blood in the bag but, thankfully, I never did see that. And I was surprised at another tube (a Jackson-Pratt catheter) that protruded from a hole in my abdomen to fill a large plastic bulb with more blood and other unspeakable fluids. Finally, a large blood-stained bandage covered the deep incision where Dr. Tracks had gone in after my prostate. My entire abdomen ached.

As my head cleared, thanks to the oxygen that I was breathing, I felt a strong urge to talk to my Mom and Dad. They had called me just about every day since I told them I had cancer and the memory of my Dad breaking down on the phone the night before loomed large in my mind. I had to hear their voices again and tell them that I was okay. It was the first call I made. They were both ecstatic to hear from me and it put my mind at ease, contributing to my growing sense of peace and emotional well-being. Dianne had already called them as well as Caralia, my office and my friends and took charge of making sure everyone was kept up-to-date on my progress. Occasionally the phone would ring and Dianne would handle those calls as well. It was just as well because I didn't really feel like doing it myself.

So let's talk about pain. I had read somewhere (one of the countless books or articles that I had inhaled over the previous couple of months) that the operation was "no big deal". Well, maybe I'm just not Superman, but this operation *was* a big deal. This was major surgery! And it hurt like hell! As the anaesthetic from the operation wore off, I experienced the full impact of the slicing and dicing of my abdomen. One of my doctors told me that Dr. Tracks had to cut through five different layers of skin, fat and muscle to get to my prostate and that each of these layers had to be sewn or stapled back together. Because the prostate rests against the rectal wall, by starting from the front of my body, he had to cut all the way through me. No wonder it hurt! But I did have some help in the form of the morphine pump. There is nothing worse than lying in pain in a hospital bed waiting for a busy nurse to come in with your pain medication. The pump solves this problem by allowing the patient to push a button to administer a measured dose of medication when the pain got too bad. It has a safety feature that only allows a certain amount to be administered within a specified period of time to prevent overdose. The device became a very close friend during the hours after my operation but, ironically, the nurses told me that I wasn't using it as much as most patients did after similar operations. While I had always feared the pain of a major operation, I found that I actually had quite a high tolerance for it. For some reason it just didn't bother me as much as I thought it would. As the days went by, I continued to use less than I was allowed and I began to feel almost comfortable with the pain. Perhaps it was because the pain continually reminded me that the cancer had been removed and that the immediate threat was gone. Or perhaps there's a streak of masochism in my makeup. Whatever the reason, I found myself saying, "It's only pain." And, for some time after that experience, this was my mantra.

As I lay in my bed, happily pushing on my morphine button and revelling in the aftermath of a successful surgery, the rest of the world started to find its way back to me. I had been inwardly focused for so long, feeling sorry for myself as I tried to cope with the fact that I had cancer and completely disconnected from what was going on around me. But, all of a sudden, I was ready to party. The private room was a great idea, because I could have all sorts of people in without disturbing anyone else. Dianne and Ruth stayed with me for the rest of day while several friends came by to see me. Nancy was in the hospital and came by to check on me. I think the doctor in her wanted to check my stitches and staples but there are certain things that friends don't need to see! Andrew came by too, which meant a lot as he was the one who had helped me most to get through the dark days. After Nancy and Andrew left, two of my best friends, Greg and Steve came by for a longer visit and Dianne and Ruth left us alone for a while. They brought me books and magazines (I received a lot of these but didn't actually read very much) and Steve brought me this garishly coloured walking cane to help me get around. While I couldn't really get up or do anything physical, I had enough morphine in me to be feeling pretty good mentally so we talked and laughed and had a great time. The worst part of it was that I was very dehydrated and my mouth tasted like a sewer. I desperately wanted something to drink, but the nurses wouldn't let me have anything except ice chips and I went through a huge supply of that. In what was one of the most memorable experiences of the day, Greg and Steve took turns spoon-feeding me ice chips, as I was too weak to do it myself. There they were, standing at the side of my bed with a bag full of blood-red urine hanging beside them, spoon-feeding me. It gave true meaning to the word friend and it is something that I will never forget (nor will I let them forget it!).

As the day went on, Ruth and Dianne started to worry about the effect that all of the partying was having on me. Ruth in particular wanted everyone to leave but is too nice a person to have said anything, and Dianne was happy to see me enjoying myself after the months of misery the cancer had dragged us through. I was clearly high from the morphine and while I was definitely feeling some pain, I was having more fun than I could have imagined. Ruth seemed to know that it was going to catch up with me and it turned out that she was right. When Greg and Steve eventually left, Ruth and Dianne started to get ready to go. Dianne had originally planned to stay overnight, but Caralia was at home sick and alone and I assured her that I would be just fine on my own. But before they could make it to the door, it hit me. A wave of nausea so intense that I could barely speak hit me like a brick wall. I had been so ecstatic coming out of the operation without a hint of nausea, but it finally caught up with me. I thought I was going to die. I would have gladly traded ten times the amount of pain for the feeling that came over me. One of the girls rushed down to the nurse's station and, within minutes, a nurse arrived with a bag of anti-nausea medication that she hooked into my intravenous line. It was amazing! Within about twenty to thirty minutes, the medication washed the nausea completely out of me and I was back to normal. Or at least back to the normal post-operative condition I was in. But the party was definitely over and I was ready to take it easy. Strangely enough, I wasn't tired either from the operation or from the medication. I thought I would just go out like a light, but I found myself laying there wide-awake.

We insisted that Ruth go home after that. She had been so great and supportive throughout that long, eventful day and I loved her for it, but she really needed to get some rest. Dianne decided to stay with me in case I was sick again so we asked the nurses to roll in one of those huge, reclining easy chairs for her to sleep in. I have no idea how old those things were or what sadist designed them, but Dianne could not get comfortable no matter how she positioned herself. And to top it all off, she still wasn't feeling that well herself. As she twisted and turned to find some minimum amount of comfort, the chair creaked and squealed like a trapped animal, the sound seeming to echo throughout the night time stillness of the hospital corridors. Before too long, we realized that neither of us was going to get any sleep. Dianne wanted desperately to stay but I insisted that she go home so, reluctantly, she packed up and headed out somewhere around 1:00 or 2:00 am. She soon found out that nothing much was going on around the hospital at that time of night. There were no visitors, no throngs of people milling around the ground floor coffee shop and no taxis lined up outside. She found a phone to call for a taxi and stood alone by the back door waiting. After about a half hour, she stepped out to see if the taxi was coming and found herself locked outside in the middle of the night, all alone in the dark! After everything she had been through that night it was icing on the cake. Eventually the taxi came and she made it home while I lay wide-awake in my hospital room, totally oblivious to her plight. What a day it had been for both of us.

Perhaps being in a deep coma during surgery used up my sleep quotient for the week because it seemed to me that I lay awake for most of the night. I had expected to be weak and exhausted so I was surprised at how difficult it was to fall asleep, although I must have fallen asleep at some time during the wee hours. I awoke with a start at the sound of a construction crew that had to have been right under my window. I heard jackhammers and saws and other machinery as I realized that it was 8:00 in the morning and the hospital construction had shifted into high gear. As I lay there waiting for a nurse or someone to arrive, I found myself clinging tightly to the teddy bear that Ruth had given me. It felt soft and familiar, in stark contrast to the stiff hospital sheets, and gave me an amazing sense of comfort, just as Ruth had promised.

With the new day came a starker realization of the trauma that had been visited upon my body. Mentally, I was still basking in the relief of having my cancerous organ removed but, physically, the pain began to become a more obvious and more intense companion. I pumped myself with morphine but it barely seemed to take the edge off. Strangely though, I felt comforted by the presence of pain as it was a constant reminder that I had done it, that I had taken the necessary steps to survive my cancer. The pain equated to being alive, a marker that indicated the start of a new chapter in my life.

Eventually, the nurse arrived to check my vitals and my IV's and to empty out the blood-filled bag that hung at the side of the bed. She spilled some of it, which grossed me out, but at least I didn't have to look at it. She gave me a shot of Heparin, a blood thinner, to keep me from getting blood clots. I received a Heparin injection twice a day alternating from my left shoulder to my right. It didn't bother me at all. I was so happy, they could have poked me as many times as they wanted to. Whatever they had to do was just fine with me.

In the latter part of the morning, I had my first visitors of the day. Keith and Gerald, two other friends of mine, brought me some more magazines and stayed for a couple of hours. As it was just us guys we had a great time talking about the wonders of prostate care and the infamous Digital Rectal Exam. I told them I had read about a guy who kept ejaculating every time his doctor pushed on his prostate. He had to bend over a table with a paper towel to catch his semen. While I had also seen something like that in a movie, a comedy where some teenagers where donating sperm for a couple of bucks, I thought it was pretty strange for it to happen during a normal, run-of-the-mill DRE. None of the doctors who DRE'd me had ever pushed or massaged my prostate hard enough to cause that reaction so we deduced that it was one of those things that some doctors did just to have some fun with their patients. Well ..... that gave us great fodder to think up all sorts of scenarios where this particular little trick could entertain the medical profession. We laughed our heads off and had a great morning. It was a wonderful start to this new phase of my life.

As the day progressed, I began to feel somewhat more alive and I gradually settled into a bit of a routine. The nurses came in periodically to check my vitals and empty my catheter bag, which was getting clearer and clearer each time. In the afternoon, I had my first hand-wash to get the antibiotic paint and bloodstains off my body. I received lots of encouragement to fart. While the nurses joked with me about it, it was a very important part of my recovery because it would signal that my digestive system was starting to work again. And they would absolutely not give me any solid food until I did. As time went on, gases were definitely building up in my abdomen and, given the state of affairs down there, an exceedingly painful pressure started to grow. And trying to fart felt like I imagined giving birth might feel! But all of this was a precursor to the real highlight of the day – going for a walk.

Walking was just as important as farting as it helped to prevent blood clots from forming and it began the long process of healing that my damaged muscles had to go through. While I was up for it, I had no concept of how difficult it would be and how much it would hurt. The first step was to get out of bed, which required me to tense my abdominal muscles to try to lift up my legs. I couldn't do it. Whether it was the weakness in the muscles or the pain, it was like a wall I couldn't break through. The nurse was expecting this and she helped me slowly get off the bed and shuffle out into the hall where my first task was to walk down to the nurse's station and back. While it was only about thirty feet, it was the longest walk of my life. The pain was enormous. Each shuffle forward brought a pain like a hot knife buried deep in my abdomen, unlike anything I had ever experienced before. But I sucked it up, punched my morphine pump a couple dozen times and made the tour. I felt like an old man shuffling down the hall literally an inch at a time, but I knew in my heart that this was part of the price that I was more than willing to pay to be rid of the cancer. By the time I made it back to my room, I was exhausted and I found that getting back into bed was even more of a painful challenge than getting out. Bending at the waist, I sort of fell backwards while the nurse lifted my legs up and swung them over. The pain was intense but the relief of getting back into bed was worth it.

Dianne arrived at the hospital around noon, just in time for my first sort-of-real meal. I can't remember exactly what I was served but it was all soft and liquid for easy digestion (because I hadn't farted yet) and although I didn't think I was hungry, I wolfed everything down in a matter of minutes. Later, Dianne had the pleasure of accompanying me on my second walk. This time, I went a little further and I remarked to Dianne that I was actually moving faster than the first time. She was amazed at how slow I was and she seemed to share every horrific stab of pain that I felt. But it was good holding on to her and I drew strength from having her with me.

Now that I was up and around and able to take oral sustenance, the nurse came and took my friend, the morphine pump, away from me. At first, I worried about what I would do without it, but the nurses had assured me that I wasn't using it that much anyway and that they had lots of other drugs to give me when I needed them. It wasn't long before I did.

I let the pain build for a while, as much to see how much I could take as to revel in the full aftermath of my surgery. The surgery had been so important to me that I considered the pain to be a very good thing, but after savouring it for a while, I finally buzzed the nurse who promptly returned with two Percocet. I had never had Percocet before and they sure did a wonderful job on the pain, but they also made me higher than a kite. I felt like I was floating around the room and half-expected to start hallucinating at any moment. This was something I would have given up my allowance for in my younger days and I could now understand how all of those movie stars and athletes got hooked on painkillers. But I was now forty-nine years old, well beyond any desire to escape reality on a chemical magic carpet, and I frankly didn't like the feeling. At least I slept for a couple of hours. The next time I needed something for pain, I asked them to bring me only one but they mistakenly brought me two. When I suggested that they just leave the other one with me for later, they looked at me like I was nuts. I guess they don't like to leave high-street-value narcotics just lying around!

The rest of the day was pretty uneventful. Dianne stayed. We talked. I tried to get comfortable. I hurt...... a lot. The nurses came and went. Dr. Tracks dropped by to tell me how great the operation went and to assure me that I was going to be "just fine". He shared with me the same details he had given Dianne the day before but it was actually reassuring to hear it directly from him. I also had a visit by one of the volunteers from the Man To Man support group. This is a great program, particularly for men who may not have a loved one to stay with them or who still have many questions. With all the research that I had done, the volunteer couldn't help me much, but I really appreciated the visit.

That night I slept with some semblance of normalcy and awoke once again to the sounds of construction and a visit from the nurse for my morning ablutions (if emptying the catheter qualifies). Randy brought Dianne down in the morning and she stayed with me for the better part of the day, helping me in and out of bed and up and down halls as I increased the frequency and lengths of my walks. As it turned out, Friday was a landmark day with several changes that suggested I was getting closer to being able to leave the hospital. I realized then that I had passed into another stage of this long journey, focusing now on getting well enough to go home. It was something I could get my mind around and it was enough.

In the afternoon, the nurse arrived and removed my bandage, revealing a puckered, purple and raw-looking wound that was held together by about twenty vicious-looking metal staples. I was expecting stitches and, while I knew that these clips would be strong enough to hold everything together, I wondered why my insides didn't squeeze out through the gaps in between. The cut stretched vertically from just below my navel down to my pubic bone and, near the top, it looked like I had a permanent fold where my slight, middle-age spare tire flipped over the top few staples. It looked a lot better after the nurse cleaned the blood from around the area but it was still pretty ugly looking.

For my next big surprise, she started working on the Jackson-Pratt catheter that protruded from a hole the doctor had punched in my abdomen with a scalpel. The bulb on the JP was filled with blood and other disgusting looking fluids, but not as much as the first couple of days so I guessed that it was no longer needed. After removing the bandage from around the hole and cleaning that up, the nurse told me to take a big breath as she pulled the tube out of my body. It felt like she was pulling out my intestines! I had thought it was just a short little thing, but it kept coming and coming and finally popped right out, at which point she put a fresh piece of gauze on the hole and pushed down on it with all of her ample weight. I don't know which felt worse, the pulling or the pushing (let's not forget the abuse and trauma that my abdomen had just been through!) I was convinced that I was going to pass out until she finally let up on the pressure and taped a bandage in place. What a relief! Next, she removed my IV line and bandaged up the hole in the back of my hand. Two more things gone from my body and one more step closer to home

Armed with fewer protuberances and better able to negotiate the hallways, albeit still very slowly, I was invited to partake of a luxurious shower. Now this is nothing like a shower at home but more like a locker room shower with only one stall - little more than a large closet. As I showered, the catheter tube and bag kept getting in the way, and it hurt to bend my body, but it was hot water, soap and shampoo and it felt very, very good. When I returned to my room, I slipped into clean sheets feeling like a million bucks. I spent the rest of that day sitting up a little more (thankful for the power bed controls), walking occasionally and eating much better. I was finally able to pass gas, never so pleased to fart in my whole life. All this meant that I could go home the next day and I was thrilled!

There was no construction work on Saturday so I awoke naturally and focused on getting ready to leave. I had another hot shower and began to pack my few belongings and was ready to go when the nurses arrived to help me replace the big catheter bag with a small one that attached with rubber straps to my leg. This was the day bag, which didn't have the capacity of the larger night bag but would allow me to walk around with relative comfort. I was given a take-home package consisting of a new night bag for home use, an extra leg bag, a staple remover and a variety of cleaning stuff, all placed neatly in a brown paper shopping bag. Fully equipped, I sat up in bed waiting for my ride home.

Dianne came close to noon with Russ and Randy who had volunteered to provide transport home. She was thrilled and talked excitedly as she helped me get ready to go. When I tried to pull my pants on without bending at the waist (quite a trick), she jumped in to do it, telling me, "You can't do that!" But when I stood up, we realized that she had put them on backwards, prompting me to say, "You can't do that either!" When we were finally ready, I used the ugly cane that Steve had brought me to begin the long, shuffling walk to the main doors, waving goodbye to the nurses. Russ helped me into the front seat of his SUV and we headed home without looking back. I checked off one more milestone on my road to recovery and it felt pretty damn good.

HOME SWEET HOME

Walking in my front door was another one of those small things that felt like a major milestone. I was coping with my cancer the only way I could, taking it step by step, so every one of those steps was a significant event in itself. I breathed in the air of the house as if I had just stepped outside on a fresh spring morning.

Dianne had pulled out the hidden bed in our living room sectional so that I wouldn't have to climb up and down the stairs to our bedroom. Walking was bad but stairs are another thing altogether when your abdominal muscles have been cut through from top to bottom. I tried to make myself comfortable sitting up in the bed, but I kept slipping down as I discovered that you actually need your abdominal muscles to sit up. Who ever thinks about things like that? So we abandoned the whole idea, folded up the bed and I just made myself as cozy as I could on the couch.

There wasn't very much that I could do at home, but I soon settled into somewhat of a routine. I sat up most of the day and tried to walk as much as possible. Walking was critical to the healing process (and probably to ensure I didn't get blood clots in my legs) but it wasn't the easiest thing to do. I shuffled around the house a couple of times and that was it. Frankly, I really didn't feel like walking at all and probably didn't do enough of it. Going outside was not an option in the middle of winter because I didn't need the added discomfort of the cold.

I wore nothing but a t-shirt and track pants around the house. There was no way I could wear underwear because the elastic waistband would sit right on top of my wound. With the catheter, I needed the baggy legs of the track pants so I could run the tube down my leg to the bag, which I strapped just above my right knee. This arrangement also made it easy to empty the catheter by just dropping my pants, leaning over the toilet and opening the release valve on the bottom, something that I had to do quite often. The bag would hold about a litre and it seemed to fill up about every hour. A full litre of pee is uncomfortably hot and as heavy as a brick. As it filled, I could feel the warmth building and, when I stood, the whole apparatus would slide down my leg. If I wasn't careful, it would slip all the way down to my ankle and tug mercilessly at my penis. A couple of times, I let it go too long. It blew up like a balloon and I could feel the pressure backing up into my bladder. I didn't tell Dianne, but I sprayed the bathroom a couple of times opening up the valve under all that pressure! Whenever my daughter got grumpy, I told her it was her turn to empty the bag for me but there are some things your children just don't want to hear!

I found it very difficult to sleep at home. Going to bed was a major civil engineering exercise because I had to switch from my small travelling catheter bag to my "night bag". The night bag would theoretically hold a full night's worth of urine so it was pretty big and had to be placed below the level of the bed for gravity to do its thing. I tried laying it on the floor, but my tube was too short, so I devised a method whereby I stuck the wide part of a plastic clothes hanger between the mattresses and hung the bag on the curved piece sticking out. This gave me enough tube length to get into bed but I pretty much had to lay on my back with the tube taped to my leg and, if I moved too much or tried to roll over on my side, the tube would pull at my penis (actually at my bladder where it was anchored). Occasionally, movement caused the whole contraption to shake and backwash, which felt like someone was firing a hose up my urinary tract! I finally figured out all the angles, lengths and proper position and just got used to sleeping on my back. The other problem I had to deal with at night was the surgical wound. Dianne accidently rolled over on me a couple of times, and I had to be particularly wary of my dog jumping up. Mostly, the three of us (Dianne, the dog and I) just found our most comfortable spots and settled in as best we could.

On December 9, I had my first visit from the Home Nurse. This is a great concept! A Registered Nurse comes directly to your home, eliminating the need for an extended stay in the hospital. She would visit every couple of days to check my temperature and blood pressure and inspect my urine for signs of infection or bleeding (I had heard that bladder infections were a possibility with prolonged use of a catheter, which was the very last thing I needed!). Dianne would meet the nurse at the door and send her upstairs to the bedroom where I would expose myself for her to check the plumbing. Dianne would hear the door closing and occasional laughter coming from upstairs and then thanked her as she left. It was a great joke for us!

Physically, the pain lessened every day and I soon got off the Tylenol 3's and onto regular painkillers. This was a real blessing because the codeine constipated me, and straining to have a bowel movement hurt enormously. When I finally did have my first one, it was like a birthday present. I shuffled out of the bathroom calling excitedly to Dianne to share the wonderful news! She smiled and shook her head. She was ever so patient with me.

When you have cancer, you become very attuned to your body, to the physicality of it. Because you focus so much on what is going on inside you, you develop a rare intimacy with all of your body's intricate mechanisms. I studied my body regularly, amazed at the extent of the surgery. The incision was longer than I expected and was very twisted and bunched at the top. I thought the disfigurement might be permanent but I really wasn't worried one way or the other. My penis was a constant source of amusement for me as well. My reading and research on radical prostatectomy led me to expect "turtling" (picture the head of a turtle disappearing into its shell) due to the shortening of the urethra, but mine actually seemed longer! And just to round out the total picture, my entire scrotum turned black and blue.

I quickly developed a number of routines around cleaning and positioning my catheter and tending to my wounds which I found oddly comforting, perhaps because it gave me back a measure of control. Or maybe it was just nice to have something more or less constructive to do. Dianne was amazed at how self-sufficient I was because she had expected to be nursing me for some time. Mind you, I was still incapable of doing anything strenuous (and felt pretty helpless about that) and we joked often about the book that said I couldn't do housework for five years.

And so it was that urination became the focus of my life at home and manipulating the catheter became my constant pastime. Urination is just not something that you think very much about normally, but it was the biggest and most complicated activity I had to deal with.

Now that I was home, many people called to see how I was doing. My parents continued to call every single day of my recovery, which helped to keep my spirits high. I thought about how hard it must have been for them to have their son dealing with this killer disease and having to experience such radical surgery. My own son Sean called eventually (from wherever he was at the time) but I still didn't think he understood what I was going through.

Occasionally, friends would drop by. Greg and Steve both came to visit and my friends next door, Helen and Gerald, dropped in often to keep up on my progress. My niece Meghan dropped by with some chicken soup and told me not to worry, that I was going to be just fine. I heard that a lot from many people and, while I knew they meant well, I was beginning to think that I might be fine, but I might not be.

One of the most enlightening visits was from a friend whose husband had developed a cancerous tumour in his nose, which was attributed to his smoking. He felt tremendously guilty and angry with himself because he felt that he had brought it on by his own hand. I remember thinking about how difficult it must have been for him to have to deal with that on top of the all the emotions associated just with having cancer! Strangely, he didn't seem to want to talk much about it and I, for one, was certainly unaware of what he had been going through at the time. It's like that with cancer. Some people think you don't want to talk about it even when you badly need to talk to someone. But, also, some people just don't want to talk about it because it scares the hell out of them!

On the lighter side (at least I found it amusing), I developed this habit of sticking my hand down my pants to touch my scar. It was a source of fascination to me as I watched it heal a little more each day and marvelled at all of the metal staples which just seemed so out of place protruding from human flesh. I did this so much that Dianne had to keep telling me to stop doing it when other people were around. She said I reminded her of Al Bundy on *Married with Children*. While I didn't really care what other people thought, I didn't want to embarrass her, so I tried my best.

I finally had my staples removed about twelve days after surgery. The Home Nurse came and, using a special tool, extracted them one by one. It hurt like hell but it was an enormous relief to get them out because the skin was starting to fester painfully around some of them. With the staples out, she then applied butterfly bandages to hold the two sides together. I kept wondering if that was going to be enough as I pictured the whole thing splitting open and my guts popping out. But that didn't happen and I tip my hat to Dr. Tracks and the entire medical profession for their skill at making repairs and putting people back together.

My next major milestone was two days later with the removal of the catheter. I was getting very, very tired of it and couldn't wait to be able to pee normally. Even though, I was feeling apprehensive because I knew that many men experienced urination control problems after a radical prostatectomy but I hoped I wouldn't be one of them. I had been doing my Kegel exercises before the surgery, but I wasn't sure if it would be enough? Dianne and I drove to the hospital, to a special Urology clinic to have the catheter removed. Both Dr. Tracks and Lee-Ann were there and I first asked if he had the pathology results on my prostate, which would tell me if the surgical margins were clear and if there had been any spread. They weren't ready yet and Dr. Tracks told me to call the office after the New Year. I was very disappointed because those results meant so much.

Although the doctor was there, it was actually a nurse who did the removal. I lay on a table, took a big breath, and out it came. There was a funny sensation associated with it but I remember thinking it was probably a lot worse going in than coming out! I had bought a package of "peeny pads" (*Protection For The Incontinent Man!*) and put one in my underwear, but I was enormously relieved when I found that I didn't need it. I wore one to bed that night just in case, but it was completely dry in the morning. After several weeks of a life revolving around the act of urinating, it was nice to not have to worry about it but, to be on the safe side, I stuffed some tissues down my pants for a couple of days. While I had the occasional squirt (especially when I tried to fart) I never had a serious problem. I feel for the guys who aren't as lucky.

As I was leaving the hospital, Lee-Ann told me to make sure that Dianne drove, that it was too early for me because my wound wasn't healed enough. Dr. Tracks came out and told me that I had to listen to her because she was the boss, at which point he got down on his knees and looked up at her like he worshipped her! This was the last thing I would have expected from a world-class surgeon but it gave me even more respect for the man.

While I could now pee normally, I got into the habit of doing it sitting down. I was way beyond worrying about how girlish that was. It was just easier to sit and relax while it drained. Occasionally, I would experience a slight turtling effect that caused me to pee out the side of the toilet. Dianne found "water" on the bathroom floor once and I honestly didn't know it was pee until it happened again. I assured her that urine was sterile, but I made sure that it didn't happen again.

Now that I was free from the urine-filled ball and chain, I felt very liberated. I could wear regular clothes (sort of – they still had to be pretty loose around the waist), and I could move around a lot more freely. To celebrate, one of my friends picked us up and drove us to a shopping mall to do some Christmas shopping. He dropped us off at the door while he searched endlessly for a parking spot during this outrageously busy season. I was surprised at just how much walking I could do in the mall. We were there for hours and, while I was pretty slow, I covered a lot of ground. While I was there, I picked up a gold teddy bear necklace for Ruth, in appreciation for her tremendous support and in recognition of the teddy bear that she had given me in the hospital. She wears it all the time. These little touches have so much meaning when you are going through such an emotional time.

By the time I got home, I was exhausted and, while I was impressed at how much I had been able to accomplish, I paid dearly for it the next day. My abdomen felt like someone had kicked me. It was back to the Tylenol 3's for awhile and I pretty much stayed in the house from then on.

Christmas came and, while at one time we had considered skipping it all together, we were determined to celebrate and have a little fun. Ruth stayed over on Christmas Eve and through Christmas Day, which was a real treat. In the evening, we had a few friends over and really enjoyed ourselves for the first time since everything had happened. Early in the evening, my son Sean showed up with a friend, seemingly oblivious to what I had gone through and the fact that he had walked out on us. It was very awkward. After about twenty minutes, he left and we didn't hear from him for quite a while.

After Christmas, I started to think about getting back to some sense of normalcy, or at least to begin the journey back. I couldn't go into work yet but I started to do some work at home, mainly through email and voice mail. I booked some meetings for January and talked to a few customers and co-workers on the phone. I had received many caring and supportive messages from friends and co-workers and even from a few of my customers who knew what was going on. I exchanged emails with one fellow where we joked about how important it was to drink lots of red wine. Ironically, I found out later that he had had a Bladder Cancer scare several years ago but that he just wouldn't talk about it.

At home, with some time on my hands, I finally got around to recording several more songs and burned my first CD which I gave out to friends and relatives (this is just a hobby, remember). Music was an important part of my life and a form of therapy for me. One day when I was feeling particularly frisky, I drove downtown and traded in one of my electric guitars for a new acoustic-electric guitar and amplifier. It was a treat for me in recognition of all I had been through. While I was not supposed to be carrying anything heavy, I secretly carried the new equipment into the house (the amp was particularly heavy), taking a strange pleasure in doing something bad!

I began to feel more alive as each day went by. The surgery was over and I was (I hoped) cancer free. I was down about twenty pounds from my BC weight and was physically feeling better overall. Emotionally, I was still on the high that I had experienced immediately after the surgery. While I continued to enjoy a certain degree of pampering, I was becoming more self-sufficient. I did more and went out more and began to actually look forward to getting back to work in the New Year. The capstone of this part of the journey was my first orgasm. While I couldn't count on an erection for some time, it was very nice to know that I still had this ability. And without a prostate, there was no muss, no fuss! It was going to be an interesting new year.

MOVING ON

As I look back upon my distant memories,
I see quite clearly how I always tried to please.
But now my life has changed. I'll never be the same
And I'm moving on.

I always tried to be the best that I could be.
I never realized just how little I could see.
Now it's time for me to open up my eyes
Cuz I'm moving on.

> *I'm moving on to a better way of life.*
> *I'm going to see all the things that I have missed.*
> *I'm moving on to the far side of the moon;*
> *To a better place than this.*

When I was young enough to think I knew it all.
I never dreamed that I would ever take a fall.
Now I've turned my back on immortality
And I'm moving on.

The world is different when you finally look around.
There's a whole new life out there just waiting to be found.
I'm facing up to all my insecurities
And I'm moving on.

> *I'm moving on to a better way of life.*
> *I'm going to see all the things that I have missed.*
> *I'm moving on to the far side of the moon;*
> *To a better place than this.*

Doug Gosling 2003

Happy New Year! I had made it through the worst part and the changing of the year seemed to signal the time for me to start looking ahead. I was feeling much better physically and was still feeling "up" emotionally. We stayed home on New Year's Eve and, for probably the first time since I was a child, I was ready to go to bed before midnight. We were just debating this when the doorbell rang. Cory and Deanna, two of my son's young friends, had left whatever festivities they were at to visit Dianne and I. They had brought me a little guardian angel token to look after me, which I carry around all the time (later I bought Dianne one to wear around her neck as she was my real guardian angel). I almost cried at their thoughtfulness and yet it underscored the fact that my own son was not around for me. We had a great time, celebrating the New Year with a glass of champagne while we watched the ball drop in Times Square. We stayed up until about 1:30 AM talking to the girls and then fell into bed feeling that we had just left the longest and worst year of our lives behind us. It was time to get on with life, whatever that meant.

As I turned my focus on getting back to some semblance of normalcy, I began to see more clearly that nothing would ever be completely "normal" again and that the cancer "experience" doesn't just end once you've had your treatment. I was still feeling pain from the surgery, although it was much better, and my mind was starting to lightly probe the question of recurrence. As Dianne and I talked about it, I discovered that she thought I was in "remission", meaning she thought that the cancer was probably going to come back. I reminded her that, with the prostate gone, the cancer should ideally be gone as well, although there was still uncertainty whether the cancer had penetrated the prostate membrane or in some way escaped into the surrounding cavity or the blood stream. This could be a noticeable spread, although Dr. Tracks hadn't seen anything during the surgery, or just microscopic particles that would float around my body with the potential to lodge somewhere and grow. Typically, the first sign of Prostate Cancer spread is in the prostate bed, which is why some oncologists will radiate that area immediately after a radical prostatectomy just to be sure (what they call "adjuant radiation therapy"). Otherwise, the cancer will appear as a metastatic recurrence in the bones or in the organs. If that happens, chances are virtually zero that it can be cured. As I said to Dianne, if it comes back, I'm a dead man. A little blunt perhaps, but essentially accurate. She was worried and, at that point, I realized that she would always worry.

On January 7, 2003, I called for the results of my post-RP pathology report. This is the most accurate reading of the extent of my cancer as they have the entire prostate and the attached seminal vesicles that they slice up and stain to do a complete analysis. The good news (great news!) was that there was no evidence that the cancer had spread outside of the prostate. The surgical margins were clear, meaning that there were no cancer cells along the incision and hence little chance that the doctor had unknowingly left some behind. It was such a relief to get this news and we were able to celebrate yet another major milestone.

With this behind me, I started to think much more about my general health. The cancer had been a terrifically loud wake-up call, probably not unlike what an overweight person has when they have a heart attack at age forty. The difference is that my medical crisis was not brought on by anything I had done to myself, through neglect or bad habits (at least I didn't think so), but by my own body turning against me. Regardless, I was determined to start taking better care of myself to make sure my immune system was strong enough to hopefully fight off any cancer cells still floating around, and to avoid other potential health problems. I was eating better already and had regained about ten of the thirty pounds I had lost in total. I quit drinking coffee (serial double espressos actually) and began cutting out carbohydrates, sweets and greasy foods. I also beefed up the list of supplements that I was taking to include just about all of the compounds that studies had indicated might help prevent Prostate Cancer. I figured that if there were any cancer cells remaining in my body, perhaps the supplements would help to fight them off or at least slow them down. There is no real proof of this but it seemed logical and gave me yet one more element of control.

That week I went back to work. My relaxing vacation was over. It felt good to arrive at the office after a month away, another major step forward. While I was uncertain how I would be treated, I was very pleased at the warm reception that I got from many people. There were still those who didn't know what to say and seemed somewhat uncomfortable, but I didn't really care too much because I was so happy to be back; so happy to be alive! Over the next couple of days I worked my way back into a routine bit by bit. I was generally fine most of the day, but started to wear down by mid-afternoon and organized my schedule accordingly. This creeping exhaustion was partially due to the physical effects of the surgery itself, but also because the anaesthetic from the operation takes a long time to wash out of your system. So I went home early a few days and vegetated the nights away.

As I went through my working day, I used every opportunity to talk about my close call and the importance of getting checked (PSA and DRE) every year. I told people in my office and more of my customers, continually amazed at how open many of them were in return. It once again emphasized how we really are all the same. I think that we sometimes lose track of that in business because people get so wrapped up in their professional status and their "expected" roles.

Before too long, however, I found myself working more and longer hours. Dianne thinks that I'm a chronic workaholic but I rationalized it by thinking that I had to work hard to get on top of things so that I could get to a point where I didn't have to work so hard; talk about a Catch 22. But Dianne was probably right.

In January, our company held its annual sales meeting in San Francisco. I was nervous about this, mainly because of the flight. I was worried about the discomfort from my surgery and terrified of the possibility that I would get stuck on the runway having to pee and not be able to go to the washroom. I had taken care to book aisle seats where I could stretch a bit and get to the washroom quickly, but the airline screwed up and put me in a middle seat, which I only discovered as I started to board. I told the gate attendant that I couldn't possibly survive the flight because I had just had abdominal surgery and she kindly upgraded me to business class. It made the flight more than bearable and I ended up sitting beside Dave, a friend from work, with whom I had a great chat about life, health and lifestyle, the first of many such conversations I was to have with different people over the months to come. In San Francisco, I was fine for the actual meetings (although I visited the washroom a lot) but found myself severely restricted for the fun parts. I turned down a team dinner one evening to climb into bed and sleep. Another evening, a bunch of us went to a nearby Irish bar to listen to a band that played all the music from my teenage years, but I had to settle with sitting in the corner singing along with the music (I knew all the words) while everyone else danced and jumped around having a ball. One afternoon, a bunch of us headed down to the waterfront to tour the area. We had a great time but after a couple of hours of walking I just stopped. I literally couldn't take another step. I was physically exhausted (although I had been keeping up a good front), but my abdominal muscles tightened up so much I couldn't move anymore. One of the guys flagged a taxi and helped me back to the hotel for which I was immensely grateful. By the end of the four days, I'd had it and I paid the extra charge for an upgraded seat on the flight back.

January 31 was another milestone. It was my first post-surgery PSA test and Dianne went with me to the hospital to hold my hand. By now, with no prostate, there should be no PSA left in my system so it is generally a major indicator of whether the surgery was successful. To my great relief, it came back "undetectable", yet another piece of good news. I also received a copy of my post-surgical pathology report with a complete analysis of my prostate and the attached seminal vesicles. These is a very informative document and I encourage everyone to make sure they get a copy and keep it, because I have found myself revisiting it many times. These are not the kind of details that stick in your mind and on the many subsequent occasions that I have been hit with *recurrence paranoia* (I'm not sure that is a generally accepted term but it works for me) I have gone back over the report and extensively researched every single term. In my report, the most striking finding was that the cancer represented 40% of the weight of the prostate. This was much more than I had expected and indicated once again how lucky I was to have been diagnosed when I did. Gleason 6 and low PSA aside, this thing was damn big! It actually scared me a lot more to discover this.

During this visit, Dianne asked Dr. Tracks what my odds of recurrence were, given all of the findings to-date. Surprisingly, he wouldn't give me any odds. Prior to surgery, he was more than happy to pull out his

Palm Pilot and punch up the Partin Tables to tell me that I had a 90% chance of cure, but now he wouldn't do it. He said that everyone is unique and that I had a great chance of a full cure but he wasn't about to give me any numbers. I'm sure that he had wanted me to have a positive attitude going into surgery but perhaps now, he was hedging his bets. Maybe it had something to do with the uncertainty created by my low PSA. But he did tell me that I'd be "just fine".

On March 17, I went for my second PSA test. Once again, it came back as "undetectable" which, for most men, would be great news. In my case, I didn't know what to think. The previous time, I was just happy that nothing showed. This time, I focused on the fact that my pre-surgery PSA level had not indicated the presence of cancer which suggested to me that what PSA I did have in my system was likely just from my prostate rather than the cancer. I asked the resident who talked to me first whether my low PSA meant that I now had no "marker" to indicate the recurrence of cancer. He gave me what I thought was a wishy-washy answer about how something would likely show. When I asked Dr. Tracks the same question, he simply said, "We don't know." I appreciated his straightforward answer, however this issue would become increasingly important to me in the months to come as I transitioned from recovery to uncertainty over my future. Turning to more immediate matters, I told him that, while I was essentially continent, I did get up in the night a lot to pee. He did a quick ultrasound of my bladder to make sure it was emptying properly (which it was) and told me to take one acetaminophen every night to cover the urge. I did try that for a while but it didn't work.

These visits back to The Prostate Centre led me to develop a very strong bond towards Princess Margaret Hospital. I felt thankful for the physical treatment and the emotional support that they had provided and I began to realize that I was now part of a very broad community of cancer patients, survivors, researchers and caregivers. This sense of community, or kinship, is important in learning to live with the reality of cancer. The fact that you are not alone and that many cancer victims have it much, much worse than you provides a little perspective to the whole thing. I ordered some blue ribbon lapel pins that I began to wear in public. I was a survivor, damn it, and I was proud of it!

On March 31, I developed a triple migraine on my way to a family get-together. I used to get migraines a couple of times a year at most and they came with weird psychedelic visual effects followed by a blinding headache, characteristic of a "classical" migraine. I had learned to take caffeine pills as soon as the visuals hit and that generally stopped it dead in its tracks but, this time, it came back two more times, something that had never happened before. It is a symptom of having cancer that anything unusual like this makes you think that just maybe the cancer was beginning to spread, in this case to my brain. I didn't do anything about it and it didn't come back over the next few days. I still don't know why it happened, but it made me wonder and, frankly, scared me a bit.

Continuing on the same paranoiac theme, I was hit again with severe back pain around April 5. Now this gave me pause. While I had been down this path before, it felt different this time and I was no longer able to just put things like this aside. After all, since my original prostate biopsy (which was not supposed to show anything) had come back positive for cancer, I had lost my confidence over such things along with my sense of immortality. This time, rather than just complain to the doctors, I did what I do best and researched the hell out of it. I learned that Prostate Cancer can metastasize directly to the spine, generally along the nerves that connect the two body parts. Because my biopsy report indicated the presence of something called *Perineural Invasion*, it suggested to me the possibility that some cancer cells could have escaped along this little road to destiny. The back pain was bad enough that it didn't go away when I lay down, which was one of the symptoms of metastasis. I asked a local Chiropractor to do a quick X-ray for me, but it didn't show anything specific in the bones, except for a mess of metal clips and staples, enough to set off an airport metal detector. This was quite a sight and I wondered if some of them were from my old hernia operation in addition to my recent surgery. The Chiropractor suggested a bone scan but this would have been virtually impossible because we were in the midst of the SARS lock-down and medical facilities were hard to get into. Dianne suggested that I go to Buffalo and pay for one, but I decided to wait. Why, I don't know. But the pain went away on it's own after a couple of weeks, suggesting it wasn't cancer-related. Sometimes waiting a little bit is the best treatment for recurrence paranoia.

I had convinced myself that my particular brand or strain of Prostate Cancer did not produce PSA. There was no medical support or explanation for this opinion, but it seemed to fit the facts. Prostate Cancer cells typically produce ten times as much PSA as regular prostate cells, so if mine was 40% of the weight of my prostate, there should have been a huge jump in my PSA. My reading of 1.26 was low even for a normal prostate. I couldn't let this thought go. Dr. Walsh, in his book "Guide to Surviving Prostate Cancer" suggests that there are several strains of Prostate Cancer and men who have low PSA levels and Prostate Cancer should look closely for small-cell carcinoma. Dr. Tracks said that their pathologists would have checked for this and I know that I would be dead by now if that were the case. But I became convinced that I had no marker. I asked Dr. Tracks, "If it didn't show before, why should it show after?" and he said, "We don't know the answer to that". He added that he had never seen any recurrence in men with PSA levels lower than 20. The way I looked at it is that my PSA could have been 5, 20 or 400 if my particular strain of cancer produced PSA. One theory is as good as another, because there doesn't appear to be any solid research or statistics on this. One-in-four PSA tests yield a false reading and I believe that false negatives (like mine) are much more rare than false positives. There probably aren't enough of us to develop good statistics or to give a decent sample size for research. A recent study, however, has suggested that the PSA test misses about 15% of cancers in older men with low PSA readings and that these are often aggressive cancers. I thought that I might need to have a bone scan each year to put my mind at ease.

When I read the reports and look at the statistics I realize just how rare my case was. Not only did I have a false negative PSA reading, but I was very young. On the Prostate Cancer news group that I occasionally visit, Dr. Walsh was quoted as saying that the odds are one-in-one-hundred for guys under fifty. This was part of a discussion on a forty-seven year old guy whose cancer had already metastasized when he was diagnosed. Poor bastard. I also checked some Canadian statistics and, when I interpolated the chart, it looked like my odds at age forty-nine were something like 0.05%. That's 1/20 of 1%! I wondered what the hell I had done to deserve this! There is also a school of conjecture that suggests Prostate Cancers appearing in younger men is much more aggressive. What if the Gleason Score was not the only measure of aggressiveness? It makes me wonder if the odds of recurrence are therefore higher for younger guys, but this is another case where the sample size is likely too small for study or for predictive purposes.

By this time (April) I was really obsessing over cancer. I couldn't get away from checking cancer web sites and news groups just about every day and I developed a burning need to talk about it. Part of this was about raising awareness, but I think it was mostly for me. In fact, maybe it was all about me. Some of my research indicated that this was a normal reaction but that it really depended on the individual. Surprisingly, there are some people who don't talk about it at all. I think I would explode if I didn't and I wonder if these people are just letting it build up inside them and that someday it will burst out in some physical or emotional crisis.

I began to see that I really was a different person. Having cancer and major surgery had a huge impact on me. I tried to act like my old self, but it was impossible. That Doug was gone forever. I had become, and always would be, a cancer survivor and life was just not going to be the same. The cancer had created an abrupt demarcation between who I was before and someone else with an entirely new perspective on life, death, physical well-being and what was really important. On a very fundamental level I understood that what I did with my new life was entirely up to me. I could screw it up, try to go back to the way I was, or I could accept it as a gift that I ought not to squander. This was to become the most difficult thing I had to deal with in the months to come.

I found that I was different at work and that I approached everything I did a little differently. My brain seemed to fill up more and I was unable to handle and prioritize the hundreds of things that I had to do. In fact, it seemed to fill up so much it wanted to shut down. I caught myself on numerous occasions staring at my computer keyboard or doing something totally mindless and unproductive. I also found that, occasionally, I was having difficulty finding words. I would be speaking to someone and suddenly experience a mental block over reasonably simple words like "confidence" or "isolated". Someone suggested that this was all probably the lingering effect of the anaesthetic but I think it was just emotional overload. Dianne suggested I try to sleep for an hour each night when I came home, but I couldn't seem to do that either. My brain was too active (if confused).

By the middle of the month, it was starting to affect my physical condition. I was feeling extremely fatigued and naturally wondered whether this was a sign of recurrence. It was probably more a result of my state of mind than anything, but I couldn't help but wonder and worry a little bit. I went to my GP, Dr. Gates, and told him that I was obsessing. I said that I knew how my mind worked and I could clearly see that I was obsessing irrationally and that I needed to do something about it. He was very understanding and did a full blood workup on me, including an old acid phosphate test that was used for Prostate Cancer indication before PSA came along. These tests eventually all came back negative but he also booked me for a series of X-rays and a bone scan to help put my mind at rest. He told me he thought it was depression.

On May 1, I had my X-rays and bone scan done at a local clinic. The bone scan required me to lie still on a table after receiving an injection of some kind of radioisotope that they kept in a lead-lined box. This is absorbed into the bones and, under the scan, damaged areas of bone (from cancer or old injuries) show up starkly. I made arrangements to pick up the pictures as soon as they were ready. The next day, I had to race to the clinic from work in order to get there by closing time. It was a Friday and I wouldn't get them until Monday otherwise, and I just couldn't wait. I arrived just at closing time and they had locked the front door, even though I could see people inside. I knocked frantically and this bitchy woman tried to shoe me away until she reluctantly opened the door and gave me my pictures. I felt like saying, "You bitch! I have cancer and this is important to me. What's the big deal about waiting another thirty seconds?" People are funny.

I ran to the car, opened the envelope and leafed through the pictures. Everything looked clear and I breathed yet one more sigh of relief. Dianne got a kick out of the pictures, particularly the bone scan which showed the radioisotope brightly highlighting my bladder and running up the length of my penis. She told me not to show it to anyone, knowing full well that I would. I seriously had no more shame!

In early May, I started to get severe stabbing pains in my abdomen that lasted for a couple of days. I wasn't sure, but I suspected they might be bladder cramps, which I had read about but hadn't yet experienced. While these eventually went away, they helped me realize that it was about time to start rebuilding my body. I had been doing nothing really physical since my surgery and my muscles had all gone to mush. I was determined to never to let my body get into the shape it was before my diagnosis (overweight, no muscle tone, a penchant for greasy foods, etc.) so I started to visit the gym where I had an on-again, off-again membership. I worked hard at it, doing vigorous circuit training three or four times a week, and quickly brought my weight back down (about thirty pounds overall) and carved off several inches all around. It would be some time before I would build up my muscles, but I was committed to this for the long haul. In my mind it was a matter of life and death, in the same way that I had to ignore my occasional cravings for butterscotch ice cream, carrot cake, french fries and other old favourites.

But even though I was getting in shape physically, there were many reminders that things were different. My scar was still quite prominent and a constant reminder every time I looked in the mirror; and the fact that I still could not get an erection was always in the back of my mind. I also had to adjust to having to scope out the washrooms everywhere I went. While I wasn't leaking, I found that when I had to go, I *really* had to go. Urination was still very much a part of my new life. Whenever I was in a public washroom and an older guy walked in, I immediately wondered if he had prostate problems or even Prostate Cancer. It's strange that I only associated this with older men and not men my age. Obviously, my anger at getting this disease at such a relatively young age was still very much with me.

Around the same time (six months after my surgery), I was still wrestling with what it was all about. My attitudes were slowly changing, but I didn't feel the major life change that I had expected and that I felt was necessary. I had been thinking about starting a support group for younger guys with Prostate Cancer because I just couldn't relate to the older guys that I kept running into. In mid-May, I asked Dianne if she would participate in a parallel wives' group, but she shocked me by saying that she just wanted to get on with life. It was a clear signal to me that she was beginning to move past it, even though I wasn't, and I was beginning to wonder whether I ever would.

Symbolically, later that day, I tossed out the organ donor card that I had been carrying around in my wallet thinking that no one would want any leftover pieces of a cancer victim.

Well, we did try to get on with things. On June 2 we bought a new car with 0% financing. Dianne brought up the idea of life-insuring the loan. For some reason this thought weighed heavily on my mind and all through the next day I had this intense feeling of foreboding. I wondered whether this was normal, because so many things seemed to be triggering these kind of feelings.

In June, we watched a television documentary on Prostate Cancer. The show followed four men who made different decisions for different reasons. I was amazed at their thought processes. A couple of them were terrified of getting "cut open". One man (actually one of the founders of Greenpeace) decided to try some natural therapies because sex was so important to him and he didn't want to lose the ability to have an erection. Of course these therapies will not cure the cancer, so he moved inexorably towards a slow death, taking hormone therapy that, in a cruel irony, rendered him impotent! He eventually died of the cancer. Another man claimed that he had no pain after the surgery. Liar!! He also said he had an erection a month after; not impossible, but I think he was lying about this too. A lot of men will not admit to anything that might reflect negatively on their manliness. The entire show was disturbing and moved both of us, bringing Dianne to tears. I find that I still get choked up when I hear of someone whose cancer has recurred with little hope of cure, thinking there but for the grace of God and my GP's gloved finger go I.

I will not try to fool anyone by pretending that my impotence (Erectile Dysfunction or whatever) doesn't bother me. I was constantly looking for signs of life in the little bugger and fretting over how long it would be before I could get an erection, if ever. Dr. Tracks gave me a sample of something called MUSE, which you inject into the urethra (lots of fun) and hope that it helps you get an erection. I had to walk around to get the blood flowing while Dianne waited patiently (which was not very romantic!) It didn't work, and it hurt like hell. It felt like someone was squeezing my penis in a vise. A couple of weeks later I tried it again out of sheer persistence and it still hurt. While there was some increase in size, it wasn't even "stuffable" (a new phrase I learned from the Prostate Cancer news group). I was starting to get a little *night tumescence* and began thinking about other devices to try, like the vacuum pump. I felt tremendously sorry for myself (and for Dianne) and angry as hell.

By the middle of June I was starting to worry about the fact that I was getting up many times to pee in the night, sometimes as many as five or six. My bladder never seemed to be full but I still had the urge to go and it never seemed to empty completely. Around the same time, I thought that I felt a hardness in my abdomen, although I may have been imagining it. It's funny how the mind works. By this time, I was reasonably confident that there wasn't anything really bad going on, but a little voice in the back of my head kept telling me that there just might be something. I considered calling Dr. Tracks again but I was beginning to feel like the boy who cried wolf so I let it go until my next scheduled appointment.

While my mind kept chipping away at my self-confidence with all manner of doubts and fears I discovered that I wasn't alone in this thinking. Dianne and I were chatting about the bathroom renovations that I was starting to plan when she told me that she didn't want any "temporary modifications". She wanted them to be permanent in case I got sick and couldn't finish the work! We talked about it and she admitted to believing that there was a good chance that I was going to get sick again. For some reason, the fact that she thought this scared me even more than my own dark thoughts. It made me realize that this was a cross that we both would carry for the rest of our lives - wondering, always wondering. I tried to reassure her, but how could I do that when I was so unsure my self?

I tried very hard to get on with life and living. While I was determined to change my life and mend my evil ways (or at least my unhealthy and wasteful ways) I certainly recognized that I still had a job to do and a home and family to provide for. And while I wanted desperately to retire immediately to a small cabin on a lake somewhere, this was just not feasible and, yes, perhaps a trifle unrealistic. So it was, by the middle of June, that I found myself slipping back into my old work habits. In my mind, I thought in terms of "work hard, make money, have choices". So here I was working evenings and weekends again with, frankly, not a lot to show for it as the software market was very, very slow. By the end of the month I was seriously approaching burnout. I was desperately in need of a holiday. In the past, I could easily handle this kind of workload, even though it was hard on me and everyone around me, but now I just didn't have the mental stamina. I also thought that perhaps I lacked the degree of focus I needed to be doing my job properly but, at the same time, everything seemed much more *artificial* and somehow less important in the big picture.

I talked to Andrew about this at length and he characterized my old way of working (and living) as "hanging on with my fingernails" and just trying to "keep my head above water". He said that having cancer makes you want to slow down and walk, to appreciate life and what goes on around you and that this is a good thing. I knew this on an intellectual level, but I was having a massively difficult time actually putting it into practice. I vowed to myself to slow down. Hah!

Some of my obsessiveness started to spill over into other aspects of my life other than work. I found that I was getting obsessive about personal health and about what I was eating, and was becoming very critical about what others were putting into their mouths under the guise of nutrition. While I was generally watching what I ate, which was keeping my weight down, I was also getting into a fairly regular and intensive exercise regime at my fitness club. I felt like I had to go to the gym at least three or four times a week and, whenever I missed a day, I felt horrible about it - like I had missed one of the most important events of my life. I realized that this was the state of mind that I had tried to achieve so many times before and failed (like many people who join fitness clubs and never show up) and was, in fact, a very positive and welcome side effect of having cancer. The irony is that people would look at me, see the weight loss and rather than saying, "Hey, you look good," they would say, "How are you feeling?" Many of them, I'm sure, thought it was the cancer coming back, and I really couldn't blame them.

In late July, about eight months post-surgery, I was taking a shower, looked down and noticed that my penis was fuller and bigger. While it wasn't firm enough to qualify as an erection, it was an indication to me that the one nerve I had remaining was beginning to fire again. I was so excited, I yelled downstairs for Dianne to come up to witness it first hand. Alas, she was doing preserves and had her hands hovering over boiling water and didn't even hear me. Since no one else was around, I ran downstairs stark naked to show it off but the cold air destroyed my creation by the time I got to Dianne who looked at me like I was nuts. But it had happened. And although it wasn't good enough to do anything with, it was just nice to know that my single nerve was beginning to heal.

I was learning that Erectile Dysfunction was near the top of the list of concerns of just about every Prostate Cancer survivor. It was discussed at each of the Man to Man group meetings I attended and I marvelled at the light-heartedness with which it was tossed around. One of the fellows joked that he had become a lesbian trapped in a man's body because all he could do was have lesbian sex with his wife. This was a crude way of putting it, but every man there understood what he meant. Another man claimed that he desperately needed to get an erection to "put my wife out of her misery!" I wasn't at the point where I could joke about it yet and wasn't sure if I ever would be, but I knew that I had a long road ahead of me, and probably a hard one (no pun intended!)

Overall, the summer was very good. I worked a lot but tried to do it from home as much as I could so that I could sit out on my back deck and enjoy the fresh air and sunshine which seemed so much more precious to me. And I was feeling much, much better physically. In the middle of August, Steve and I went on an incredible five-day kayaking trip following the old fur trading routes down the French River and out into Georgian Bay. It was wonderful! The weather was great and, with the kayaks, we were able to go places where there were no powerboats and no other people. Physically, I was in great shape, so the paddling was easy and the portages bearable. Mentally and emotionally, it was truly a spiritual experience; a pilgrimage to the great outdoors that I love so much. I needed it badly and I returned more relaxed and in a better frame of mind overall. Since getting the cancer, I had been so focused on it that I felt like I was in a bubble, not really noticing or caring what went on outside of it. On the water, in the middle of the great outdoors, that bubble burst and my world enlarged to take in all of the beauty and peace around me. I became a part of it, as I always did.

While on the trip, we totally missed all the excitement of that summer's widespread blackout. When we arrived back in civilization we wondered what the big deal was. We had been without electricity for five days! It emphasized to me just how "artificial" life in the big city was and how dependent we had become on things like electricity. It served to further reinforce my desire to get out of the city.

Unfortunately, the summer had to come to an end and I needed to get back into the groove at work. Activity picked up in the software business and the workload increased significantly. I found it very difficult to keep up, partly because I wasn't really up for it yet, and partly because I desperately wanted to avoid slipping back into my old ways. But I really had no choice. I had responsibilities as well as a need to be doing *something*. Life goes on even when it changes violently.

September 30 was another scheduled check-up with Dr. Tracks. As it approached, it loomed very large in my mind, even though I didn't think my PSA test would show anything. Each time I had an undetectable PSA test, I felt like I had dodged another bullet. It was strange and somewhat inconsistent that I felt that way considering my strong belief that my cancer would never show up on a PSA test. I needed to tell Dr. Tracks that I was feeling fatigued and urinating frequently (although I really didn't expect him to have any particular answers for those symptoms). I was growing impatient as I waited in one of the examination rooms, until I overheard Dr. Tracks telling a guy across the hall that he had Prostate Cancer. The guy responded with a number of questions (most of which I couldn't hear) including, "What is my life expectancy?" I found this deeply disturbing because I remembered agonizing over this very question. It triggered a crazy, paranoid image where I thought that I was being kept until last because I was going to get some bad news of my own. As I waited, I imagined how he would tell me and how I would feel, contrasting that with the memories of my initial diagnosis. But I worried for nothing because, once again, my PSA was undetectable. I still left with a hollow feeling knowing that, in my case, an undetectable PSA didn't rule out cancer. But I also left with a prescription for Viagra!

I had asked for the Viagra, not because I was getting overly impatient (I knew it was going to take a long time), but because I felt it was necessary to exercise my penis - to get the blood flowing into it. I didn't know if there was any scientific support for this but I'm sure I had read something about it on my news group. A few days after my appointment, I tried it for the first time. It actually got a bit bigger and I was pleasantly surprised that there was no pain, as I experienced with the MUSE. I didn't get a complete erection, but we had some fun with it and it was nice to see that there was still some life left in the old appendage.

Andrew and Jeanette, from PMH, had an interesting perspective on Erectile Dysfunction related to Prostate Cancer treatment. At a Man To Man awareness evening in the fall they presented the results of the couples study that Dianne and I had participated in, covering this topic among others. They discussed two perspectives on ED:

1) Use it or lose it (early treatment).

2) Wait and see (later treatment).

Clearly, personal feelings will determine which of the paths an individual might choose, but the really interesting fact they presented was that 50% of men stop treatment for their ED (drugs, injections, vacuum pumps, etc.) in the first year. Wow! What's that all about? They suggested that a number of psychological factors are at play, including conflict in the relationship, anxiety, longing for spontaneity and loss of sexual interest, but also point out that these things can be modified with counselling and other forms of psychosocial treatment. Regardless, this generates a lot of stress and distress. It's not easy. A lot of couples have trouble with the whole idea of using sexual aids and partners don't know how to help, as much as they might want to. In fact, many couples have difficulty re-starting sexual contact. While this is all very difficult for the guy who has to deal with the loss of something that defines his overall maleness, it is also difficult for the woman who misses the intimacy and spontaneity that was such a big part of their pre-cancer relationship. Dianne is very glad that I am alive, but she mourns the loss of what we had. I do too, but she has confided in me that, at times, she feels like she is not attractive to me. Although I've assured her that this is not the case, it is probably a very natural reaction and one that I need to be sensitive to because she is truly the most important part of me. There is an onus on both of us to find a way to get some of that intimacy back, especially if I were to never regain my potency. Thinking about this made me extremely angry at what the cancer had done to both of us.

Finally, October 15 came - the one-year anniversary of my diagnosis. It is as big a milestone as there could be on this wild journey. Wow! What a difference a year makes. One year-plus-a-day ago, I was healthy (I thought) and going about minding my own business. And here I was now, a cancer survivor, thirty pounds lighter and emotionally screwed up.

The day itself turned out to be quite eventful. My new car got hit and a huge tree came down in my back yard. Rather than celebrating that evening I was outside in the dark, with help from my friend Russ, trying to keep the tree from crashing into my neighbour's roof. I damn near broke my thumb when a large branch I was cutting swung down at my head. I resolved to spend all future October 15ths locked in the house. Strangely, for several days afterwards, I couldn't shake a general feeling of unease and depression. I attributed it to what I call "emotional memory" as my subconscious mind unearthed the feelings of a year ago. It was the same effect that always made me think of new books and chalk boards every September, long after I had finished school. It didn't help my overall state of mind, but I was alive and my tumour was gone.

I desperately wanted to turn my cancer experience into something positive, to do something that was cancer-related that would help others facing the same horrible situation. Writing this book was one of the things I decided to do, knowing that it would be as therapeutic to me as much as I believe it will be helpful to others. The other thing I decided to do was to volunteer as a member of the PMH Community Advisory Committee. I became aware of this through one of my acquaintances, whose wife Susan was on the committee, another example of the extensive network that you can tap into when you join the ranks of the cancer community. I looked at it as a way to give something back to the cancer community in general and to PMH in particular. It was a tremendous experience to attend my first meeting and meet so many others who had experienced cancer themselves or through the suffering of their loved ones. One fellow was a Prostate Cancer survivor and another had an inoperable brain tumour that he had been living with for some time. The strength of these people was truly amazing and inspirational. I still feel humbled in the presence of people who have been or are going through experiences that seem so much worse than mine.

As the days passed by, I hit other milestones that served as a constant reminder of how much my life had changed. On the morning of November 18, I woke up thinking that I needed to have an abdominal CT scan because I was experiencing some pain. When I checked later, I discovered that it was exactly one year ago that I had my first CT scan at PMH! It is truly strange how the mind works. A couple of weeks later, on the anniversary of my surgery, I was one year cancer-free (as far as I knew). I wasn't sure how I would feel and, as the day arrived, I didn't know how I *should* feel. In fact I did feel pretty happy - again probably some of that emotional memory thing. A couple of people remembered and commented to me (which meant a lot) but not many. Then again, why should they remember?

With the passing of the one-year anniversary of my surgery, I took stock of where I was physically. My wounds (I thought of them as battle wounds) were seemingly healed, I was showing no PSA (for what that was worth) and I was still impotent. I was also experiencing pain in my abdominal area and, while exercising, I felt a weakness in my right side which seemed to stem from my lower spine. I made an appointment with Dr. Tracks in December to check on these symptoms and to also see if I could try something other than Viagra, which didn't seem to be working well enough for me. I was starting to think about penile injections, which gives you some indication on how much this was bothering me.

Dr. Tracks didn't seem to be worried about the weakness, suggesting it was probably just the result of aging. I got a laugh out of his philosophy on this. He figures that men are programmed from birth to reach their peak at age twenty and then get mauled to death by a tiger before they reach fifty. Anything beyond that is just gravy! We compared aches and pains for a bit but, for some reason that I can't explain, I didn't mention the pain in my abdomen. I think that subconsciously I knew that it was probably something else and didn't want to seem like a whiner. For the erectile dysfunction, he recommended that I see a Dr. Wang who specialized in this area and who ran a clinic at the PMH Prostate Center once a month. He also booked me for a cystoscopy to see if there was some reason for the frequent need to pee that we had discussed before and that I continued to experience. The problem was not just the frequency, but also the variability of it - the fact that, at times, it would flow like a tap and, at other times it worked like a pinched hose. I didn't really ever want to have a cystoscopy, but it seemed like a good thing to do and I thought that I would feel better if we actually had a look around inside. Dr. Tracks thought I might have a loose surgical staple in my bladder that moved around while it built up with whatever mineral deposits you find in the bladder.

I went for the cystoscopy on February 3 at the hospital clinic. It felt a bit surreal as I undressed and hopped up on a table to allow the nurse to clean my penis, thinking I would never again be embarrassed about showing my privates to the entire health care profession. There was a sign on the wall prohibiting the taking of pictures that made me wonder just who would want to do that, but it was a nice touch. Dr. Tracks did the actual procedure, which was not nearly as bad as I thought. First, he anaesthetized the tip and then inserted a long tube containing a fibre optic camera straight through into my bladder. It was a bit uncomfortable but didn't really hurt. On the television screen you could see that the entire urethra and bladder was perfectly clear, so clear in fact that Dr. Tracks remarked that it didn't look like I had had any surgery at all, except for the fact that I had no prostate! I think he was kind of proud of himself at that moment, as he should be. It sure made me feel better, except that there didn't appear to be any explanation for my urinary problems. We discussed ways to better manage my water intake and how to mentally manage the urge. Apparently this was another thing that I was probably going to have to live with.

So that was one more thing down, but I wasn't finished yet. I had asked Dr. Gates to arrange for a colonoscopy for me, just to check out my bowels. I didn't really think that there was anything wrong up there either but, in the same way that men should be tested for Prostate Cancer, I felt that I should as least screen myself for other forms of cancer (I think everyone over 50 should be tested). As I've said previously, my confidence had been shattered beyond repair and my sense of immortality (which I had never really acknowledged before) was completely gone. A lot of people cringe at the thought of a long tube snaking up their rectum but, as I said to the nurse when she asked me if I was nervous, "I had a radical prostatectomy. Nothing scares me anymore!" Besides, they give you a sedative so while you are not entirely out cold you have no conscious recollection of the procedure. I had a vague memory of talking to the doctor while I was under but that could have been a dream. Regardless, I did it and everything was clear; one more checkmark.

Shortly after all of these procedures, I met with Dr. Wang to review my options for dealing with my ED. He told me that I really shouldn't expect anything for at least 18 months but he gave me a prescription for Cialis, one of the new Viagra-type drugs that was supposed to last several days, and made me another appointment in two months time to discuss injections, pumps and implants. Well, the Cialis didn't work either and it gave me a blistering headache for three days. It would seem that I was heading for a lot more headaches on this incredible journey. I hoped that I had the stamina for it.

THE ONGOING EMOTIONAL
TOLL OF CANCER

I think I will be a hypochondriac for the rest of my life. I used to get a kick out of all my Dad's complaints (he could be a big baby at times) but I always felt that this concern over his health would keep him alive for a long time, which it did. Nothing was going to sneak up on him! Now it's happening to me. Ever since my cancer diagnosis, I worry about every little thing that happens to me. I don't really expect every little ache or pain or funny lump to be from cancer, but I never even had to think about this before. In the past, if I had back pain, it was just back pain - from lifting, from sitting in one position for too long or from just getting older. But now I know that there is always a chance that it *could be* related to my cancer. So, to this day, I worry about every little thing and I get everything checked out. I have to. And there is always some expectation, however small, that it will turn out to be something bad. Because I had such bad news before, it seems like I have developed an expectation of bad news. In fact, at times, it seems I almost look forward to "getting it over with." I know this sounds crazy, but there is a feeling of inevitability that I can't shake. There are days when I feel like I am just biding my time.

Some of this paranoia is directly related to the physiology of cancer in the sense that recurrence *can* happen and can manifest itself in many ways. The rest of it is more of a secondary impact of having cancer. I felt like I'd dodged a bullet but, for some strange reason, my body was trying to kill me! And if it didn't work the first time, well … there are many more ways to skin a cat. Irrational isn't it? And a little sad. But that's the way this works. At times, I feel that I'm overreacting and I feel embarrassed about it, like I'm being weak. But it's not just me. Dianne always worries about me to such an extent that I wonder whether I should even tell her when I'm not feeling well. I'm convinced that, deep down inside, she thinks I am riddled with cancer. I try to reassure her but, as I've said before, it's hard to be convincing when I'm not so sure myself.

I've talked to Ruth about this many times, usually when I think that I'm being stupid and paranoid. But she has the same thoughts. She is convinced that her cancer will come back some time because it was just too serious a case and she gets panicked whenever she gets sick. In the case of Breast Cancer, there are no markers to warn you that it is recurring, so she has to rely on symptoms. One of the reasons we relate to each other on this subject is that I don't have a reliable marker myself. So we're kind of in the same boat. Ruth hates it when people tell her not to worry, that she'll be okay. I know exactly what she means. People mean well and really want you to be okay, but they just don't know enough.

It's always on my mind to some extent. Not that I worry every day, but from time to time something happens to make me think about it. Sometimes, I realize I haven't thought about it for a couple of days and that's excuse enough to think about it. The thing is, it's not in my nature to just worry and not at least *try* to do something about it. It's easy to just trot off to the doctor and see what he says, but I have a compelling need to review and research things to better understand what could happen and why. For example, every once in a while I will pull out my post-surgery pathology report and go through it again. There's no guesswork here (as there is when interpreting biopsy results). The facts are the facts.

My pathology report indicated that I had an adenocarcinoma (tumour) that was 40% of the weight of my prostate. It also indicated that it was "nodular throughout" which means that there wasn't just a single tumour but many of them scattered throughout the prostate. So how do I interpret this? Well, it suggests to me that well over half of my prostate was likely involved (because the 40% would be spread around), which would differentiate the cancer as Stage T2c rather than T2b. This, in turn, slightly increases the probability of recurrence based on the Partin tables. Number games, mind games. This is how we think.

The report also indicated the presence of *Perineural Invasion* (or Perineural Extension), which means that the cancer had penetrated the nerves within the prostate. While some studies have shown that there is no difference in outcomes with or without the presence of Perineural Invasion, there is another viewpoint that cancer cells can travel quite freely along nerve pathways and thus is a potential mechanism for spreading. As you can see, this type of information can be interpreted different ways and the fact remains that there are no definitive causal links that have been proven between specific findings and recurrence. It's all based on statistics, and statistics deal with large numbers. They are not dependable for minority situations like mine, where I was too young and had a false negative PSA reading. So I can choose to go with what the broad statistics say, or I can choose to worry that my peculiar status negates or minimizes the relevance of these studies. It all depends on how paranoid I happen to be feeling at the time. It also proves the point that there are some things better off not knowing, but it is not in my nature to be ignorant.

I surprised myself one day when I found myself wondering if maybe I should have had radiation instead of surgery. This is stupid for many reasons. First of all, I believed then and still believe that surgery was the best route for me in my situation; get it all out and (hopefully) be done with it! Secondly, because of how and where the tumour was protruding from my prostate, it may have been difficult to do radiation anyway. Thirdly, and most importantly, you should never second-guess choices as important as this. You make the best, most informed choice at the time and go with it. Once it's done, you can't change it, and worrying about the choice you made just adds more unneeded stress to your life. So I pushed this thought aside and scolded myself for even thinking about it.

It did, however, make me wonder about the fact that Dr. Tracks did not remove my lymph nodes. Often, during surgery, the doctor does a quick pathology on a couple of lymph nodes to see if the cancer has spread to them. If the pathologist says they are clear, the doctor proceeds with the surgery. If they show signs of spread, they sew you back up and leave your prostate intact, because removing it won't cure the cancer, which is what the surgery is all about. In my case, Dr. Tracks inspected them visually and by squeezing them, relying on his vast experience to feel confident that they were okay. I would never second-guess him on this because he is so damn good, but I still wonder (during my more paranoid days) if there might have been microscopic traces of cancer that might have been detected by a pathologist. I don't dwell on this any more (and to this day, my lymph nodes are still clear), but it did give me pause at one time.

So I'm resigned to the idea of always worrying about changes in my health and general well being. It's a very real symptom of having cancer and it's something that all cancer survivors must deal with in one way or another. It's yet one more thing that makes us different from the rest of the population.

The emotional impact of having cancer manifests itself in so many, many ways. I find myself thinking about it at the strangest times - on a plane, listening to someone talk about something I'm not that interested in, or sitting with a bunch of guys having a "normal" conversation. I think about it whenever I think of old age or death, particularly when someone talks in an off-hand way about someone dying of cancer. Recently, I heard about an old boss of mine who dropped dead at the age of forty-three while running on a treadmill. It sent shivers up my spine when I heard about it and bothered me for weeks. It wasn't that I was really close to the guy, but it just seemed so .... unfair! In the fall, my daughter was in a high school production of *Fame* and there was a part where one character talks about having Testicular Cancer and another boy makes a joke about it. I found the scene disturbing, but then Caralia told me the boy playing the part used me as his inspiration (remember that the entire school knew about me). I'm not sure how true that really was, but I was very touched. Later in the play, the husband of one of the teachers was dying. She didn't say what he was dying from, but I felt a tremendous welling up of emotion and was on the verge of tears right there in the school auditorium. The idea of death is so much more personal to me now because the cancer forced me to confront my own mortality and to imagine my own death. I thought for sure that I would be a wreck when my own parents died.

One evening, Dianne and I were watching *Entertainment Tonight* and they were talking about the movie *The Hulk* and the old television show of the same name. I hadn't known this previously, but Bill Bixby, the actor in the television series, had died of Prostate Cancer. It had not been detected until after it had metastasized and he had slowly withered away. The pictures of him in his later months were heart-rending and it was a stark reminder to me of just how serious this disease was and how unforgiving it could be. It was so strange to hear about someone dying from a disease that I had and it filled me with an overwhelming sadness and a deep fear. Dianne cried.

The initial, crushing blow of a cancer diagnosis and the ongoing burden of cancer survivorship should never be carried alone. There are many times when I feel very much alone and isolated from the rest of the world and it's far too easy to withdraw into myself and try to deal with it as a highly personal cross that I have to bear. But it is important to use the resources and support network around you to help you deal with all of the emotions and fears that are an inevitable part of your survivorship existence. Family and friends are the most important source of support and I consider myself very lucky to have a wife who is my best friend and closest confidant, a wonderful daughter who consistently lends her quite support, a son whose love I still feel from afar, and a couple of close friends and even not-so-close friends who are willing to talk to me about how I'm doing. And of course my Mom and Dad (until my Dad died) continued to call all the time. Through all of this, they were my biggest fans and my biggest worriers and it's strangely reassuring to know that my Mom still wants to parent me after all these years. I think about both of them all the time too and try to call Mom every couple of days. I know she appreciates it and it's an important connection for me. My brother and sister called occasionally to check on me and, more recently, have begun calling regularly which means a great deal to me.

I spend a fair bit of time on the Google Prostate Cancer newsgroup (alt. support.cancer.prostate) where Prostate Cancer survivors post questions and answers regarding treatment, after-effects, coping, etc. There are several regulars who freely answer any questions from newbies or from other long-time survivors. To me, these guys are true heroes and, although they know me only from my postings, they have helped me through some difficult times. It's a great place for me to post questions about some of the odd concerns that I have in order to substantiate that I have found out all I can about a particular problem. I'm always thrilled when I can add my own two cents to a discussion thread and wish I could spend more time with this virtual support group.

Earlier, I discussed the local Man To Man support group. Support groups are a mainstay in the world of cancer survivors and serve an incredibly important function. The emotional weight of cancer would be unbearable without the support of others who have been through the same thing as you. But I have always felt a little left out because of the age difference between me and the typical Man To Man member. Earlier in my recovery I thought it would be great to have a sub-group or even just an informal gathering of guys closer to my age to discuss issues that are particularly relevant to us. I wrote up the following note and forwarded it to the President of the local Man To Man group, hoping to get it published in their monthly newsletter. It encapsulates my sense of the difference age makes in Prostate Cancer diagnosis.

"We're looking for a few good men!"

In Canada, the average age for diagnosis of Prostate Cancer is 65. Once considered an older man's disease, this has changed considerably with heightened awareness and improved testing. Men in their 30's, 40's and early 50's are now being diagnosed and treated successfully thanks to early detection.

While a diagnosis of Prostate Cancer has a tremendous impact on anyone, it can be even more devastating to younger men, in several ways.

- *There is a feeling of being hit before they are in the "risk" zone - like being hit by a car on your front lawn. They have to face their mortality a lot sooner than expected.*

- *They are typically in mid-career and are suddenly faced with a life-changing event that could threaten their career aspirations and their whole attitude towards work.*
- *Many still have children at home, some very young.*
- *Incontinence and impotence have much longer-term implications for younger men.*

All of these factors can lead to serious depression and a high degree of stress, which can be very destructive.

Support groups like Man To Man have proved to be a valuable source of information and support for men diagnosed with Prostate Cancer and we encourage all men to take advantage of this wonderful resource.

We are now reaching out to men in their younger years who would be interested in talking to other men in similar situations, whether newly diagnosed, undergoing treatment, or coping with life after treatment. The intent is to provide an informal forum for information sharing and mutual support.

If you are in your 30's, 40's or early 50's and would be interested in attending an initial meeting, or if you have any questions, please contact Doug Gosling.

I eventually spoke to the group president when I cornered him at a Man To Man Awareness Night. He told me that they were starting to get younger men coming out to their meetings so he felt it wasn't necessary to have a special group. I know that younger men would attend to find out as much as they could when they were first diagnosed but I wonder how many of them, like me, don't return because they felt out of place. Having said this, I certainly don't want to undervalue the tremendous benefit of this group, but there is a definite gap. I haven't pursued this any further, but have offered myself as a resource to PMH to talk to younger guys. I've had several referrals and I found it very satisfying to be able to share my own knowledge and experience with others in the same boat.

As the new year arrived, I found myself doing a lot of soul searching with what I thought was a degree of objectivity that I didn't have a year earlier, just after surgery. I found myself thinking about things a bit more analytically. I was still wearing a Prostate Cancer blue ribbon on my jacket like a badge of honour and talking openly about my experience with anyone who would listen. But one day, I walked into work with a PMH envelope and a copy of Lance Armstrong's latest book (a Christmas present from Dianne) and found myself feeling somewhat self-conscious. I was beginning to wonder whether people would think that I was obsessing over the whole cancer thing (which I was) and also wondered whether they would start to think less of me. I asked myself, "Am I weak for having cancer, or am I strong because I survived it?" - a question that still comes back to haunt me from time to time. And what do others think? And does it matter?

I was struggling more and more with the whole "meaning of life" question. I had come to realize that it was going to be impossible for me to go back to living my life without worrying about the future. Because I now had a new appreciation for the whole concept of dying, I wondered what the meaning of life really was when we all die eventually and are remembered only by a few people whose life goes on without us and who will also be dead before too long. A hundred years from now, who will even remember? At the extreme, you can wonder why you we should do *anything* when we're all going to die. These are age-old questions and the stuff of myth and religion, but there really are no answers except what we find to be meaningful to ourselves. I remember a statement in one of the books that I read, "The meaning of life is life itself." That's actually a pretty good start, but I know that I need to keep working on what I do with my life and the relative importance that I place on health, happiness, material goods, friends, family, work, and everything else.

Occasionally, I attain some great insights into life. For example, I attended another one of my daughter's high school plays in February (no cancer references in this one) and enjoyed it immensely, feeling very proud of her. I remember sitting there thinking that *this* is what life is all about! At times like that, I feel tremendously lucky to be alive.

One of the problems associated with not having a clear idea of what is important is that other roles and situations tend to eat up your mental and emotional energy. Early in the new year I realized that I still hadn't found a way to reduce my workload and the excessive hours that I was putting in at my job. It seemed that I was just not making the right choices and that I desperately needed to start thinking seriously about making some big changes. As soon as I started down this path, I realized that I needed to get out of my current company, which was over-burdening me with administrative work in a bad market, and I made a move to a much smaller company. I had been working every evening and weekend and didn't have a lot to show for it. I had been unable to take any Christmas holidays because I was working on an important proposal and the workload showed no signs of lessening. My boss was doing his best for me, but there was only so much he could do. I held a great deal of loyalty to the company for their support in the past but I truly felt that I was killing myself. I had no choice but to make the move.

Moving to a new job had immediate benefits. I was making more money, working with some old friends and was immediately engaged in more productive sales activity. Overall, the environment was much more positive and I felt that I was really contributing to something. This was significant because work can be a major source of stress and unhappiness and in making the change, I vowed not to let it eat me up as the previous job had done. Of even greater significance was the *act* of making a conscious decision to change my life and then following through with it. Changing jobs is a huge decision and, in doing so, I was telling the world and demonstrating to myself that I was back in control.

Before I started the new job, I decided to take the family on a much-needed and long-overdue vacation to Cancun, Mexico. We had a great time almost in spite of ourselves. With Caralia there, we couldn't just "relax in our room" in the evenings. She pushed and prodded us out the door and forced us to participate in all of the hotel events. For some reason, I kept getting called up on the stage by the hotel entertainment crew and, in one night, I was voted "Mr. Macho" and danced the Mexican Hat Dance with a professional troupe. Mind you, it took a couple of Margaritas to get up enough guts to do this, but it was actually a lot of fun. The old Doug was far too reserved to do anything like that.

I started my new job the Monday after we returned from Cancun. As luck would have it, I picked up some kind of bug and lost my voice for the entire first week on the job. My throat was raw. I was coughing, feeling extremely fatigued and just plain *blah*. If it wasn't for the fact that Caralia had a similar bug, I would have been seriously worried about cancer. I visited my family doctor and he sent me for a chest x-ray at the clinic in his office building. As I waited in the x-ray room, I realized that I could see the video screen through a window as the technician checked the picture quality. While I couldn't see very clearly, I found myself straining to see if I could detect any spots on my lung and I had an image of the doctor calling me back in to tell me that. The fear was always there, just under the surface; something that I was going to have to live with for the rest of my life.

As it turned out, I had what they call *atypical pneumonia*, which means pneumonia without the chest congestion. I was sick for over four weeks, working all that time. At night, I would come home exhausted and often went right to bed. A couple of times I made my way to the gym for a workout but that was too much for me and I dragged around even more for the next few days. It took me so long to recover that Dianne was beginning to worry that it was a sign of the cancer coming back and I found myself thinking the same thing because I had been so healthy for quite a while.

As I got past these immediate physical concerns, I realized just how depressed I had become without really knowing it was happening. It was as if I had slid steadily down a long slope that had started at its high point immediately after my surgery, but there had been no levelling off at some "normal" state of contentment. While I was at work, I was occupied enough to keep any other thoughts at bay but at home, where I was more relaxed (Dianne says home is our "safe place"), I was becoming more and more depressed and increasingly afflicted with negative thoughts. The cancer had forced me to look forward and I kept thinking about how little life was left. To me, the glass was now half-empty when I really should be looking at it as half-full and should be damn glad it was! I worried about retirement and whether I would have enough money to do what I wanted to do, something that most everyone worries about but for which I felt a particular sense of urgency. Time seemed to be so short all of a sudden.

At least I wasn't doing this alone. Dianne and I talked a lot about it and agreed to forget about the past and all the mistakes we had made. We promised each other to look to the future and to move forward individually and as a couple with a more positive outlook. Most immediately, we both had to deal with my increasing depression and we were concerned that our relationship was lacking the intimacy we once had. It was extremely complicated. I'm sure that my continuing inability to get an erection had a lot to do with it because it is a known fact that a man's penis is hard-wired to his brain. And an erection is a pretty important part of intimacy, particularly from a man's point of view. Dianne felt very strongly that this was a big contributor to my depression because I had lost, hopefully on a temporary basis, a big piece of what defined me as a person and as a man. She was probably right (even though she constantly told me that she only cared that I was alive and able to share my life with her). I'm sure this is very similar to how women feel when they've lost a breast - a symbol of their womanhood - to cancer. But the depression itself also has an impact on your sex drive and your ability to feel passion, so it tends to feed back on itself in a closed loop that can be devastating. I'm depressed because I had cancer; the cancer caused me to have ED; the ED reduces my ability to be physically intimate; I feel worse emotionally because I have ED; the depression reduces my sex drive; I become more inwardly focused and perhaps less sensitive to Dianne's needs and our personal relationship; the lack of intimacy makes me more depressed ...... around and around we go and where we stop, nobody knows. It was clear that we had to find a way to bring the intimacy back into our lives in a way that didn't involve me having a raging erection.

As I always did, I tried to analyze the nature and cause of my depression. I am a very self-aware person in that I know intellectually what is happening to me, even if I don't always know what to do about it. Perhaps I have always had a generally depressive nature but I had been successful in managing this in the past and generally enjoyed life. The cancer was a trigger, plunging me into a dark place when I was diagnosed and now seemingly coming back to haunt me. I attributed it to the lack of confidence in my health, the loss of my wonderfully juvenile sense of immortality and my ED, compounded by a bad year at my old job. I had reached the year-and-a-half point in my cancer journey where signs of recurrence could begin to show (even though it could take many years). My brain could not hide from this fact and it was increasingly on my mind, particularly when I experienced some illness or new pain. It was becoming a real problem because it attacked the root of who I was and severely eroded my overall level of confidence in myself as a human being and as a functioning member of society. I needed my confidence to get control of my life and to do well in my new job which was not just a way to pay the bills but my vehicle to a more secure future.

As I began to wallow more and more in this dark pit of depression I also started to experience minor panic attacks. This worried the hell out of me because I had never experienced anything like it before. It was small things, like a fleeting feeling of panic as I strapped myself into my seat on an airplane. Worse, it could be triggered by the most innocent thing. I would switch on a light and suddenly find myself thinking about the cost of electricity, and then all the bills I had to pay, and then start to think about losing my job and all the horrible things that would entail. In a matter of minutes, I was imagining everything falling down around me like a tumbling house of cards. Irrational, yes, but it frightened me half to death. I tried to explain it to Dianne, but it is a very difficult thing to understand unless you have experienced it yourself. She told me I needed professional help. As usual, she was right on.

I booked an appointment with a psychiatrist who immediately started me on a course of anti-depressants. I have never liked the idea of being medicated, but I was smart enough to know that I needed something to help me deal with the depression and the panic attacks. I needed to start thinking more positively or I was going to go crazy. The doctor asked me if I really felt that the cancer would recur and I initially said, "No". I said that I knew it could happen but that I did not expect it to happen. Later that day, I thought about what I had said and came to the realization that I was lying to myself. Some part of me clearly felt that recurrence was likely and I was definitely scared. I had been fooling myself with a fake confidence.

Strangely, while I worried about recurrence and the horrible death it could bring, I found myself becoming increasingly afraid of old age, even without recurrence. It was all related to the idea that I had little time left. I started to think about things that I had never really thought about before, such as what happens when you die. Do you go to some better place or do we come face-to-face with God? Is your soul embraced by some omniscient energy life force that is the true existence? Are we reincarnated? Or do we simply cease to exist - a notion I found difficult to accept? I needed to find some deeper meaning to life while I was on the planet as well as an even deeper meaning to man's existence in the cosmos. Heady thoughts with no easy answers.

The depression was always there but, as the medication began to take effect, I stopped having the panic attacks and seemed to be better able to push bad thoughts out of my mind. Things were looking up. On June 18th I had a wonderful experience. Annually, the Canadian Cancer Society runs a *Relay for Life* which is an all-night event where teams of people run, walk or otherwise move around a track to raise money for cancer research. One of these events was held near my home and Ruth had asked if Dianne and I would join her in the *Survivors' Lap* that kicks off the event. Each relay begins with a group of survivors, wearing a special t-shirt, walking around one lap of the track while an announcer reads off their names. Survivors who participate can also invite their care-giver to walk with them. For Ruth and I, that was Dianne, and I know she was as thrilled as we were to have her join us. It was an incredible feeling to walk around that track, Dianne tucked in between Ruth and I. The track itself was surrounded by "luminaries" (candles in a bag) with notes to loved ones lost to cancer (I had, in fact, purchased one for Dianne with a note to her sister Judy). I felt honoured and somewhat humbled to be with such a large group of fellow cancer survivors led by a couple of children who my heart went out to. Just as we started to walk, the rest of the crowd in the stadium unexpectedly broke into applause. I felt like I was going to cry as a whole host of emotions welled up inside of me. All the highs and lows and fears and sadness that I had been facing day after day seemed to bubble up from deep within and I felt uplifted. These people, all of whom had some connection with a cancer victim or survivor, were applauding us because we were survivors. Here was a group of people who seemed to recognize, as best they could without going through it themselves, the tremendous toll that cancer had on us as individuals and the strength that it took to get through it. And while I didn't often feel very strong, it was a reminder to me that I should feel damn proud of myself for getting through it and damn lucky to be there to walk proudly with the rest of the group. It was made all the more special to share those very special few moments with Dianne, who had stood by me through it all and who suffered as much as I in her own way, and with Ruth who had been my rock and advisor - my cancer buddy! I can honestly say that this was the first time that I really understood what it meant to be a survivor and the first time that I fully realized what a big deal it was to be one. It was an epiphany of sorts and felt very, very good!

As I began to mellow out and feel like I was getting more control of my life (thanks to the miracles of modern medicine), I started to look outside of myself. Each day I drove past the lake on my way to work and felt a strong pull, a longing, to be out on the water in my kayak where I would feel free and close to nature. I felt the incredible draw of the outdoors which, to me, was a place of refuge and represented the best of life. I was looking forward to the summer when I could spend more time with Dianne. Thinking about this was something positive that helped take my mind off the everyday stresses of my working life. I was also able to focus and spend more time working on this book, which has forced me to re-live everything, for better or for worse. Writing it has been a very therapeutic experience as I reached back to remember all of the tragedies and triumphs on this long journey and tapped into that emotional memory that I know will always be there. It's funny how the mind can bury the details but can't hide the emotions. If I hadn't kept a detailed diary throughout the ordeal, I couldn't have done this book justice. I would encourage anyone going through a similar experience to keep a diary of events and emotions for a couple of reasons. First and foremost it provides a way of revisiting your experiences which can help you get through some of the inevitable rough times ahead. Second, it's something you can share with your family and friends who want to understand what you have gone through and what you continue to go through. Unless you have gone through it yourself, you can't fully appreciate what cancer does to you emotionally as well as physically, so this is a way of giving others a glimpse of what it's like, in your own words. Besides, you could always write a book!

In May (a year and a half after my surgery) I felt a lump in my neck that appeared to be a swollen lymph gland. Normally, a swollen gland is not something I would think much about, but by mid-June, it was still swollen and there was nothing else going on to explain it, such as a sore throat, sinus infection or dental problem. I made an appointment to see Dr. Gates, who took some blood tests and told me to come back in about a month if it was still there. I had an appointment coming up with Dr. Tracks (my regular PSA test) so I decided to ask him about it.

The visit with Dr. Tracks turned out to be another of several small epiphanies that I have had along this journey. A week before the actual appointment, I had gone in for the usual PSA blood test, still convinced that it would never show anything. For my appointment, I brought a list of things that I didn't think were necessarily signs of recurrence, but that I wanted checked out - just in case. As is often the case at a teaching hospital, I was first checked over by an associate of Dr. Tracks. I showed him my swollen lymph node and described the pains I was having in my abdomen from time-to-time. I also told him how tired I was. He felt all of my lymph nodes (the one's he could anyway - there are lots of them) and he asked several clarification questions before leaving to confer with Dr. Tracks. When they both came back about ten minutes later, Dr. Tracks said, "You're doing fine. We don't need to see you back here until next spring", which was about nine months away. I said, "What about all the symptoms I described to your associate?" He told me they were *non-specific* and likely not related to my Prostate Cancer, particularly since the cancer was contained in my prostate and my margins were clear. I explained my belief and fear that, without a reliable marker, all I had were my symptoms. He said, "You know, you're allowed to have other things wrong with you". Interesting point! But I must admit I was taken aback by his casualness and his seeming *dismissiveness*. Didn't he realize how these fears plagued me? Wasn't I right to wonder? Wasn't it normal to worry?

I thought about this on the way home and came to realize a couple of very important things (this was the epiphany). First of all, he really had nothing else to go on but my PSA and the results of my radical prostatectomy. All of the statistics and his years of experience strongly suggested that my cancer wasn't likely to recur and certainly not this soon. Second, and most importantly, if something specific were to happen, he would deal with it appropriately at that time. There was really nothing he could do but run a lot of expensive and probably useless tests. At the most fundamental level, he knew I was depressed about it and he was just trying to be very positive to make me feel better. He had done the best job he could and the rest was up to my body. I realized then that I was making a symbolic break from my reliance on PMH or, at least, on Dr. Tracks. An important stage of my journey was finished. From now on, all I needed to do (could do) was to monitor my health, take good care of myself, and rely on my family doctor. I would go for the regular PSA tests (I would be foolish not to, just in case) but that would be just one more of the periodic reminders of what I had gone through. I wasn't going to forget anything, nor was I capable of putting everything behind me, but it was clearly time to move on. I needed to think some more on the lessons in this.

In keeping with this new perspective, I enrolled in a special study program at PMH on the relationship of nutrition and eating habits to cancer recurrence. This would not take a lot of time (a couple of questionnaires and interviews) but I figured I would get some valuable information out of it and perhaps help to advance the cause a bit. I also booked another appointment with Dr. Gates to continue to pursue my symptomology. By the time of my appointment, I had had the lump in my neck for about eleven weeks, which I felt was a long time. Gates felt it again and told me that he didn't think it was anything *pathological*, but he made me an appointment with another specialist to check it out, or rather to put my mind at rest. I appreciated his sensitivity a great deal, but I couldn't help but think back to the fact that both he and Dr. Bones initially didn't think the bumps on my prostate were anything either. I will never just assume that these things are nothing until I have had all the proper tests done to prove it. That's just the way things were going to be from now on!

A month later, I finally managed to get in to see Dr. Hall, a local surgeon who had done my colonoscopy a while back. He checked the lump on my neck and told me that it wasn't a lymph node but rather a "submandibular" gland, one that makes your mouth fill with water. Finding out that it wasn't a lymph node was an enormous relief for me, but I felt angry that I been walking around for almost three months thinking that it was. And it wasn't just me. Dianne carried around her own fears about it all summer. For cancer survivors, any problem with the lymphatic system is a cause for worry - it just goes with the territory. No one else had corrected this impression so I sweated it out unnecessarily for all that time. Nonetheless, Dr. Hall was very kind and sensitive. He assured me it was very natural for cancer survivors to worry about every little ache, pain and bump and that it was all right to check things out. In fact, he offered to send me for a bone scan to put my mind at ease about another bout of lower back pain that I had been experiencing for several weeks. While I didn't expect that it would show any metastatic progression (and it didn't), I would feel better knowing for sure.

As I look back on the emotional roller coaster that I had been on for the past year-and-a-half, I began to see that there were two very distinct stages that you go through when you are diagnosed with cancer - one associated with the initial diagnosis and treatment, and the other when you are past all of that and fully face up to the possibility of recurrence. Each of these stages have their own "cycle" of shock, denial, action and acceptance and each one requires different approaches to coping. In the initial stage, it's all about dealing with the immediate threat to your life and the direct impact it has on everything you have ever known. In the later stage, it's all about making the adjustment to life as a cancer survivor and trying to look forward. In some ways, the second stage seems a lot like post-traumatic stress syndrome where the memories and fears that you first felt and had dealt with come back to haunt you in different ways. There is also an element of mourning to this second stage. It's like when you have lost a loved one and, well after the initial shock and the funeral, you think back to what you used to have with that person and feel a real emptiness and sadness. For a cancer survivor, time provides distance from the initial shock but you begin to realize just what you have lost. Life can never be the same and there is a profound sadness in facing this loss of innocence. But, as my psychologist Andrew says, you mourn with the purpose of healing.

As I pondered these feelings and wrestled with adjusting to my life as a cancer survivor, I came to realize that cancer was really two diseases in one; a physical disease of the body and also an emotional disease – a cancer of the mind, if you will. It's a two-for-the-price-of-one special for those unlucky enough to have their bodies turn on them, particularly if they are in the prime of their lives. It is clear that the physical effects of different cancers can vary widely and some people are in much worse shape than others. But it is equally clear to me that the emotional impact of having cancer can be even more devastating than the physical effects. Women are left without breasts, men with problems of incontinence and impotence and, in the worse cases (short of death), people are left with horrible physical handicaps. But any of us can be left with a severely impaired capacity to get on with life and to enjoy the fact that we are still alive. In the very worst extreme, you can become an emotional cripple, preoccupied with the inevitability of death and lacking the perspective to make your life meaningful and worthwhile.

I was not going to let this happen to me.

CHANGING MY LIFE

My mind is an open book.
All you've got to do is look.
And you'll find the answer to
The mystery of my life.

Just take a look at me,
A look at my reality.
And tell me that you can see
The truth of who I am.

> *And so we carry on each day*
> *Without a plan to guide our way.*
> *And we won't know what tomorrow brings*
> *Until the new day dawns.*

I know that you will understand.
I only want to take your hand.
And you can depend on me
To keep you by my side.

I don't want to take you down.
I just want to turn around.
I only hope that I can find
The meaning of my life.

> *And so we carry on each day*
> *Without a plan to guide our way.*
> *And we won't know what tomorrow brings*
> *Until the new day dawns.*

Doug Gosling 2003

While I was going through the worst experience of my life, the rest of the world wasn't doing much better. We were all living through the aftermath of 9/11, sending people off to obscure wars in obscure places, dealing with new fears brought on by SARS and the new reality in which we were all living. To top it all off, the software industry continued to barely sputter along, adding to the everyday pressures that I was faced with. I turned fifty just four months after my surgery and what should have been a significant milestone in my life went virtually unnoticed in the shadow of an even larger, albeit unexpected, milestone - my cancer. The fact is that either one of these milestones could have been enough to trigger some serious soul-searching about what life was all about and what I should be doing with whatever number of years that I had left.

Around the time I was recovering from my surgery, an interesting little story was circulating around the Internet with the title, "*The Mexicans may just have this figured out....*" I have no idea where it originated but it was one of the most illuminating things I had read since I was diagnosed. The story goes like this:

> *Welcome back to the Rat Race (anonymous)...*
>
> *A boat docked in a tiny Mexican village. An American tourist complimented the Mexican fisherman on the quality of his fish and asked how long it took him to catch them.*
> *"Not very long," answered the Mexican.*
> *"But then, why didn't you stay out longer and catch more?" asked the American.*
> *The Mexican explained that his small catch was sufficient to meet his needs and those of his family.*
> *The American asked, "But what do you do with the rest of your time?"*
> *"I sleep late, fish a little, play with my children, and take a siesta with my wife. In the evenings, I go into the village to see my friends, have a few drinks, play the guitar, and sing a few songs...I have a full life."*

*The American interrupted, "I have an MBA from
Harvard and I can help you! You should start by fishing
longer every day. You can then sell the extra fish you
catch. With the extra revenue, you can buy a bigger boat.
With the extra money the larger boat will bring, you can
buy a second one and a third one and so on until you
have an entire fleet of trawlers. Instead of selling your
fish to a middleman, you can negotiate directly with the
processing plants and maybe even open your own plant.
You can then leave this little village and move to Mexico
City, Los Angeles, or even New York City! From there
you can direct your huge enterprise."*

"How long would that take?" asked the Mexican.

*"Twenty, perhaps twenty-five years," replied the
American.*

"And after that?"

*"Afterwards? That's when it gets really interesting,"
answered the American, laughing. "When your business
gets really big, you can start selling stocks and make
millions!"*

"Millions? Really? And after that?"

*"After that you'll be able to retire, live in a tiny village
near the coast, sleep late, play with your children, catch a
few fish, take a siesta, and spend your evenings drinking
and enjoying your friends."*

It's amazing where motivation can come from. It was clear to me that
working my ass off could kill me. I was a workaholic before I was
diagnosed and I had found myself slipping back into those habits. That
had to stop, because I believed the stress could weaken my immune
system and increase the chance of recurrence (I wasn't really sure of
this but I wasn't taking any chances), as well as opening up the door to
all sorts of other problems. The flip side of this was that I was having
trouble finding the meaning in what I was doing. If you're going to
spend most of your waking hours at a job (like I was) it had better be
something that is meaningful to you. What was the use of chewing up
all those precious minutes, hours, days and years if, in the end, you felt
that you had missed out on really enjoying life?

So I started to question what was really important. What was the sum of my life up to this point and what would it be when I finally lay on my deathbed and looked back on the years that I had spent on this planet? Would I be able to say I lived a good life? What is a good life? What is life really for? It was time to make a change and I was beginning to think that maybe I got this horrible disease to *make* me change.

When I was a kid, I felt that I was destined for some kind of greatness. Perhaps many kids feel this way or perhaps my ego was trying to overcome my childhood insecurities. I was a reasonably smart and well-read kid and hadn't yet had to deal with the emotional stresses of being a teenager nor the realities of adulthood. My heroes were people like Leonardo da Vinci, who had used his intellect to make a difference in the world. I thought I would be a scientist when I grew up, maybe even a famous one. Well none of that happened. I haven't touched a physics equation since high school, nor would I want to! But in these later years, with the incredibly loud wakeup call that I had received, I wondered how to make the most of the time that I had left. I knew I had to start with getting a grip on who I was now, so I called Andrew at PMH.

Andrew is a wonderful human being and a very insightful and practical psychologist. He had helped me immensely during the dark time between my diagnosis and surgery and I felt he could help me get a handle on this. I had to talk to him on the phone because, at the time, the hospital was still locked down with SARS. I called him from an empty office at work. Andrew told me how men were having their Prostate Cancer diagnosis delivered by alien-looking doctors in gowns, masks and plastic face shields and weren't even allowed to have their spouse with them for support. I couldn't imagine how horrible that must have been for them.

Andrew described to me how I was actually two people - who I really was and who I projected – and that I had to find a balance between the two. There were times, like when I was at work, that I had to be someone different from who I really was. This was okay because I had to work. But I needed to be true to myself and ensure that this persona didn't dominate my life. Because I was in the midst of experiencing the depression that can go hand in hand with being a cancer survivor, he cautioned me that it was perhaps the worst time to be reviewing my life. Depression makes it very difficult to deal with global issues such as the meaning of life. I had been through a huge change and had to deal with fifty years of habits that I had developed and that were deeply ingrained in my brain. He said that I was like an abused woman who returns to what she knows, even though it is bad for her. I sure felt abused and he was right - I was definitely reverting back to what was dangerously comfortable.

He gave me some ideas on how to cope with the depression so that I could begin to get on with my life and start to address the big issues. He recommended meditating ten minutes a day but I never could seem to get the hang of that. When I had "bad thoughts", he told me to write them down and reflect on them the next day. I actually did this for a while and it helped. He also told me to find other things to do to distract me from my depression. What I was going through was normal, and I had to realize that, but I couldn't let it dominate my life.

As a Type "A" personality, he pointed out that everything tended to be black or white to me and also that I tended to be risk-averse, in fact avoiding any real risk whatsoever. I had never really thought about that before but it was very true. What I needed to do was to realize that other things in life were just as important as my job and my cancer and that I needed to find the time to pursue other interests. I needed to set goals and work towards them but I also needed to realize that the *journey* was much more important than reaching the actual goals.

I had no goals. I was on a journey, but it had no purpose and I just was just being dragged along. If I was going to change my life, it really was time to start.

But how do you do this? How could I begin to get a handle on what was important to me and what I should do with my life? I had never done anything like this before and I didn't know how to start. I needed help.

Sue, a good friend whom I had worked with for several years, recommended that I try the FranklinCovey system, based on Stephen

Covey's well-known book, "The 7 Habits of Highly Effective People". She walked me through her own version of the system and I thought it might do the trick.

At first glance it seemed to be just another time management system, but there is a part of the system that forces you to think carefully about what was important to you with the ultimate goal of defining a personal mission statement that would govern everything you do. I found this to be one of the most valuable things I have ever done and I would like to share some of the key observations and statements that help to describe who I really am.

One of the key steps in the process is to define the *Values* that govern your life. It forces you to articulate what has value for you as a human being and describes the key influences on what you do in your life and how you do it.

It should come as no surprise that *Health and Fitness* was the first value I defined. I then broke it down into several short statements that help to clarify what this really means to me.

- *I must prevent recurrence of cancer.*
- *I will eat proper foods and take appropriate supplements.*
- *I will strive to minimize stress.*
- *I will work out regularly.*
- *I will attain/maintain a high level of fitness.*

The next, obvious value I defined was *Family*.

- I love my family.
- I have a strong sense of duty.
- I will be there for my family.

Since most of us have to work, it's important to have a value around *Professionalism and Career* and I had been doing a lot of thinking about this anyway in terms of where it should fit in the big picture of my life.

- My career is a means to an end.

- I enjoy doing high quality work
- I am damn good at what I do.
- I will work hard but will not allow it to consume me.

I began to think a lot about *Friends* as well. About what a friend really was and about who were my "real" friends. I believed that I had ignored my friends and had discounted the value of friendship for many years. Not good.

- I will make time for my friends.
- I will be more social in general.
- I will focus on a few friends.
- I will be there for my friends.
- I will avoid toxic people.

One of the problems with being a workaholic is that you just don't have time for anything else, including friends, which means that you miss out on so much. The experience that I had with the friends who stepped up to support me during my worst times taught me how important it was to make the time to be with them. But I also recognized that I had to be selective in who I spent time with. I knew now that life was too short to waste on meaningless or toxic relationships.

A new value that I had come to realize was very important, was *Balance*. I had done a lousy job of attaining this so far in my life. Now it was time.

- Balance is important to my health.
- I will strive to achieve balance.
- I will work smarter and be more organized, effective and focused.
- I will not let one thing dominate my life.

A big value that I had lived with for all of my life was my love of the *Outdoors*. With my new perspective on life, it was taking on even more importance. To be a bit "new age" about it all, I was beginning to realize that life in the city, surrounded by concrete walls, was not what human beings were intended to do. We have been given this beautiful, wonderful planet to live on and we continually push it back and purposefully shelter ourselves from it. It was a very important part of my life growing up but I had distanced myself from it as I grew older. I wanted to recapture some of that to reorient myself.

- I love kayaking and wilderness camping.
- I will share this love with family and friends.
- I derive spiritual health from being in the outdoors.
- I will make time for this.

Many of these values are very personal and inwardly focused but it is vitally important to look after yourself in many different ways. But it is equally important that your values extend to relationships and interactions with others. A very strong value of mine was *Respect and Integrity* which, in my mind, was a two-way street.

- I will work and live with the utmost integrity.
- I will respect others.
- I will respect myself.
- I will earn the respect of others.
- The past is gone; only today and tomorrow count.

Life can be pretty serious at times so it's important to have a little fun and *Humour* is a key part of that.

- Humour is healthy and relieves stress.
- I will keep my sense of humour at work and with friends and family.

Community has been an important part of my life ever since I was a teenager and community work was always something that gave me back as much or more than I gave. I had gotten away from it in the past several years but it was time to get back into it, albeit in a balanced way.

- I have given much to my community.
- I will help where and when I can.
- I will focus on cancer related activities.

My cancer was a call to action for me personally, but it has also given me a focus for my need to help. This book is a very important part of that.

And finally, the most neglected value was *Life* itself. This was the most fundamental of my newly formed value system.

- I will live life fully.
- I am not afraid to die but I do not want to.
- My life has meaning to others.
- When things look bad, I remember that *I am alive!*

There are many other important steps in the FranklinCovey system – defining your various roles and answering critical evaluation questions about yourself – and through these you start to get a very good picture of who you are and what is important to you. The final step then is to define your *Personal Mission Statement*. Here is mine.

- I will live with integrity and strive to be a positive and creative force in the lives of others.
- I will be healthy and encourage others to live healthy lives.
- I will live for today, focusing on what is really important.
- I will be part of nature.
- I will paddle hard and true.

While the last bullet may seem a little confusing, or perhaps even corny, it is the one statement that encapsulates the essence of how I wanted to live my life moving forward. Paddling hard and true embraces my love of the outdoors, especially kayaking, and the hard and true applies to everything I do. I will work hard, with purpose and integrity, but with direction. I am going somewhere. Now I just have to make sure that I know where that is!

I read a lot of other books that promised to show me how to take control of my life and be successful. I finally read "The 7 Habits of Highly Effective People", which reinforced the lessons of the FranklinCovey exercise. I read a book for an effectiveness course called "Strategic Coach" that stressed how important it was to schedule time for yourself, something I have always had difficulty doing. And I read the famous

"Who Moved My Cheese?" that emphasized in very simple terms how we all need to take a chance and be a little adventurous if we want to improve our lot in life. To me it meant breaking away from the bad habits of my past, which were not getting me anywhere, and not letting the fact that I had cancer stop me from moving forward and living my life.

These readings and exercises helped immensely in my efforts to put some structure around my life and to become more focused in how I approached the day-to-day challenge of living. I concentrated on trying to work smarter (which helped me to work less) and to make myself do things for *me*. I felt that I needed to unleash my creativity because it was so much a part of who I was and I had been neglecting it for so long. I got back to playing my guitar and wrote three new songs in four days, songs that talked about how I was feeling and my hopes for the future. If felt good. And certainly, writing this book was going to be a positive, creative activity, but it was much more than that. I love to write and it has always been my dream to be able to make a living at it. I thought that perhaps it would stimulate me to write more and to put the effort into getting published. We have all heard how the best career in the world is one that allows you to do what you love. Well this would be mine. I could clearly picture myself living in a comfortable small place on a lake somewhere and writing for enjoyment and for a bit of a stipend on which to live. My expectations are certainly not as high as they might have been in the past, so I don't feel the need to be a best-selling author. It's something to think about and perhaps a goal to pursue.

I started to change other things in my life in keeping with my emerging new self-image. I had my hair cut in a less sober style and messed it up in a funky kind of way when I was not at work. It was a small thing but it made me feel younger, freer and more in control. I stopped putting up with toxic behaviours from people around me, even from people I formerly liked. I didn't need it and there just wasn't time enough to waste on that type of negative interaction. I remember a particular advertisement for Scotiabank that was on television recently with the tag line, "Life is your most valuable asset." I understood this now and was determined not to waste it.

I began to realize how much of a rat race I was in, living in the city and working in an uncertain, high stress job. To live in a big city, you need a more substantial income than if you lived elsewhere and, while you can do anything and find anything in a big city, you had to fight the traffic and spend lots of money on things you probably don't really need. People kill themselves just to live in the city and I sure didn't want to be one of them. Whether I could make a living at writing or not, I would love to live in a small town near the water, such as on Georgian Bay or on the west coast. Dianne could teach painting and I could do design, carpentry or just work in the local hardware store. I always found that my mind was very clear and at peace when I was working on projects around the house and I was beginning to wonder if I was meant to work with my hands. I honestly felt that, if anything happened to Dianne, I would move to that place on a lake (with my dogs) in an instant. I could picture myself running a small bait shop, growing my hair long and driving a Harley-Davidson around on the dirt roads. Dianne bought me a small model bait shop, along with a toy Harley and kayak, to remind me of this dream and to help me keep my perspective. Dianne and I both realized that we had to plan for our future - to find something that would fit both of our dreams.

I continued to find inspiration in strange places and I found some one day while sitting in the dentist's chair having my teeth cleaned. Lucy, the dental hygienist, had just been married and was talking about the future. She said the simplest thing that resonated loudly and clearly in my own mind, "The best is yet to come." I couldn't get it out of my head for days. I turned it over and over again in my mind thinking about what a wonderful view of the world it represented. Here I was, struggling with the sudden realization that I had a limited time on the planet, wondering what I was going to do with myself, thinking that the glass was half-empty, and then along came this idea that "the best is yet to come". If that was true, if one could truly believe in that simple thought, then everything that happened in the past was just less important and we could look forward to what was going to come our way, to the *better* things we were going to experience in the years to come. And why shouldn't that be the case? Why couldn't the future be as good as we want it to be?

I have always recognized that I am a product of my past; of everything I have done and everything that I have seen, heard, experienced or had done to me. There really is nothing earth-shattering in this statement, but perhaps it is the wrong way to look at who you are. The past is past and there is nothing we can do about it; so defining ourselves in terms of something we can't change doesn't give us very much flexibility, nor much to look forward to. Perhaps we are really defined by what we do today - right now - and that in turn starts to define our future selves. And if that is true, there really is nothing holding us back from becoming all we can be by making choices today that are dictated solely by who we can be rather than who we were. This is tough for a cancer survivor whose memories and self-image are dominated by the fact of cancer. But perhaps it is a fundamental truth that we should all come to grips with. If the best really is yet to come then let us not allow the past to prevent us from breaking away and experiencing a true freedom that we have never allowed for ourselves.

Almost immediately I noticed a change in the way that I approached my job and my personal life. I was getting some fire back in my belly and was more confident and direct in my dealings with customers and co-workers. For a while I seriously considered the idea of making a wholesale career change, but I convinced myself that this wasn't the right time. I was in a new job in a new company where I felt like I was an important part of their future. I was excited and energized and I found that I could work hard and be successful without consuming every night and weekend. What a concept! I was having fun at work and now had time to do other things.

My personal life began to change now that I had the time to think about it; now that I allowed myself that luxury. I started to become interested in current affairs again, something I had completely abandoned so I could concentrate on my own little world, dominated by my illness and my fears. I started to listen to new music again, having previously slipped back into the safety and comfort of those golden oldies. Even my reading habits changed and I started picking up books that dealt with history, current affairs and more serious things. The world was coming back into focus for me and I began to care what was going on around me. It wasn't all about me anymore. I just had to let myself go. It was a wonderful feeling of freedom to be back in the world of the living. I would still be who I was but I finally knew that I was in control of who I could be.

It was a year and a half after my surgery when Dianne signed up to work as head cook at a summer camp. It was something previously unthinkable that had a profound impact on both of our lives. Our kids had been going to a summer camp a couple of hours out of Toronto for most of their childhood and teenage years, both as campers and as counsellors. We always knew that it was a wonderful experience for them and, when Dianne got the opportunity to sign on as the head cook for the summer, we both thought it was a wonderful idea, even though most of her friends thought she was crazy. As our daughter, Caralia, was going to be working at the camp, it would be the last opportunity to spend time with her before she headed off to university. It was going to be a big change for both of us. Dianne had not worked outside of the house for a long time and had never cooked for so many people. And I was going to be totally alone for the better part of each week. Quite a change, but we both realized that this was just the kind of thing we needed to be doing to shake us out of the doldrums of the past and to make positive changes in both our lives. For my part, I arranged to take Fridays off for the whole summer so that I could join her up at the camp. I even brought my kayak up and parked it near the water.

It proved to be an eventful summer. The job was much harder than either of us realized as Dianne found herself working twelve or thirteen hours a day with only one day off each week. At first I just relaxed while I was up there and she was in the kitchen, but soon I found myself working beside her for many of the meals just to help her out and to be able to spend time with her. As a bonus, Caralia worked for Dianne in the kitchen during the first part of the summer so our little family unit was together quite a bit, in a totally foreign environment. There were ups and downs as Dianne had to deal with all the drama that unfolds when a bunch of young women (the camp staff) were together in such a closed environment, but that just added colour to the whole experience.

It was wonderful! As hard as it was on Dianne, she rediscovered a great deal about herself. She developed a renewed confidence in her ability to do a very hard job with horrendous hours and to do it well. Her sense of independence grew enormously. But even more important, she developed very close relationships with many of the camp staff; teenagers who we had seen grow up as campers with our own kids and become confident young adults and leaders. Several of the kids took to confiding in her and she literally became one of them, an amazing feat given the huge gap that often exists between adults and young people. They lovingly called her the "Queen of Hearts". While I didn't get as close as Dianne did to the kids, I grew very fond of them and they gradually began to reciprocate. When I would go up on the weekends, I was greeted with warmth and lots of hugs that meant so much to me, particularly since I used to be somewhat aloof in dealing with young people. And just being there was a profound experience. I would work all day on Thursday, talking to bankers and co-workers about all sorts of serious things and, a couple of hours later, I was in the camp dining hall singing camp songs along with the staff and campers as they jumped up on their chairs and screamed at the top of their lungs! There is nothing like it to make you immediately forget about work, traffic jams, and all the other worries that afflict you in the city. I looked forward to the weekends and to being back at camp. This was what life was really all about. This was living as we had never done it before. We realized why our kids were so connected with the camp and how close they had become to their camp friends.

Even more amazing was that many of them were now our friends too. We threw an after-camp party and invited all of the camp staff to our house before the Labour Day long weekend. To our great pleasure, most of them came and all of the ones that were closest to us. We had a ball and were so pleased to find that we could sit and talk to the kids as if we were "one of the gang". As the evening wore down, we sat with several of them, talking about boyfriends and other problems. They listened to what we had to say. We had found some rare and wonderful balance where we were treated as peers, or at least friends, and yet they accepted our adult advice. For Dianne and I, it was a cathartic experience and showed us that there were so many new dimensions to the world and gave us hope that we truly could find the best things in life.

Even though this was a wonderful, even magical summer, we couldn't completely get away from the dark cloud of cancer. I had to deal with the lump in my neck, spending most of the summer thinking it was a lymph node. That, combined with the lower back pain that plagued me all summer, ensured that nagging doubts followed me around every day. Dianne worried constantly about me, particularly since I was alone a good part of the week. We got through it, but I couldn't help thinking again that this was a glimpse of what my life was going to be like for some time. As usual, my "cancer buddy" Ruth put it into perspective for me in a card she sent me towards the end of that summer.

Doug, Just to let you know that I enjoy talking to you about what you and I struggle through. Dammit! I hate some of the things that we must endure because of cancer! We'll probably never be able to make all "the bad stuff" go away, but we can enjoy each day as best we can, and I truly believe there remains lots of good living yet!

SURVIVORSHIP AND SPIRITUALITY

Do not stand at my grave and weep.
I am not there, I do not sleep.

I am a thousand winds that blow,
I am the diamond glints on snow.

I am the sunlight on the ripened grain.
I am the gentle autumn's rain.

When you awaken in the morning hush,
I am the swift uplifting rush
Of quiet birds in circled flight.
I am the soft stars that shine at night.

Do not stand at my grave and cry.
I am not there, I did not die.

A Hopi Prayer

After all I had been through, I knew that I needed to continue with the process of getting on with my life, building on all of the insights and strengths that I had developed. But I found that getting on with life was not that easy when you have been through a life-changing experience such as cancer. In my case, it took a good four years before I could honestly say that I had dealt as best I could with all of the challenges that my diagnosis and treatment had brought.

I had eventually come to the realization that I had to adjust to being a survivor, to allow the cancer to become a past thing, a big bump in the road, a wake-up call ... whatever. But I couldn't let go. Something was bothering me, something very deep down in my psyche. By this time, I knew myself well enough to realize that I would not be able to move on until I discovered what this was and dealt with it. But I knew I couldn't do it on my own. I needed help, and who else could I turn to but Andrew.

Over the course of several intensive sessions, Andrew and I explored the feelings that I was experiencing, the questions that kept creeping up from deep inside and the impact this was having on my ability to achieve some degree of peace and to move on. Andrew again emphasized how significant an event my cancer diagnosis was and helped me to step back a bit and look at myself more objectively. He helped me to better understand how my mind worked. I tend to over-analyze everything to the point where I experience real mental and emotional stress if I can't understand, categorize and explain what is going on. This is not a bad thing; it's just part of who I am. It's why I am good at my job and good at whatever I try to do. I read, I research, I model, I sort, I categorize and reach conclusions or form opinions and then (and only then) do I feel any degree of satisfaction. Andrew pulled this out of me, gently urging me to articulate the questions that were bothering me, and then forcing them back on me to answer. He enabled me to have a dialogue with myself that allowed me to work through the confusion and to finally understand what it was that was bothering me. It was very simple. I had come face to face with my mortality – the reality of my own eventual death – and I realized that I had absolutely no idea of the true meaning and value of my life. There, at the root of all that I was feeling, was the age-old, ultimately unanswerable question, "Why am I here?" I was now in the realm of the truly spiritual because there is simply no provable, factual answer to that question. For anyone!

I was raised as a Christian, but was not a regular churchgoer. My belief in God was wrapped up in what I had been taught about the bible, but religion was simply not a big part of my life. I believe that I have always had a sound moral foundation to my character and to the way I lived my life, but it was not something that I "refreshed" regularly through religious worship. In fact, I had become very disillusioned with the modern church, feeling that the trappings of the church and the secularism of religion were a complex man-made veneer over much more fundamental things. God was not going to save me from cancer or talk to me and give me the answers to my questions. So where was I to get this? I recall telling Andrew that I actually envied people who were deeply religious because they knew what their purpose in life was (to serve God and prepare themselves for Heaven) and they knew what was waiting for them after they died. To me, this was the fundamental attraction and perhaps the most beneficial thing that religion can offer an individual. To be able to have such certainty in your beliefs seemed to me to be a tremendous gift. Unfortunately, I just wasn't built that way and was going to have to figure this out for myself. But where was I to start?

As it turned out, my discussions with Andrew were the starting point for all of this. We talked at length about what it meant to live and what it might mean to die. Andrew wasn't trying to lead me in any particular direction but he coached me through my own mental journey, helping me to uncover the nuggets of ideas that could be polished and arranged into something that began to make sense. Along the way, I discarded some of the old beliefs and ideas that were actually more about me then about God or destiny. We talked about different religions, particularly the Eastern religions, and their concepts of where we come from, why we are here, and how we move on to higher planes of existence. While fundamentally, these had some greater appeal to me than the traditional Christian religions, they were old belief systems and had therefore built up their own secularized trappings and traditions. It was the core of their beliefs that I was interested in and I couldn't see the answer (for me) in diving in and becoming a follower. So I took what I could, without great study, and used it to reinforce the foundation that I was building,

Around this time, I began to read a very interesting book by Ernest Becker entitled "The Denial of Death" for which he received a Pulitzer Prize in 1974. Ironically Becker died that same year of Colon Cancer at the age of 49, the same age at which I was first diagnosed. This is a complex book that is not for the faint of heart. With the risk of understating this great work, Becker tells us that the fear of death haunts us all and drives us to adopt "heroic" roles that allow us to deny death and define some kind of meaning for ourselves. He mentions that some primitive cultures celebrated death as a kind of "promotion" but that most modern people do not really believe this so we are driven to focus on the roles that we adopt to somehow avoid the finality of death. He doesn't have any answer to what happens after we die, just that we will die, and he clearly understands that facing up to this fact is exceptionally scary and difficult for anyone. I wonder how he felt at the end of his life.

Dianne was not very happy to see me reading a book about death. Understandably, she thought that it was very morbid and feared that I was focusing far too much on the subject. This was a scary thought for her given all of her experience with cancer and she didn't need to be reminded that cancer could take her husband. She also didn't want to see me become even more depressed than I had already been by thinking too much about it. I understood this and I loved her for her concern, but I needed to wrestle this thing to the ground if I was to ever find peace.

I spent many months contemplating and even agonizing over this subject. My discussions with Andrew had allowed me to get past my fear that life had no meaning – that, since we all die, what's the use of doing anything? This was far too bleak a view of life and one that I realized I just couldn't accept. And in getting to this point, I saw the emergence of an important realization that I could believe *something* even if I couldn't *know*.

I read a few more books to try to get some other perspectives and I did a bit of research on Hinduism and Buddhism. One of the books that finally helped me to coalesce my thoughts around all of this was "The Active Side of Infinity" by Carlos Castenada. I haven't read all of Castenada's books and I wasn't focusing on his life as an apprentice to Don Juan, but it was the first book that made me think about the broader Universe and how it exists beyond us and forever beyond our short existence on this planet.

And so it was, while sitting on a rock in Georgian Bay on one of my week-long kayak trips, that I achieved a true spiritual epiphany. This was not a revelation from God or anything as dramatic as that, but it felt like I had finally found my way through the heavy fog that was surrounding my life into the light of understanding. I found a belief system, or at least a way of describing our place in the Universe, that felt comfortable enough to me that I could use it as the basis for understanding and perhaps living my life. I fully accepted the fact that I could not prove anything whatsoever about life, death or eternity and that this was okay. And since I couldn't prove or disprove anything, I had complete freedom to define a spiritual view that made some sense to me and that I could live with. It was the ultimate religious freedom. I did not need to be bound by anyone else's beliefs. I knew that I needed something, so I created it.

In a nutshell, I choose to believe that we are all part of a great Universe that is all energy and that has intelligence. I do not believe there is a master plan that guides us except that the Universe is all about growth. We (or the spark of energy that is us) are somehow "installed" on this planet to spend time learning and growing and, through interactions with others, help them to learn and grow. And in the end, we all go back to that Universal field of energy contributing to and becoming part of the whole. So while we are here, we can adopt roles (as Becker suggests) that allow us to function, but that ultimately allow us to grow. Our purpose is simply to sample life and interact with others. And since I choose to believe that good is better than evil and that joy is better than sadness (and that these positive things help us grow), I can define a role for myself that does good and gives me joy. My purpose in life and the meaning of my life are defined in these simple choices, and I can live with that … even thrive. I don't know what happens after death, whether we retain any concept of self, but that's okay. Energy cannot be destroyed and I am energy and will return to energy having added something to the whole.

I have since read many, many books that seem to support this idea of the Universe and our place in it and I am thankful for the reinforcement this gives me. But the choice is mine. I am comfortable with what I choose to believe and it has helped me immensely. I no longer fear a death that is inevitable and I can now live my life as fully as I want.

In April, 2007, my new beliefs were tested when my father passed away at the glorious age of ninety-two, having led a full and happy life. He had been steadily declining for a couple of years and, in the last few months, it was clear that it was only a matter of time. While he never really lost the sharpness of his mind, he seemed almost too tired to communicate most of the time and I felt that he was finally choosing to let his body shut down. He had been living with a lot of pain for several years and perhaps it was becoming too much to bear.

His passing was a tremendously enlightening experience for me. There had been several false alarms when he had contracted pneumonia and the hospital had told us it was near the end. Many times, he had proved them wrong, but each time he recovered it was only about half-way to where he had been. As a result, I had time to think about the fact that he was going to die and to adjust to the idea. Even more importantly, I had a chance to talk to him about it. One day, when I visited my parents in their retirement home, I took my dad for a stroll in his wheelchair and parked in a quite area. We didn't mention death at all but we both clearly understood what we were talking about. I told him that I loved him very much and that I was very proud to have him as my father. I also told him that he had been truly blessed to have lived a long and wonderful life. When I asked him if he had any regrets he said he had only one - that he hadn't met my mother sooner. They had just celebrated their fifty-ninth anniversary! It was a wonderful, sharing experience that gave me, and I hope him, a sense of closure.

I saw my father two more times after that. He had been admitted to the hospital after taking a turn for the worse and he lay in bed hooked up with an IV, catheter and oxygen tubes, too weak to do much more than make small noises and occasionally move his hand. When I went to leave after several hours I leaned over to kiss him goodbye and, surprisingly, he grabbed my arm, lifted his head to kiss me, and said, "Thanks for coming." It was the first and only thing he said that day. I almost cried. The next time I saw him was a couple of days later, the night before he died. He had become a withered shell of the big, powerful man who had raised me and it was clear the end was near. I had a few minutes alone with him before I left and, as I stroked his hair, I told him that it was okay to let go and that we would take good care of my mother for him.

The retirement home called me the next morning to tell me that my father had passed and they gave me the opportunity to tell my mother, which I was very grateful for. I called her and told her that it had happened and that I would head down there right away. She said she would wait for me so we could go to see him one last time together. It was a sad day but the sadness I felt was mostly for my mother who, after all of these years, would be alone. I was sad for myself as well, but I had already accepted his death and I felt good that he was finally free of all the pain. I stayed with my mother that night, actually sleeping in my father's hospital-style bed. As I drifted off into a restless sleep, I had the distinct sense that my father was in the room with us. I saw, in my mind, his gentle face in a cloud of energy floating near the ceiling. He smiled at me and said, "Thanks for coming." Then he was gone. In my heart I choose to believe that he really was there, that the energy that was his essence came to me on his way back to becoming part of the Universe once more. I can't prove that, of course, but I don't care. It was profoundly comforting to me.

My father's funeral was, unlike any other I had attended, a true celebration of his life. His many friends and all of our family members gathered to say goodbye, to praise the good man that they had all known, and to comfort my mother. For my part, I felt truly uplifted. I spoke about the great, long love affair of my parents, about wonderful memories that I had, and about the support they had given me when I was diagnosed with cancer. I told everyone how he had cried for me on the phone the night before my surgery. Somehow, I made it through my speech without breaking down myself. The look in my mother's eyes when I finished touched my soul. I had faced my father's death and I knew with certainty that I could face my own when it finally came.

Looking back on this spiritual journey, this intense voyage of great discovery, I see how essential it was for me. I realize that, without it, I would never have been able to achieve the degree of acceptance and understanding that I needed to move on with my life. It was something that I just had to get through. And for a while, I thought it was just me, or people like me. But I soon discovered that this was a very common stage that many, if not most cancer survivors go through. I was introduced to a program called "The Healing Journey" that has been around for some time as an aid for cancer patients. This program is a series of interventions (group discussions and self study) that focus on the many aspects of survivorship including coping with stress, developing a healthy lifestyle, changing attitudes, and on developing a spiritual awareness. The spiritual component is all about discovering the self, finding meaning, and ultimately achieving peace and acceptance. This is everything that I had gone through on my own and here it was offered in a program! In my own case, it was probably good that I did it my way, but it is reassuring to know that help is available for other cancer survivors. And it is always good to know that you are not alone in what you face.

And so it was that I was able to get on with defining, rather than finding, a life that had meaning. I had my critical roles to play as husband, father, breadwinner and friend, and these would always be the biggest part of me, but I felt that I needed to exploit my role as a cancer survivor in a way that would help others. I had already started writing this book and I knew it could be of some help to others, but I wanted to reach out in other ways. So I threw myself into the development of a web site that would take advantage of the latest communication technologies and potentially reach a wide audience.

There are over twelve million cancer survivors in North America and, if you take into account only the immediate family, the number of people who experience the *emotional* disease of cancer, the "cancer in the mind", that number swells to thirty-six million. Adding extended family and friends to this number can blow it way up. In all of my own research on the web, looking for information and support, I found very little dealing with the emotional aspects of cancer, so I decided to focus my website on that. And so *talkingaboutcancer.com* was born. With the help of my own psychologist, Andrew, and my cancer buddy Ruth, the site was launched in the fall of 2007 using the concept of blogging to allow for interaction with the ever-growing community of web-savvy cancer survivors and their families and friends. Immediately, we started connecting with people from all over the world who thanked us for sharing our thoughts and who provided their own very personal and insightful comments. The site will grow over time and all of the blog posts and comments will always be accessible, gradually building the content of the site and providing a wealth of knowledge on how cancer affects people emotionally and how other people have dealt with it.

So I have become an author and a blogger. Who knew? I have chosen to accept my role as a cancer survivor and to build something good on the foundation of knowledge and insight that it has given me. My work has importance and I truly believe that I am helping people. And I will continue to do so for so as long as I can.

My life has meaning.

THE WOLF AT MY DOOR
RECURRENCE

It is useful sometimes to think about our lives in terms of chapters. Like a book, we open new chapters of our life as we make new decisions, make significant changes or when we are faced with major events in our lives. I felt that I had been through several important chapters during the four-plus years since my initial diagnosis and that I was, in fact, well into the post-cancer chapter of my life. I had been through an intensely emotional journey that had left me with many scars, physical and psychological, but I had emerged a new and better person. I had faced my mortality directly and had defined myself and my place in the Universe with a new spirituality. I had embraced my survivorship in a positive way and was trying to give something back to the world, to make a contribution by helping others deal with their cancer diagnosis.

But I came to realize that having cancer is like having the proverbial wolf at your door. You sense that it is out there waiting to jump you if you open the door at the wrong time and you always worry that one of these days it is going to huff and puff and blow your whole world to hell. And sometimes, when you think everything is safe and sound and you're feeling very secure, you hear the screeching of sharp claws on the other side of the door and it all comes flooding back. The fear, the uncertainty and the gnawing doubt that eat away at all of the precious hope that you have so painstakingly built.

On September 24, 2007, the door came crashing in on my home and the wolf reared its ugly head.

A few days earlier, I had gone to PMH for my annual PSA blood test. It had been almost five full years from my initial diagnosis and, since my surgery, my PSA reading has always been <0.05, considered undetectable. My appointment on the 24th was with Dr. Tracks and, as usual, he sent one of the residents in first to give me the good news. I was expecting the same old undetectable but, this time, I was told that my PSA reading was 0.13. The resident told me that their lab had changed the assay method for measuring PSA and that they were getting some odd results, such that they couldn't be sure whether my reading was indicative of recurrence. At that point, I asked to see Dr. Tracks who told me that 10-20% of his patients were getting strange results and that he was not happy with this. He suggested that I have another test done and see him again in three months.

I was in shock and not at all happy with the explanation. Had the cancer returned or was this some spurious result? There was no damn way I could wait another three months so I suggested that I have another test that day. Dr. Tracks said this was a good idea and that I could call for the results on Wednesday.

Coincidently, I had seen Andrew pass by while I was in the clinic so I went to see him as soon as I had left the consultation room. I told him how shocked I was and how angry I was with the explanation I was given. He promised to look into the testing situation for me and told me to call him after I got the new results. I left the hospital in a daze and was halfway home when I realized that I had left without getting the second blood test. Talk about denial! I called Dianne and told her that I had bumped into Andrew and had left my briefcase in his office, then turned around and went back.

I couldn't tell Dianne. When she asked, I said that everything was fine. In spite of all we had been through together, I kept it from her, partly because there was uncertainty around whether this was a valid result, but mainly because I was heading out of town for an overnight trip as soon as I got home. There was no way I was going to dump this on her and then leave like I had when I was first diagnosed. It seemed to be the lesser of two evils. I hated to do it, but I felt that it wasn't fair to blow up her world without more facts. I carried the burden alone, trying to feel good and applying all that I had learned about the mind. I awoke that evening at 2:00 AM in a strange hotel, unable to sleep anymore.

Two days later, on the Wednesday, I received the news from my second PSA test. This time, it was 0.15, close enough to the last one to be more or less the same. I was still worried and confused about the so-called "strange" results that Dr. Tracks mentioned so I made an appointment with Dr. Goodman (who had since become my family doctor) and asked him for another PSA test at a different lab. Even though I was back from my business trip, I still didn't want to worry Dianne so I told her that I was experiencing some vertigo and wanted to check it out. She is scarily perceptive. First, she asked me if I thought my vertigo was from brain cancer. Later on, out of the blue, she told me that she didn't want to lose me and when I asked her how, she said she was terrified that my cancer would return! That made me even more afraid to tell her until I knew for sure. Even though she had chided me for trying to protect her in the past, I still couldn't do it.

On Thursday, I called Andrew and made an appointment with him for the following Tuesday. He told me over the phone that I needed to tell Dianne soon or she would never trust me again, and I promised to do that on the weekend. Andrew called me back later in the day and said that he had spoken to Dr. Tracks specifically about my case. Dr. Tracks said it was possible that this new test was so sensitive that it was showing a level that had already been there and perhaps it was defining a new baseline level of "undetectable". He said we wouldn't know anything until the next couple of tests. If my PSA was stable, then it may be a new baseline, but if it increased even a bit, he would do salvage radiation to "make sure I get my thirty years". I wasn't very convinced about the new baseline idea and frustrated by the uncertainty surrounding this. Given my low PSA before, I felt that anything was a sure sign of recurrence. I needed to validate the results at another lab and, in fact, Andrew suggested that I have a monthly PSA test through my family doctor.

I researched and read anything I could find on the Internet to see if there were any other reports of "strange" PSA results or if there were new thresholds being established. There was nothing, absolutely nothing, and I felt that if some new testing protocol was redefining PSA levels, that it would be all over the Internet, particularly on the news groups that had been so helpful to me in the past. At the end of the day, Dr. Goodman's office called to tell me that the other lab sent back a PSA reading of 0.14. I didn't give a damn about new testing methods and "strange" results. Something was definitely there and I had to tell Dianne.

I found some time to be by myself to try to get my head around what was happening. I was okay. Not great, but okay. While I was researching PSA testing, I found a wealth of information on recurrence suggesting that catching and treating it early could potentially put me into long-term remission. If the treatment didn't work well, based on what I had read, I figured I could still have eight to fifteen years. I can do a lot with fifteen years. I could make it meaningful, but I was utterly horrified at the thought of leaving Dianne early. She had recently posted on my website that she is terrified of losing everyone close to her and not having anyone left to look after her. I hated the thought of doing that to her.

Life was going to change yet again. Big time. I wondered what tomorrow would bring?

Tomorrow came fast and I finally gathered up the courage to tell Dianne. She took it well, all considered, but was clearly afraid. As I expected, she was a bit angry with me for not telling her right away, but understood why I had waited. She had definitely suspected something and knew the moment I sat down with her that there was bad news. In fact, she said she had suspected something when I told her I had left my briefcase in Andrew's office, something which I never do. She also confided to me that she wondered if the cancer had metastasized to my brain, causing me to be forgetful! How's that for sensitivity?

I told her everything I knew, what I didn't know, and what I thought, and I assured her that from then on, the two of us would face this together. Later, I drove to my daughter's office and sat down with her in the lobby and told her what was going on. I didn't want to wait because she always seemed to know when something was wrong, and I wanted to tell her in person and treat her like the intelligent, mature young lady she had become. She took it stoically as usual, but I could tell she was very worried. That night, I told my son Sean over the phone. He told me he loved me and to call him any time I needed to talk, which was sweet. I hated to bring this dark cloud over all of us.

On the following Tuesday, Dianne and I met with Andrew in his office at PMH. He explained how the emotional impact of a recurrence could be just as significant as my initial diagnosis and that I needed to deal with it in much the same way. He carefully explained the options and sequence of treatments that I faced, which I think really helped Dianne. We were both okay until we got home and I experienced an enormous weight descending upon me, forcing me to bed where I slept for a long time. I realized that it was finally starting to hit me.

On Saturday, I visited my mom in the retirement home and told her. She didn't really want to talk about it but I knew that she would worry. It must be scary for a mother to think her son could die before her. Dianne stayed home and missed me, but she felt it was better that I talk to my mom alone. She talked to Ruth for a while and cried her heart out. She worries about everything now and my heart aches at what this is doing to her, after all she has been through with Judy, Ruth and me.

I was finding that it was really starting to affect my sleep. I would wake up in the wee hours of the morning unable to get back to sleep. Even when I slept, I dreamt about cancer and PSA. I kept going over it in my mind. We were looking at a biological system (me) that never had a PSA level above 1.26 with an intact prostate and a 40% tumour volume so, with the prostate completely gone, a PSA of even 0.15 had to be very significant. I had been researching the link between tumour volume and recurrence and found studies that showed it to be a predictor of recurrence even though the research subjects had tumours much smaller than mine. I thought that perhaps my situation would teach the hospitals to red flag big tumours.

October 15 was the five-year anniversary of my initial diagnosis. It was a very bad day. On every other anniversary, I could celebrate being cancer-free and be thankful for all of the positive changes that the experience had given me, but not this time. I felt like I had been kicked in the teeth. I couldn't focus at work and later, talking about it with Dianne, I broke down and cried. The stress and heightened mental activity, combined with the lack of sleep, were beating me down. I was feeling tired all of the time and finding it hard to concentrate. The other cancer - the "cancer in my mind" - had me in full force. I could work, but would drift away every once in a while. When I was out doing simple things like grocery shopping I would have to stop every now and than as that now-familiar weight descended on me unexpectedly. One night, Dianne and I went out with our good friends Pete and Elli to see a comedy. We had dinner and laughed a lot, but it was mostly small talk. I love both of them and it was a special night for Dianne and I, but neither of us really enjoyed ourselves. I thought at the time, it would have been better to talk about what was happening, but that really wouldn't have been fair to any of us. It seemed that this black cloud followed us around all the time. It was just like before and I began to wonder how we were going to get through it this time.

On October 24, I received the results of my latest PSA test from Dr. Goodman. This time it was 0.12, which was still within a reasonable range of error of that second decimal place (PSA doesn't go down on it's own). The fact that it hadn't gone up significantly was a good indication that the cancer could be slow growing. I felt I could live with that, as it would take many years to grow and I could stretch out my treatments. It made me feel a bit better, but there was still a possibility that, since my original cancer expressed very little PSA and was very large, that this small amount of PSA could be indicative of a larger than expected growth of new tumour. I needed to verify or disprove this. Dianne spoke with her friend Ann, who had experienced a recurrence of breast cancer, and she insisted that I have a CT scan or MRI to address my concerns. I called Ann myself and also spoke to Ruth who both agreed that I should get whatever tests done that I felt I needed. I had to be my own advocate and try to get some control back. I called Andrew and made another appointment.

I met with Andrew on November 1. He understood perfectly and suggested that I meet with Dr. Tracks and present my case. He said he might not agree with me, but I needed to do it and it was the right place to start, so I booked an appointment for the next Monday morning. I would ask him to do a CT scan, a bone scan, another blood test, and give me a referral to a radiation oncologist. I couldn't wait for three or six months to see what my imperfect marker test would say. I was still too young and I wanted to treat this aggressively. I began to research salvage radiation therapy (SRT), hormone therapy (HT), and even orchiectomy which involved removal of my testicles to completely eliminate testosterone production. I was deadly serious about this.

I met with Dr. Tracks and explained what I wanted to do. To my surprise, he said that he would do the same thing if he were in my shoes. That was a real bonus! All I really wanted was the tests and the radiation consultation, but hearing him say that made me feel so much better. He booked me for the bone scan and CT scan and put through a referral to a radiation oncologist to discuss SRT. I was beginning to think that I should have SRT done sooner rather than later to give me some odds of killing this thing. According to what I had read, SRT has a 40-50% success rate, depending on whether the recurrence is limited to the prostate bed or whether it is systemic. This wasn't as good as I wanted but it was better than nothing. It gave me a chance that I didn't even realize I had five years ago.

Later that day, believe it or not, I went for a job interview. I don't know how I handled all of that, but I got through it. I was exhausted when I got home and in retrospect I probably didn't to that well in the interview. I never did get the job (I wasn't really that interested in moving, and it wasn't a great fit anyway) but I also realized that starting something new when I was facing SRT was maybe not such a great idea. I was finding it hard enough to concentrate at work and people were starting to ask me if I was okay. It was really hard not to tell people but I was trying to shield myself from the prejudice that people with cancer face in the workplace. Dianne said that hiding it was the worst kind of stress so I struggled enormously about what to do.

The day of my bone scan was tense for both of us and we were both a little testy on the way down to the hospital. After the injection of the radioactive isotope at 10:00 AM, we went to a nearby mall for lunch and a bit of shopping. While I was in Sears, I heard some people greeting each other and one of the women introduced an older gentleman saying he had just turned seventy. It suddenly hit me that I might not make it that far. I stopped in my tracks as I considered this. Was I being paranoid? Realistic? It surprised me to feel this way but there was an element of truth that I couldn't avoid and the fear gripped me even tighter.

At 2:00 PM, I returned to the hospital for the bone scan. It took about an hour and, for a bit of time, I could see the image on the monitor but I couldn't make out whether there were any obvious hot spots. My mind was tripping over the potential implications of the scan and, when I finally got home, I was exhausted and felt really horrible. I kept feeling like I could cry. There was too much going on in my life and I really needed to become stronger somehow.

A couple of days later, I had a major meltdown over nothing, storming out of the house and driving off. Clearly, things were getting out of control. I eventually cooled down and we had a decent evening. Ruth and our friend Janice came over to watch a movie and talk, which helped to bleed off the tension, and Ruth and I had a chance to chat a bit in the kitchen, which was very helpful. After they left, I apologized to Dianne. She understood what had happened and insisted that I talk to Andrew. She told me that I really needed to get my shit together. Once again, she was right.

My session with Andrew was great, as it always was. He emphasized that this time around was no less impactful than the first time and he pointed out that it had taken a good two years to integrate it into my life back then. Not only that, but I had grown from a deer-in-the-headlights cancer patient to a "teacher" of sorts (writing a book, starting a website, speaking with newly diagnosed men) so falling back to being a cancer patient again was a huge fall. He said I was in shock rather than depression but that we would watch out for that. He described my life as driving along with a three-quarter-full cup of coffee in the car and how each event (the job interview, going for tests, etc.) was like adding a thimbleful. The recurrence was like dumping another half glass in, and that the cup was now overflowing. The meltdown I had was something quite normal and he said he would have been worried if I hadn't shown signs like this. It was my mind telling me that this was a huge event. Just because I had been through it once before didn't mean that I could handle it any better this time. I still needed to integrate it into my life and into who I was. He urged me to continue doing what I had been doing - my research (an excellent coping mechanism for me), my website and even my job interviewing. He said I needed to move forward in good faith, focusing on the moment and dealing with what happens *when* it happens. He told me not to try to crystal ball the future because we just don't know. The only thing we really know is that, when the time comes, we will probably be in the middle of doing something that we want to get accomplished. What I needed to do was prioritize the things I was doing to make room to integrate this thing.

On November 19, I had my appointment with the radiation oncologist, Dr. Mills. He was a great guy and was the Director of Research at PMH. I first met his resident first who did a DRE and told me that my bone scan was clear (great news!) and that the CT scan would hopefully show nothing in the lymph nodes. If it did, they wouldn't do SRT. I really thought it would be okay, but I'd learned to never say never anymore.

Dr. Mills explained that I would be doing a standard dose of SRT – sixty-six Gy over thirty-three consecutive days every day except weekends, Christmas Day, Boxing Day and New Years Day. The really good news was that I was able to sign up for a clinical trial for Image Guided Intensity Modulated Radiation Therapy (IG-IMRT)! I had thought this was routine, but apparently not for recurrence. For this, they use a radiation machine with a built-in CT scanner so they could do a scan every day before they radiate. An added bonus was that they would do an MRI at the same time as my CT scan for targeting, which would give them a more precise look at my prostate bed. The more precise targeting that this allowed would also reduce the side effects of radiation treatment on my bowels and urinary system. In addition, I would get all the benefits of a clinical trial with the extra attention and follow up over five years. I was absolutely thrilled about this. I was getting the best and latest treatment at the largest and one of the most modern radiation facilities in the world! It was, nonetheless, a brutal day stress-wise and, as usual, I was exhausted. It was starting to feel so much more real. But at least it had started. Things were moving forward. I was building my brick house to keep the wolf at bay. I hoped it would hold.

Two days later, I went for the CT scan of my abdomen and pelvis that I had requested, which required drinking that tasty Barium at night and again in the morning. The scanner was brand new but the technician was a butcher with the IV needle and left a nasty bruise. As I lay on the table, I asked myself, "What the hell am I doing here?" It was so real yet surreal at the same time. Afterwards, I slept for a couple of hours feeling sick and unable to get warm. I thought it could have been a bug or something to do with the test but it may just have been the stress. Dianne was pushing me to get on meds but I resisted because I felt I needed to get my mind around it as completely as I could rather than suppress it.

A couple of days later, I got the results of the CT scan. I called Dr. Mills' office at 11:30 but they didn't have them ready, saying that there was something supplemental. The results had been reported but the secretary seemed hesitant and asked if I had talked to one of the doctors, which I hadn't of course. She said she would leave a message for Dr. Mills to call me. I hung up feeling extremely apprehensive. Dianne was very upset and insisted that I call back later, which I did at 4:00 but still couldn't speak with the doctor. Finally, around 6:00, Dr. Mills called and told me that I had a three millimetre kidney stone in my right kidney but that it probably wouldn't bother me. He also said there was a "fullness" that the doctor who interpreted the scan couldn't quite explain, but he told me not to worry because it was in the field that they were going to radiate so, whatever it was, it would be taken care of. The good news was that there was nothing else showing outside that area, which was a huge relief. I realized after that I had been very worried, especially with the hesitation of the secretary.

I slept well that night and woke up early feeling so much better and full of energy. I felt that I had eliminated as much of the uncertainty I could and I was absolutely ready to move on to the next step – Salvage RT. Since there was nothing visible (although I still wondered about that "fullness"), there was a good chance that it hasn't metastasized or, if it had, it was very slow growing. That would buy me some time. Steve invited me over for a movie that night which I found very relaxing and I really appreciated it. Pete also called to see how I was doing. With everything that was happening, it felt good to have my friends keeping an eye on me.

I was ready for the next step, but it wasn't going to be uneventful. The following Tuesday afternoon I was hit with the worst migraine attack in recorded history. They kept coming and coming and nothing could stop them. Dianne and I were out but I couldn't drive the car home because I couldn't see straight. When we finally got home, I collapsed onto the bathroom floor and lay there for a long time. At some point, I crawled into bed but it was impossible to find any position where I felt even remotely better. The attacks wouldn't stop coming with skull-splitting headaches, numbness in my face, arms and hands, and the worse nausea ever. At one point I honestly thought I was going to die. A shroud of blackness began to fall over me, blocking out my vision and hearing and I remember thinking that it was just so damn inconvenient to die right then. I also thought how ironic it was that I was going to die from this instead of the cancer. But it wasn't to be and, around four in the morning, I was able to sit up and eat a couple of crackers. The next day I just stayed in bed with a horrible migraine hangover, unable to do anything. Dianne was convinced that it was the relief of pressure from my clear scans that triggered it. Maybe she was right but, if so, I thought it was so unfair.

On Thursday, November 29, I went to the hospital for my targeting scans. I wasn't prepared well enough for the CT scan so they made me empty my rectum again and fill my bladder some more (I drank a full two litres of water). They built up a form around my hips to help position me, and placed three tattooed dots on my sides and front which would help the technicians line up the machine for the combined scan and radiation treatment. After the CT scan, I had my first ever MRI. I was given an injection and subjected to a dozen different loud noises, which lasted about forty minutes. Interesting but not too stressful, although I admit to thinking several times that they could find evidence of tumour growth on these scans. But that was what we call "scanxiety", something every cancer survivor experiences, often for the rest of their lives. I had been poked, prodded, tattooed, injected, scanned and mapped and now I was all set to begin my radiation treatment regime. I was as ready as I could be.

If you think back to earlier chapters of this book where I discussed the fear of recurrence, you might have thought at the time that I was being paranoid. I certainly did. My numbers weren't too bad and all signs pointed to the surgery being successful, but I had accepted a degree of paranoia as something I would just have to learn to live with. Was I right to be paranoid when I presumably had a good prognosis? Should I have worried so much about something I really had no control over? Well, it really doesn't matter. Fear of recurrence will always be there. It is part of the cancer journey. It goes with the territory. But paranoid or not, unfortunately, I was right.

Dianne and I talked a lot about the recurrence and how it could perhaps be a blessing in disguise because it would push me to do the important work that I know I can do. It definitely put the brakes on the progress I had made over the previous five years but, now that I was starting treatment, I knew I had to work hard to start moving forward and find a way to live. "Living well" is what Rob Buckman calls it. *Thriving* rather than surviving.

The wolf was loose in my house, its fangs and claws exposed. I was deeply frightened, but I was ready to fight.

ROUND TWO

I was now looking forward to thirty-three days of radiation therapy, with only weekends, Christmas Day and New Year's Day off. I wouldn't be finished until near the end of January. It was a hell of a way to spend the holiday season, but I wasn't going to wait. It did, however, create another problem. It was going to severely impact my work. My job required me to travel to customer sites for meetings and presentations and, In fact, I had several coming up and there was no way that I could physically do them. I was, however, very reluctant to tell anyone at work because I didn't know how they would react and I feared that it could hurt my career. I was sure the company would look after me, but I wondered where I could go from there now that I was marked a little more permanently with the stigma of cancer. It was a recurrence, after all, so it was a much different situation than it was five years ago.

Initially, I told my best friend at work, Richard, as much to have someone to talk to as having someone cover for me, but I felt tremendously guilty about placing such a burden on him. I knew I would have to tell more people because there really was no way to hide it and I certainly didn't want to lie to anyone about it. I finally told my boss that I had been treated five years ago but that there appeared to be something still there that would require thirty days of radiation. I promised to continue working, but would have to get others to back me up, particularly for off-site meetings. He was shocked to hear it, but he took it very well and told me to do whatever I had to do and not worry about it. It was a great relief to get it out in the open and, interestingly enough, we never really spoke of it again. Over the next several days, I also spoke to the people who would have to be on-site with my customers without me being there. They are all great people and they deserved to know why

I wasn't going to be with them. To a person, they were very supportive and ultimately did a great job on my behalf.

On Thursday, December 6, I got the call that I was to start treatments on Tuesday. I was very excited to get the call but that was when it really hit me. It was very real now and I promised myself to take as much time off as I could while continuing to work my active deals and to work from home as much as possible. I needed to find some down time while I was going through this and would also try to find some time to work on my website and on the survivorship initiatives that I was hoping to get off the ground through my relationships at PMH. I thought that this would be a positive thing to do while I wrestled with the all of the emotions caused by the recurrence and what would soon prove to be an arduous treatment schedule.

Dianne was very pleased that I was going to be around more over the next seven or eight weeks and that we would be trying to make the most of the holidays, but we were both feeling apprehensive about the treatments. Dianne, in particular, seemed very down and anxious and even cried a bit (she is a very strong woman and her tears were just her way of dealing with everything.) For my part, I was beginning to go into that tomorrow's-the-big-day mode – calm but more than a little apprehensive. We planned to go down to PMH together and, as luck would have it, there was an information session on Radiation Therapy that we could attend right before my first treatment. I told Dianne that I wasn't really nervous about the treatment, that I knew there were side effects but that I hadn't internalized that part yet. We would see how it goes. Meanwhile, we agreed to do some shopping after to see if we could get into the Christmas spirit.

My first treatment was on Tuesday, December 11, 2007. We had made it down in plenty of time to attend the information session but there were a lot of interruptions and, at one point, Dianne started to shed a few tears as the reality hit her hard. After the presentation, we headed down to register in the treatment centre two floors below ground level. I would have to scan my green card to check in each day and, every Wednesday, the computer would spit out the times for the following week. The waiting area was very nice but very busy. This was, after all, the largest centralized radiation therapy centre in the world and there were lots of people going through treatment.

For each treatment, I had to have an empty rectum to keep it from pushing too far into the radiation field, and I had to have a full bladder. The bladder was going to be hit regardless, but if it was full, it would stretch out and a smaller, thinner area would get radiation. It was all about minimizing side effects. Unfortunately, I overdid the bladder and was in such severe pain that I wasn't sure I could make it through the full treatment. My abdominal muscles went into spasm and, by the time I was finished, they were so tight I could barely get a decent stream. But what an incredible relief it was when it finally let go!

The treatment itself was very interesting. The machine – a particle accelerator with a built-in cone CT scanner – was very large and high-tech looking. The team of technicians ran everything from computers outside of the room which was enclosed with three-foot concrete walls and a lead door. They lined me up on my molded form and matched several laser beams with my tattoos and then did the first 360-degree CT scan. After some minor adjustments, they did the actual treatment which involved sixty different blasts of radiation on seven different planes, all guided by computer settings based on my targeting scans. After the treatment, they did an additional 360 scan which they would do for the first three treatments and once a week thereafter along with a thirty-second scan of me breathing to see if anything moved (all part of the study).

It quickly became routine for me, although I was finding that the trip down for treatment and back could easily take a three or four hour chunk out of my day. It was making it very difficult to accomplish much else and I understood why some people just took the whole period off from work, something I realistically could not do. Sometime after my first few treatments, I realized that my surgery anniversary date of December 4 (2002) had gone by completely unnoticed! I used to celebrate that as my cancer-free date, but knowing that this was no longer true, it had just slipped my mind. As I thought about it, I realized that it wasn't ever going to be something to celebrate any more.

As the days went by and the thirty-three treatment days counted down, I began to experience side effects in the form of bladder spasms, urinary frequency (I was getting up three or four times during the night) and some problems with my bowels. My biggest issue was the fatigue that seemed to get progressively worse every day and that affected my mind as well as my body. It became increasingly difficult to focus at times, particularly at night. It was as if my mind had been fractured like a broken glass into a million tiny pieces and I couldn't seem to piece them together into anything coherent. I think it was the stress of everything that was making it so difficult to focus and I felt almost panicked because my mind is normally much more orderly.

Christmas came and went. I brought a card and a box of chocolates to the Unit 9 team who were treating me and was thrilled when one of the girls came out and gave me a hug and kiss. Those little touches of humanity meant so much. One day I saw Santa Clause walking through PMH. It was just a guy in street clothes wearing a Santa hat and a real beard, but I thought if Santa was getting his treatment there, then I was certainly in good hands!

Most of the time, Dianne accompanied me downtown for my treatments and it meant the world to me that she wanted to share the experience with me as much as she could. She had her own issues to deal with at the time, but she essentially put her life on hold for me. One day, the team invited her into the treatment room to watch me get set up on the equipment and then let her observe everything on the television monitors and computers outside of the room. It really helped her to understand what was happening to me and, while it saddened her to see me like that, I know it made her feel much better knowing what was going on behind those brick walls and lead doors. My daughter Caralia also went with me a couple of times and several of my best friends (Janice, Steve M. and Pete) were kind enough to accompany me on numerous occasions. I wondered for the hundredth time how anyone could do this alone.

Over the holidays, I spoke to a number of people – friends and relatives – about my recurrence and radiation treatment. I don't know what it is, but so many people feel that sharing this very personal information is an open invitation for them to tell me about everybody they knew who had cancer, particularly if they had died or were dying. Why do they think I need to hear this? Do they think that it helps to remind me that cancer is a terrible disease that kills people? I had figured that out already! A friend of mine, Lori Hope, whom I met through the cancer blogging community, has written a great book entitled, "*Help Me Live: 20 things people with cancer want you to know*", that deals with this very subject. Through her own experiences with cancer and interviews with numerous people, she shares the many things people say that can really hurt someone dealing with cancer and, conversely, the things we all like and even need to hear. I wish everyone could read this book. It resonated so well with my own experience.

As much as I tried to get through it all with my chin up and a positive attitude, I hated almost everything about it. Each day carved several hours out of my otherwise productive time and twenty dollars out of my wallet for parking. While the waiting room was comfortable enough, there were many times when unavoidable delays resulted in my having to wait up to several hours. When they were ready for me, I had to strip off everything below the waist and put on the ugliest wrap imaginable (tartan if you can believe it!) and sit waiting in a hallway with the cold air blowing up around my privates. When I was eventually called in to the treatment room, I had to climb up on the table to be "positioned" by two or three technicians (male and female) as they lined up my tattoos with several lasers. It was all so intrusive. Everybody was nice enough, but I really wished I didn't have to be there.

The treatment itself was not painful and, in fact, was the fastest and easiest part of the whole routine. I passed the time by counting the revolutions of the CT scanner and the buzz of each shot of radiation, imagining it burning away the tissue of my prostate bed and hoping against hope that it was killing any and all of the cancer cells that remained in my body. I hoped that was what was happening, but I knew the odds weren't that great for me. While I hated it, and while it turned my life upside down, I knew it was the right thing to do. In fact, it was the only thing I could do. I had to be doing something and this was the only real option I had available to me. The next step was to admit that what I had was incurable and deal with everything that this entailed. I had made the right choice – an informed choice – and I had to see it through to the end, for my family's sake as much as mine.

By the middle of January, I was on the home stretch. I was finally starting to get back into work more intensely even while I was still undergoing treatments, but I felt good having something to concentrate on, even if I was tired all the time. Some days I felt very positive and other days I was pretty down, but I soldiered on and things started to happen that made me think better times were coming. One day, I gathered the confidence to speak with my boss about a Vice President job. He said he would definitely consider me, which made me feel good and gave me back a little dignity. Around the same time, the CEO of a new company called me to talk about a job. Another ego boost! At a PMH Advisory Committee meeting I presented a proposal on wellness and survivorship which was very well received. A huge ego boost! I was complemented on my vision and one person even called me inspiring. Wow!

But in spite of all of this, I was still feeling "off". There was always a dark spot on my mind no matter how happy or up I was feeling and I was getting very tired of the whole thing. One morning I woke up early and had some time to think. I recognized that I had allowed myself to become a victim yet again. I was coming to the realization that I might (probably would) have to live with this disease so I had better get back on track. I became determined to find ways to boost my self-confidence and get moving. There was much I could still do with my career and there were things I could do in the area of cancer survivorship that would have a positive impact on many, many people. I strengthened my resolve, held my head up high, and turned to face the world.

On January 29, 2008, I was finished. Thirty-three treatments! As important a milestone as it was, it ended rather uneventfully. I brought some chocolates and a thank you card for the Unit 9 team and exchanged some heartfelt hugs. The side effects were still with me and had actually gotten worse the final few days. The bladder spasms, which had eased off, were back with a vengeance and it hurt like hell to poo. It felt like I was passing sandpaper. In addition, I was still experiencing tremendous fatigue but had learned to doze off whenever I could and to sleep in on mornings whenever my schedule allowed. In fact, Dianne insisted on it (and how could I say no to her?!). These side effects of radiation treatment can continue for several weeks after the final treatment, so it was going to be two to four weeks before things started to return to normal. I could live with that, especially since I no longer had the daily commute to PMH and could get back to work full time and even travel when I needed to.

It was over. I had been treated twice now for this disease and had written a major new chapter in a life that was turning out much differently than I could ever have imagined. My first treatment didn't cure me and, frankly, the odds weren't that great that this one would. But I had faced it straight on, with no sense of denial and with, I dare say, a degree of grace that I couldn't have mustered five years ago. Cancer had changed me. The recurrence set me back a bit - maybe a lot - but I did what I needed to do and I continued on to the next chapter in this incredible journey. I was now living *with* cancer, and while I knew it might finally get me, I was still a survivor. And I had hope.

HOUSE OF WOLVES

It seems that it wasn't meant to be. The wolf was breathing down my neck, its fetid breath a reminder that mortality can be such a fleeting thing.

On April 21st, 2008, I dropped by PMH for my 3 month, post-SRT PSA test to see if the radiation had worked. This wasn't as routine an event as it once was because I knew that anything could happen now. A week later, I had an appointment with Dr. Maynard, one of the rising stars on the PMH radiation oncology team. I was really hoping for good news but what I heard really set me back. My PSA was 0.15, the same as it was before I started SRT! I knew that the odds were less than 50% that SRT would work, but I had allowed myself to hope and that hope had turned into expectation. It looked as if the radiation had no impact at all, or that maybe it had killed some local tumour and, had it not, the number would have been much higher, but it didn't really matter because, either way, there was still cancer in my body. Dr. Maynard said that it sometimes takes longer for the effects to show, although that was rare. I truly didn't think that was the case, but I agreed with her suggestion to give it a few more months. I knew my options and I could have insisted on starting hormone therapy immediately, but I didn't want to mask what might be going on. If my PSA fell, I wouldn't really know if it was a delayed effect from the radiation or from the hormones and I really needed to have as much knowledge and control over what was going on as I could. So I waited, trying to put it out of my mind until my next appointment on July 14. But it was hard not to think about it all time. The implications were enormous. In fact, they were potentially fatal. I was scared.

The week before the appointment, I stopped into PMH for another PSA test on my way to a meeting. As they drew the blood from my arm, I thought to myself that this was it; this was probably the most important PSA test I had so far on this journey and it knocked my apprehension up a notch. When the 14th finally came, Dianne and I sat in the consultation room holding hands, waiting anxiously for the news. It was not good. In fact, it was horrifying. My PSA had risen to 0.49 and this was over only two and a half months! At first, we sat there in shock. While still a relatively low number (compared with "normal" PSA readings), this was more than a third of my pre-surgery PSA of 1.26 which had accompanied a tumour that was forty percent of my prostate! On top of that, it represented a three hundred percent increase over a period of less than three months which implied an incredibly fast doubling rate, a sure sign of aggressiveness. Dr. Maynard pointed out that small numbers and changes in small numbers were difficult to interpret and, while I understood this, it did little to quell the gnawing fear in the pit of my stomach. I was numb, so Dianne quickly took over and started firing off all of the questions that I should have been asking. I was exceptionally proud of her as she wiped away her tears and took control. Dr. Maynard told us that she was worried and wanted to send me for a bone scan and a CT scan of my abdomen and pelvic areas as soon as possible.

Several times throughout this long journey, I had experienced lower back pain and had demanded scans that routinely came back negative, but for the last couple of months, I had been experiencing a great deal of back pain that seemed to getting steadily worse. Because my past scans had been negative, I was cautious of being too paranoid, but this time seemed different. The pain would come on fast and strong. My Chiropractor didn't help, stretching didn't help, heat and cold didn't help. In fact, nothing seemed to touch it. It hurt when I was walking and even when I was laying down. At times, when I was out walking in stores, I had to stop and squat down on my heels to relieve the pain before I could go on. I told Dianne that shopping seemed to be the culprit so we shouldn't do that anymore, but she didn't laugh. Neither of us was finding anything funny at that time. Dianne had insisted that I ask the doctor for an MRI and, when I relayed the story to Dr. Maynard, she immediately ordered a bone scan and an MRI, deferring the CT scan for later. We asked her about hormone therapy and she explained to us that they usually didn't start it until there were visible signs of the cancer spreading. We knew it was there, in my bloodstream as micro-metastasis, but they wanted to see visible tumours in the bones or in the lymph nodes before starting hormone therapy (HT). Part of the reason for this, was that HT would only last for so long so they wanted to wait presumably to give me the most time (there is some controversy over this approach, but it made sense to me at the time). Dianne asked how long I had and Dr. Maynard told us that the median number of years to death was four to five following the first visible signs. Median, of course, meant half would be less and half would be more. Where would I fall? We had no way of knowing.

We left the hospital in a state of shock, both of us angry and scared to death at the implications. We now knew that the cancer was back and that we were at the point where we had to accept that it was incurable. It staggered our minds. Our thoughts now turned to questions of how fast and how long. The scans would, perhaps, give us some indication of this, but we hoped fervently that they would not show anything.

My scans were booked for the last week of July, not too far away, yet not soon enough for us. But timing is everything and, on the weekend, I left for my annual kayaking and camping trip, this time to the French River with three close friends. It was perfect for me as I loved being back in the outdoors and on the water and it gave me time to decompress amidst the camaraderie of good friends. We talked a little about what was going on, but it is a hard thing to talk about. Besides, while the news was bad, we were still waiting for the full story. As we paddled along amidst the beauty of the river and camped at night under the trees, there was always a dark cloud that seemed to follow me around, dulling the normally therapeutic value of the trip. But it was still worth it and I came back refreshed, if somewhat apprehensive.

At one point on the trip, I suggested to my buddies that I wanted them to scatter my ashes over the Bustard Islands, my favourite Georgian Bay destination. While my best friend Steve jumped at the idea and loudly proclaimed his personal guarantee that this would happen, I think it took the other two by surprise and, in a way, made it seem more real to them. It definitely ended the conversation! Later, when Dianne heard the story, it made her cry because it meant that she would not be able to visit and talk to me when she was feeling sad and lonely. She had always assumed that we would be buried side by side, resting together forever. I also think it hammered home for her just how much love I had for the outdoors.

The following week, I had a business trip overseas and, as I arrived back home, to my great surprise, Sean showed up at the door, all the way from out west. When he walked in the door, I almost cried (well ... I actually did cry) as I gave him a huge hug. Apparently, he had been missing me horribly and his friends threw a little fund raiser for him, arranged with his boss for some time off, and bought him a ticket home! I was floored! I was even more amazed that Dianne could have kept this a secret. What a gift this was!

With Sean here for the week, he was able to accompany me to both my tests. The first was a bone scan, which I had done twice before, so I was becoming a bit of a pro. As the scan progressed (it takes about an hour), one of the technicians asked me if I had been experiencing any pain in my shoulders. I said no, but it scared me because I realized they must have seen something. When it was finished, the technicians left to confer with the radiologist and, when they came back, they did an extra 360 degree scan of my lower back. They said it was because I had been complaining about my back pain, but I wondered what they had seen in the first scan that made them want to do this extra scan which I had never had before. It made me extremely nervous, but I was able to compartmentalize it knowing that I would be getting the results soon and that they would be what they would be.

On July 31, I woke up poor Sean at 5:00 am to head downtown for the MRI and my follow up PSA test. To his credit, he didn't complain at all and just having him with me gave me some strength. It was, in truth, starting to really get to me. Once again, I was becoming a slave to the medical system and it was beginning to dominate my life. I tried to push it all to the back of my mind so I could continue to function, but it was becoming harder and harder to do this. By the time Sean had to leave, he had received a small taste of what my life was like and I'm sure he had enough.

Finally, on August 14th, Dianne and I found ourselves once more sitting in a hospital room waiting for the penny to drop. Our good friends Pete and Elli had volunteered to drive us down and to be with us in case the news was bad. One of Dr. Maynard's associates came in before her. He was very pleasant and began by reviewing the history of my case. We both nodded politely, but exchanged glances knowing that this just didn't feel right. We had both arrived hoping for some good news for a change – clear scans and no further change in my PSA. But something was wrong. The doctor asked to examine me and had me pinpoint the spot on my back where the pain was the worst. He then stood back and told us that, unfortunately, they had found a hot spot on my bone scan. It was like a shot between the eyes, compounded when he told us that my PSA had risen to 0.62 in just three weeks! This was now half of my pre-surgery PSA and moving up very quickly. Dianne started to cry and I just looked at him. At that moment, Dr. Maynard stepped in and the associate told her that he had "just dropped the bomb." That was when it really hit me. My coping mind had been waiting for some kind of "but" that would make it better, but there it was. Dr. Maynard offered her condolences and the resident told her that the hot spot corresponded exactly with the central point of pain in my back. They explained that cancer that metastasized to the bone was of two kinds – osteoblastic, that actually grows denser material on the bone (and is most common with prostate cancer), and osteolytic, that dissolves the bone. In my case, it was lytic and the lesion was actually eating into the bone of my sacrum, at the base of my spinal column very close to the sacroiliac joint. The associate wondered whether we should do a biopsy just to make sure, but Dr. Maynard pointed out that the pain, the bone scan and the rising PSA confirmed that I had Metastatic Prostate Cancer. I didn't say anything at the time, but I remember thinking there was no way that anyone was going to go sticking a needle into my cancer-eaten spine. It was just not going to happen. No freakin' way!

The doctors took us out to another room to see the actual bone scan image on the computer, which showed up like a bright flashlight shining out of my lower spine. Seeing it made it seem so real; there was simply no doubt anymore. It was there in black and very bright white. It was at that moment that it really hit me. This was my death sentence. This was the visible, physical evidence that the cancer was really, truly there; that it was growing and growing fast. This was the start of the next stage of the journey and the countdown that would inevitably lead to the end of the line. It was a life-changing moment.

In a much more sombre mood, the doctors brought us back to the other room and talked with us for a long time. Dr. Maynard said that she would book me for radiation treatment on my back to hopefully lessen the pain and stop the growth of the cancer in that spot. She also wanted to start me on hormone therapy right away, which would (also hopefully) slow down the cancer and stop the development of more metastases for some time. I was all over that! I wanted to do anything and everything I could to slow this down and I certainly didn't want to wait a minute longer than I had to. She wrote out a prescription on the spot and sent me down to the hospital pharmacy to pick up a syringe of Lupron and two weeks worth of Casodex.

As we left the offices, we sat down with Pete and Elli who had been sitting patiently in the waiting room and had sensed that something was wrong when were taking so long. They had also seen our faces when we changed rooms and I remembered that I had waved half-heartedly to them at the time. We told them the news and exchanged some hugs. It felt really good to have them there. Dianne then stayed with Elli while Pete accompanied me to the pharmacy. The drugs were unbelievably expensive and I hoped that my medical insurance covered them, but it didn't matter because I needed them. When we came back up, a nurse gave me the Lupron injection in my ass and I was given follow up dates for the radiation, the abdominal and pelvic CT scan, and my next injection in three months time. I would also have a PSA test at that time to confirm whether the hormone therapy was working.

Let's talk about the hormone therapy for bit because this was going to be a big part of my life from now on. To be perfectly clear about it, Metastatic Prostate Cancer is incurable with today's medicines and treatments. There is lots of research going on and everyone is hopeful, but all that can be done now is to slow the cancer down to buy as many years as possible. Lupron is one brand of a class of drugs called LHRH agonists which are designed to stop the testicles from producing any testosterone which the cancer cells, in turn, need to survive and grow. This is called "medical castration" (as compared to surgical castration from oriechtomy). The Casodex, which is an anti-androgen, stops the body's response to testosterone and is given the first couple of weeks to counteract an initial flare in testosterone levels from the Lupron.

But unfortunately, this treatment (also called Androgen Deprivation Therapy or ADT) doesn't work forever for two reasons. First of all, there are two kinds of prostate cancer cells – those that are hormone-sensitive (and thus affected by HT) and those that are hormone-insensitive. Regardless of what happens to the hormone-sensitive cells, the insensitive cells will continue to grow and spread and ultimately will kill me on their own. On top of this, cancer cells continue to mutate and even the hormone-sensitive cells eventually learn to live without testosterone. At this point, HT ceases to work and the cancer is free to grow and do the job it was designed to do, spreading throughout the rest of the body, creating its own blood supply and lodging in various places (bone, liver, etc.) to grow tumours. This is called Hormone Refractory Disease (always good to have a label!). While there are some chemotherapy agents available when HT fails, at this time they are of limited value and, at best, extend life by a couple of months. The statistics (in general) give men with metastases two to ten years with fifteen percent dying around two years, fifteen percent around ten years, and the rest spread out over that period with a median of four to five years. This is a lot better than some cancers but, at my age, it's definitely not good. One study I read put the mortality rate at seventy-five percent at five years. Much depends on the relative portions of the two types of cancer cells at the start, which is impossible to know.

The other joys of HT are the side effects - those annoying yet equally inevitable things I would have to put up with to extend my life. HT essentially puts you into male menopause and, as an educational by-product, helps men to understand what it is like to be a woman. Here are the side effects listed on my Lupron fact sheet:

More Common
- *Sudden sweating, feelings of warmth (hot flashes)*
- *Decrease in sexual desire or impotence*

Less Common
- *Chest pain, irregular heartbeat, shortness of breath*
- *Constipation, diarrhea*
- *Dizziness, headache, blurred vision*
- *Loss of appetite, nausea or vomiting*
- *Swelling of feet or legs*
- *Swelling or tenderness of breasts (gotta like that one, guys!)*
- *Tiredness, trouble sleeping*
- *Weight gain (another one to really look forward to)*
- *Bone pain, numbness/tingling of hands or feet*
- *Increased pain or difficulty in urination*

Additionally, in rare cases, you can get blood clots causing sudden pain and shortness of breath and, I suppose, death (this would qualify as an emergency situation). And over the long term, the loss of testosterone causes your muscles to atrophy and brings on osteoporosis, making your bones porous and brittle. Sounds pleasant, doesn't it? Lots of wonderful things to look forward to but, considering the alternative, I was happy to face it all, or at least was resigned to it.

With all of this roiling around like a storm in my head, we left the hospital, feeling like we had just woken up in another country where all the rules were different (an excellent analogy borrowed from Andrew). Pete and Elli drove us home, but first, we took them out for dinner to thank them for their kindness. I'm really glad we did that because they had been so sweet to us and it helped to take our minds off things for a little while.

When we finally got home, we both sat down and stared at each other. I was in shock. Dianne was in shock. She cried. I sincerely wished I could but, for some reason, the tears wouldn't come. I think, in some ways, I had been waiting for this for almost six years since my initial diagnosis. Not that I was expecting it, but just that I knew it was always a possibility. Each annual PSA test was a stark reminder of what could happen. In some ways it was like being on trial for six years, hoping to get off with time-served. The verdict had finally come down and I had been given a death sentence.

There was no silver lining to this. No upside. But I did feel a certain sense of vindication, if not satisfaction, when Dr. Maynard's associate said that I must be a "non-secretor", meaning that my cancer did not secrete (or express) PSA. This is what I had been saying all along, with the further implication that there were other factors to consider other than Gleason scores and PSA that would indicate aggressiveness. No longer was anyone going to tell me that I would be "just fine" because my numbers were so low, or that I had plenty of time because it was slow-growing. But there was no solace in this. It was nothing to cheer about. I could say, "I told you so," to the world but it didn't change the fact that I had a confirmed terminal disease. But at least I could now feel that I was working with the system and not against it, always having to push for more aggressive testing and treatment than my numbers called for.

That night, we called our family and close friends to share the bad news with those who cared the most. They had all been hoping, and even expecting, good news and were all terribly shocked and saddened. I know it was difficult for all of them to come to grips with what it all meant. And with more tests to come and additional treatments to take, many of them continued to express hope. It was hard for them to understand or accept that this was incurable and terminal with today's medical knowledge and I eventually brought home a copy of my bone scan to help explain it (as it had helped us). With all of their best wishes, there was hope only that I could slow it down. But their thoughts meant so much to both Dianne and I and we realized even more than ever how important friends were going to be.

I was desperately worried about Dianne. We talked a lot that week, more than we ever had before. And we talked about many things for which there was no immediate answer. We avoided words like "death" and "dying" and talked about "after". How would Dianne live on by herself? Could she keep the house? Could she handle two dogs? Would she have to go back to work? Could she ever be happy without me? These were all important questions but we understood that we weren't in a position to deal with them while this was so fresh. We knew that it would take time to absorb and come to grips with this new reality and assured each other that, in time, we would tackle all of these questions directly. I promised her that I would make sure that she was okay, but it didn't stop her from worrying. And, of course, I would never stop worrying about her.

It was a defining moment in our relationship when we really opened up about how we felt inside and towards each other. There was nothing to hide any more. I couldn't protect her from the fears of what might happen because it had happened and there was no turning back or running away. She cried and let me comfort her. She explained to me, and I believed her, that she cried because she dealt with things emotionally and that it didn't mean she was weak. I told her that it was okay and that I would respect this and let her work through it in her own way. And I asked to her to accept that I would have some down days, some good days, some angry days and that I needed to be able to work through them too. It was good for both of us to get this out. We knew that it would help us to communicate and that it would bring us even closer together, something we badly needed as we faced this biggest challenge of all. At one point, Dianne asked me what I really wanted to do. The truth was that I didn't have any great dreams or "things to do before I die" (a bucket list – like the movie). All I really needed - all I really wanted - was some down time. I had been running so hard, for so long, that I never seemed to have time to just do nothing. That was what I longed for most at that time. Other things would come and I would pursue other "dreams", but I just wanted to spend some quiet time with Dianne and occasionally by myself. I felt that I had earned it. Both of us had.

We spent the weekend doing things with friends. Pete and Elli took us on a little field trip on Saturday to St. Jacobs (a quaint little Southern Ontario town). I remember it so well because Pete asked me whether there was anything I wanted to do before I died. He said, personally, he would just sell everything, buy a motorcycle, and drive all over the continent. I really appreciated his comfort with asking the question and told him so, although I really didn't have an answer for him. On Sunday, our good friend Gayla spent most of the day with us. Over the past few years, she had truly become family and we love her very much. She knows the two of us better than anyone and she helped us work through much of what was clouding our minds. I talked to my mom and my brother several times. Both of them took it as well as could be expected but I knew that my mom would worry terribly. Colleen didn't call until Thursday and we didn't actually connect until two weeks after. I knew she would have heard from my mom but I think she just didn't know what to say. Sean called several times to see how I was, which was very thoughtful. Caralia asked a few questions, but she didn't seem to want to talk about it very much. She's has a very stoic personality (like me) which can be a bad thing, and I worry for her.

Well, there is time for talking and there is time for treatment. I was now married to the medical system for the rest of my shortened life. On August 14th, I went to PMH for my targeting CT scan, where they marked me up with more tattoos in preparation for the focused radiation therapy on my bone metastasis. Dianne accompanied me and I remember telling her how strange I felt in the CT scanner, realizing that it was the first time I was sitting in one of these machines without hope for a cure. There wasn't one. It was now all about symptoms. I felt the same when I went for my abdominal and pelvic CT scan a couple of weeks later.

On the 18th, I started five days of radiation treatment at double the dose I had been given for SRT but very focused on exactly where the bone met was. It only took a few minutes each day, so I was able to go into work (although Dianne thought I was crazy to do this). It was a rough week. I felt nauseous all the time and I had ongoing bowel problems, probably resulting from a combination of hormones, radiation and sheer stress. I was starting to get hot flashes as well and, while they were a bit of a novelty at first, they quickly became annoying. Dianne, who had been going through menopause for a few years, laughed and said, "Welcome to my world." From now on the two of us would be opening windows, throwing off the covers and turning the air conditioner on in the dead of winter! While I could laugh about this too, it came with the knowledge that, some day in the not-too-distant future, the hormones would stop working, the hot flashes would go away, my bones would be brittle and full of more holes, and I would be back for more radiation and perhaps other kinds of treatment.

While I probably have anywhere from two to ten years left, I cannot be naively optimistic. It all depends on how aggressive my cancer is, how it reacts to the hormones, and the relative proportion of hormone independent versus hormone sensitive cancer cells. There are still lots of unknowns, but it is the truth that I always seem to be on the bad side of the numbers. Yes, I know that this makes me sound like a "glass-half-empty" kind of guy, but that's just the way it's been. Let's review a bit.

- I was diagnosed at an age that had an extremely low probability.
- My tumour was unusually large.
- In most cases, both nerves can be spared with surgery, but I lost one of mine.
- My PSA showed a false negative, which is very rare.
- With a contained tumour and nothing in the lymph nodes, the odds of recurrence after surgery were very low, yet it recurred.
- There was a good chance, based on my numbers and the time to recurrence, that the recurrence was local and that SRT would work. It didn't.
- It usually takes many years from a rise in PSA before metastases to the bone. Mine took about eight months.
- Etc........

Not much to make me believe I was born under a lucky star, is there - at least where this cancer is concerned? So it's hard for me to really believe that I will be one of those guys you hear about who are still walking around after ten, fifteen or even twenty years. I can't even bring myself to hope for that. I suppose I can be cautiously optimistic, but that's the best I can do. I think it's more like two to five years, and I do very much hope that this is enough time for the medical breakthrough to occur that will cure or indefinitely postpone my disease. That is the hope I have and, if you want to pray for me, pray for that. It's my best bet.

I saw Andrew for a one-hour session that Friday morning. I was confident with the relationship we had developed over the past six years that he could help me through this. In fact, he was very blunt (respectfully so) and I appreciated him for that. He told me how important it was to have hope because when you lose hope, that's when you die. And then he jumped right in with the hard-hitting, to-the-point advice that I had come to expect from him.

The most important thing I needed was to integrate this into my life. I couldn't deny it nor hide it from myself. He described the three phases that I would have to deal with and that he would help me through. The first would be the time between now and when I die, whenever that would be. The second would be the actual time of my death and everything that surrounded that. And the third would be the period after I die. I was unsure what he meant by this last one, but he told me it was really about loss of future and that we would deal extensively with that as we progressed. Dianne was really taken aback by this because it seemed so blunt, but we both agreed it was good and necessary to deal with it head on. Even now, Dianne can't talk about my death without crying. But I know that Andrew has seen this many times and has personally attended way too many funerals. I have complete faith in his ability to understand and to help me cope. I was scared for both Dianne and I, but I certainly didn't envy Andrew's job at that time.

We talked about acceptance and I told him that I had really been working through this for the last six years since my initial diagnosis. I always knew what could happen and that it might happen, so this was, in a strange way, just a realization of that fear. For this reason, I felt that I had already accepted it, at least intellectually, and that now I had to learn how to deal with it, which was not going to be easy.

Andrew pointed out that this was only a small part, in terms of time span, of my whole life. Yes, it was a huge thing, but I couldn't forget about the rest of the life that made me who I am and that brought me to this point in time. I needed to find ways to enjoy life, however much I had left. It wasn't necessary for me to climb a mountain or to do everything I possibly ever dreamed of. I just needed to enjoy every minute of time that I had left. I needed to enjoy the small things, like having dinner with Dianne. That was what life was all about. He pointed out that I was, by nature, a problem solver and this was one problem that just couldn't be solved. I needed to accept that and get on with it. Not an easy thing to do for a guy like me.

I had actually been thinking a lot about all of this already, perhaps too intellectually and not enough emotionally, but that was just me. I explained to him that I had three levels of fear. My first fear was that I would die too soon. I felt that I had maybe two-to-ten years left and that five would be okay (ten would be much better, of course) but I really didn't want it to be any earlier. I wanted to ensure that Dianne was going to be okay both financially and emotionally and I needed some time to ensure that was the case. I felt strongly that five years could do that.

Secondly, I worried about my actual death and how it would happen. I knew that Prostate Cancer was the second most painful cancer and I had seen what happened to people like Bill Bixby in his final days. I am horribly afraid that I will have a year or more of extreme pain as my body gradually gives in to the cancer. I didn't want to die that way.

Thirdly, I worried about death itself and what that would be like, but I said that I was prepared to deal with that later.

As always, Andrew addressed these fears directly, in sequence. He told me not to worry too much about paying off the mortgage and other financial matters to the extent that I could not enjoy my remaining years. He pointed out how sad that would be and that it was certainly not what Dianne would want for me. I had to face up to the fact that the world would go on when I was gone and that Dianne would be all right. He was perfectly right about this but, to be honest, even writing about it makes me want to cry, particularly when I think of the things I might miss. I wonder if I will be here to walk my daughter down the aisle and dance with her on her wedding day. I want to see both my kids have their own children. I really want to be here to give them advice and to enjoy their lives with them.

In terms of my death, he told me that, in most cases, when people die, they have only a couple of really bad weeks as everything starts to shut down. He reminded me that there were some very good drugs to combat pain and assured me that I would not be bed-ridden for a year, just waiting to die. It made me feel a hell of a lot better about it at the time and I thanked him for it but, as I found out later, that wasn't necessarily going to be the case.

Andrew had lots of good advice for me that I want to share with you because it's really important at all stages of life. He told me to write a journal every day because writing was a big part of how I cope. I reminded him that I was actually writing these new and final chapters for this book and that it was definitely helping. He told me to do something personal and relaxing every day as well, like playing my guitar, which I promised I would try to do this as much as I could. Eating well and exercising was absolutely critical to minimizing the side effects of my treatment and extending my life as well, so I convinced myself that every half-hour of exercise I did extended my life by another day (I don't know whether that was true but it did provide me with some motivation). And he told me to try to push the bad thoughts from my head, something which is a lot easier to say than do. But he gave me a great tool to help with this that I would like to tell you about.

A DAY IN THE LIFE (a brief interjection) ... If you could indulge me for a few minutes, I would like to depart from this line of discussion and relate something to you that may help to appreciate what this is like for me. As I write this chapter, I am sitting in a plane over the Atlantic Ocean on the way home from a business trip in The Netherlands. Squished into an economy seat beside some charming older ladies (suffering through constant hot flashes – me, that is), I was typing away while listening to my iPhone, when one of my own songs came on – one that I had written and recorded several years back. As I listened to it, my mind filled with the idea that this was something of me that would exist after I was gone. I imagined my mother, Dianne, or my kids listening to this and remembering (with fondness and sadness) their dear old son/husband/dad and, I think for the very first time, I realized that I would not be here. I cried. In public and for the first real time, my eyes filled with tears, I stopped what I was doing and I cried. How strange and unpredictable it is that this would trigger my emotions in way that I had not yet experienced. I cried (discretely, I hope) through my meal and as I downed a couple of glasses of wine, not caring what anyone else would think of me. No one knew what was on my mind and, frankly, I didn't really care. I wanted to be home and to be with Dianne. And at that moment, I felt an extremely sharp pain in my back, just to remind me of what was happening to me. Past all the tears, it scared the hell out of me.

Now back to my story. Yes, Andrew once again gave me a great tool to use to help me manage the bad thoughts that were constantly floating around my head (case in point, on the plane). He told me to imagine that I had a green recycling bin in my head for all my cancer thoughts. As bad thoughts, fears and anger popped into my head, I was to place them firmly in my green bin, shut the lid, and get back to doing what I was doing. This wasn't like compartmentalizing or blocking because this was a recycling bin that I would open once a day when the time was right, maybe in the evening or just before I went to bed. I wasn't ignoring the bad thoughts, I was just putting them aside with the knowledge that I would absolutely deal with them when I was better equipped to do so; when I wasn't in the middle of an important business meeting or a pleasant moment with Dianne. At the appropriate time, I could take them out and process them properly, giving them the attention they deserved. When I mentioned this to Dianne, she told me that she had a garbage bin that she tried to put her bad thoughts in with the intention of never opening it at all. I thought I would try it both ways and see what worked best.

I would see Andrew much more over the coming months and I knew I needed it badly.

My next appointment (my life was quickly becoming an endless series of doctor's appointments) was with Dr. Maynard. She was just checking up on me and offered to refer me to a medical oncologist to see what the latest investigative treatments and clinical trials were. I thought this was a great idea and was, in fact, something I was thinking of doing so that I could educate myself and keep ahead of the curve in preparation for the next stages of my treatment. She also promised to see me the following week to give me the results of my CT scan, which I knew would not change my current treatment choice but would give me a better idea of how aggressive my cancer was. I was coming to realize that there was no end to this, that there was only the next appointment or the next test or the next result. The real ending would come with my own end and I was wedded to the system until then.

It was at this point that I came to the realization that I needed to confide in someone at work. I didn't want my boss to know yet and I didn't want my workmates looking at me with pity, but I needed someone to talk to on those days when I was feeling down or when I just needed to vent. I went to lunch with my friend Richard and told him the news, showing him the picture of my bone scan so he could see it for himself. He was shocked to say the least. He knew about my recurrence and had already proved himself to be a good friend by listening to me and by helping me out at work. I knew him to be a kind and compassionate person who had taken his brother into his own home for the last year of his life as he died of ALS. It helped so much to have these conversations and Richard was always there when I wanted to laugh a bit about my hot flashes or complain about my pain. It helped to bridge the gap between my work life and what was happening to me and I needed that because work was going so well and I didn't want to jeopardize it. I needed the salary and the benefits and, perhaps more importantly, I needed something positive to take my mind off things, even for a while. I remember thinking how horrible it would be to go through something like this while working at a job I hated. It would make everything seem that much worse.

That weekend Dianne and I just laid back and did nothing. We were both reeling from the events of the past couple of weeks and were too tired to do anything. Steve came over on Saturday and brought dinner, which allowed us to have a nice, relaxing visit without having to go out or even near the kitchen. You can't help but love the guy. He's so thoughtful. When Ruth called and invited us over the next day, though, I said no, truthfully because I really just wasn't feeling up to it. This was something I would never have done in the past but I was way beyond doing anything that went against the grain of how I was feeling. So for the rest of the time, I lay on the couch while Dianne gently massaged my head. I wanted to cry and came close many times. My back seemed a little better, which gave me some hope but, more importantly, I realized how badly I needed that down time and pledged to ensure that I gave myself permission to do just that.

This just seemed so unfair, the more I thought about it. I'm a good guy. I don't deserve to have cancer and I don't deserve to die before my time. And neither does Dianne deserve to have to deal with any of this. We hold each other a lot more now and always make a point of kissing each other good night. While I look forward to the night time when I can just black out and forget everything, Dianne finds night time the hardest because, for her, it means the end of the day and one less day that she has with me. And while we are both very, very tired at night, neither of us can sleep without sleeping pills - more drugs to add to the medical soup in my bloodstream.

I'm beginning to look at everything differently now, truly appreciating the simple things that I had been taking for granted all my life. I know I've said that before in this book, but this time was remarkably different. I look more closely at the clouds again and see the shapes and patterns that I did when I was younger. I feel wonder at the whorls and eddies in the water and feel the breeze more intensely on my face. When Judy was dying, she asked Dianne to take her outside because she wanted to feel the breeze on her face and I now realize what she meant. It makes me sad. I feel like I am now existing in another world, that this one is going on and passing me by, just as it will when I am gone. I always knew that, but I feel it more strongly now. I have lost all interest in politics or anything else that is distant, material or petty. I don't even want to bother cutting the lawn (I know I have to get over that). Only living is important to me now. I just want to concentrate on enjoying my life and being with my family and friends. That is all that really matters.

But that didn't keep me off the Internet! As I had done many times in the past, I shared my story with the Google prostate cancer group. In the post, I went through my whole history, focusing on the fact that my low numbers didn't really mean anything, given what had happened to me. I knew the group would find it interesting and I wanted to post it as a warning for anyone who had a similarly low PSA, telling them to aggressively pursue all options and not rely on the "average" or "normal" statistics. I received a large number of posted and personal replies which I found supportive and helpful. In fact, it generated a fascinating debate about whether one should aggressively throw everything at the cancer (hormones, chemo, radiation) as soon as it spreads or follow the current standard of care which is more sequential. I can't say that there is a clear answer to this debate so all I can really suggest is to do what you feel is best. As we all know, everyone is unique and there are no guarantees. The debate did, however, help me with my own decision making as the various options were presented to me.

On August 25, I went for my abdominal and pelvic CT scan which was to see if I had any visible tumours in my lymph nodes or organs. It was very fast and uneventful but it created an additional bit of uncertainty that I had to deal with because it would give me some further indication of the aggressiveness of my case. For the next few nights following, I struggled with trying to sleep and was forced to use sleeping pills to get by. But I used the sleepless hours to research more aggressive treatments in case the results were bad. This was the way I handled all of these appointments and milestones. I wanted to be prepared to ask the right questions and make immediate decisions on the next steps whether that was further tests, treatments or referrals. I shared all of this with Dianne who, like me, was still feeling like this was happening to someone else. We talked a lot about the uncertainty, how it was eating away at both of us, and how, in some ways, it was even worse than actually knowing. At least when you know something, you can deal with it and move forward. Until then, you worry constantly about all the horrible things that could happen, wanting to make decisions, but being unable to do so. I don't think people really understand how debilitating this can be. For both Dianne and I, it was crushing us emotionally and made it extremely difficult to function. Some of our friends could sense this, but they had no way of knowing how bad it really was.

On August 29, we saw Dr. Maynard once more and got the news that the scan was clear. This was a tremendous relief for both Dianne and I, and we felt like we could finally breathe. It seemed like such good news even though it was really a case of no-bad-news, but it removed a huge chunk of uncertainty. The doctor also told us that she was going to take my unusual case to the PMH Tumour Board, where she would present it to a multi-disciplinary group of oncologists to see if they had any ideas. I was so glad to hear this because it might result in something positive, but it was also further vindication of my long-held belief that I really was different.

Armed with this good/not-bad news, we immediately got on the phone to tell all of our family and friends who were waiting to hear. Like us, they were hungry for anything positive to celebrate. In fact, our good friends Gerald and Helen offered to take us out for dinner, which we appreciated so much and enjoyed tremendously. They are really good people and have always been very kind to us, and I hope they could see how much it meant to us. It is these little gestures that demonstrate the importance of friendships at a time like this and how something as simple as a dinner out can shine a bright light on an otherwise dark situation. And the darkness is never far away. That night I struggled through a never-ending series of hot flashes, which found me tossing off the covers every hour or so. The next day I felt sick to my stomach, suffered with headaches and dizziness, and burned with more hot flashes. I knew that most of these symptoms were side effects of the hormone therapy and that, hopefully, most of them would disappear as my body got used to it. Unfortunately, the hot flashes were not going to go away. I was going to get them at home, at work, and whenever I travelled (imagine sitting on a stuffy plane with your body going thermo-nuclear), so I was just going to have to learn to live with them for as long as the HT was working.

A few days later, Dianne and I watched a great television special called Stand Up 2 Cancer. It was an awareness builder and fund raiser featuring an hour of celebrities, many of whom talked about their own cancer. It was the first time since this latest chapter began that I was exposed to the broader community of cancer survivors and I opened up to it like a hungry man. This disease eats away at you so much emotionally, particularly if you become inwardly focused, as often happens. But it's strangely comforting when you can feel part of the (unfortunately) broader cancer community, even through the media. You feel less alone and can derive a kind of strength that comes with numbers. Watching the show helped to make my own situation very real for me. Seeing all of those people in their yellow survivor shirts, many whom I knew so well from movies and television, moved me in a deeply profound way which I can't really explain. When Patrick Swayze came out on stage, visibly deteriorating from his cancer, it hit me hard. I thought, "This is what it looks like near the end." And I saw myself like this, perhaps not too many years from now. It tore me up inside. While I didn't say anything to Dianne at the time, I knew she was thinking the same thing and I hated the idea that one day she would have to watch me fade away like that.

Neither of us slept well that night, but the show did give me hope, hearing about all of the recent medical advances in cancer treatment and seeing what they wanted to do with the money they were raising. For the first time I realized that there really was something to hope for. That even if my disease was incurable with today's medical treatments, something could come along that would enable me to prolong my life even if it wasn't a full-blown cure. It was something. It was hope. And I desperately needed hope to get me through.

Not too long after I had started on HT, I began an exercise program using the treadmill and weight equipment I had set up in the basement. My routine was simple – 10 minutes on the treadmill and 20 minutes on weights – but I knew it was necessary to minimize the bone and muscle deterioration from the hormones. As I said earlier, I had told myself that each half hour spent doing this would add a day to my life and it did help with the motivation. Initially, it didn't seem to bother my back very much so I felt that I wasn't doing any damage but, after about a week, it started to hurt like hell. In fact, it seemed worse than it had before the radiation treatment. And as it persisted, I found that the pain and accompanying fatigue began to really stress me out. I was anxious all during the day and was finding it hard to concentrate so I stopped exercising immediately. I had an eight hour flight to Helsinki coming up and I wasn't looking forward to it. Dianne sent me to bed early the night before I left and I slept for twelve straight hours.

The flight was not too hard on my back, which says something about the ergonomics of the seats on the plane, but by the end of my first full day in Finland, the pain was as bad as it had ever been. In desperation, I popped some Tylenol 3's that I'd saved from some time ago but they didn't even touch the pain. So I got on my email that night and sent a panicked note to Dr. Maynard back at PMH, who answered me right away thanks to the time difference. She booked me an appointment with her and with the Pain Clinic for the day I returned, which I was extremely grateful for. I also emailed Andrew to book an appointment to talk. I was becoming panicked at the thought that the hormones might not be working and that the metastatic lesion on my bone might be growing. It was becoming clear to me that the radiation treatment had not worked. At the very least, I needed to find a better way to manage the pain.

The Pain Clinic, I discovered, was part of the Palliative Care Program at PMH. I understood intellectually that the term palliative means to treat symptoms, but I also knew that Palliative Care was where you went when you couldn't be cured anymore - when all they could do was keep you comfortable until you died. I certainly wasn't thinking I was at that point yet. I knew it would happen someday, but I found it incredibly unnerving to be requiring palliation so soon. The doctor was very kind and understanding. She asked me to describe the pain and relate it to a scale of zero to ten. I told her it was like I had a knife stuck in my back. The pain was always there at a two or three level even if I wasn't moving. Then it would spike up to a seven or eight as if someone had grabbed the knife and wiggled it around. At other times, it would be as if someone had taken hold of the knife and shoved it in again and the pain would shoot up to a ten. As if to prove the point, this very thing happened while I was describing it to her, bringing tears to my eyes for the first time.

The doctor described the different levels of pain control that you can get from various medications which included the morphines at the top of the food chain. There was straight morphine and various forms of synthetic morphine. These were opiates, derived from the same drugs that give you opium and heroin. They would gradually lose their effectiveness over time and have to be increased. If I was ever to come off them, I would have to reduce very gradually because I could go into withdrawal. She was very careful to explain that this was not like an addiction, where you desire a drug for the high. It sure sounded like it to me, but she emphasized that getting something you need that you wouldn't normally want was different. But, ultimately, it didn't really matter to me. I was beyond worrying about taking drugs or even becoming addicted. The pain was going to destroy what life I had left and I was, by now, willing to do whatever it took. I also realized that withdrawal was probably not going to be an issue as there was surely more pain to come such that I would never get off medication. If I was going to be an addict, so be it. I later joked with my friends that I should reserve a sidewalk grate to sleep on for when I was really hooked but nobody thought it was funny. The doctor sent me away with a prescription for 30 mg slow-release morphine that I was to take twice a day to maintain a steady level of pain control, plus 10 mg of fast-acting morphine for the "breakthrough pain" (another new term for me). She also told me to take two extra-strength acetaminophen four times a day as they added some additional pain control without interacting with the morphine. That night, although I started taking the morphine right away, I was still in tremendous pain and Dianne had to help me get undressed for bed. I wondered if that small act was a harbinger of things to come. It unsettled me and probably Dianne too, although she didn't say anything.

That same day, I spent another hour with Andrew. He could immediately see that something had changed. He told me that I was still leading a double life but that now it was different. Previously, there had been the one Doug who had just been diagnosed with metastatic cancer and the other Doug who calmly and coolly did all the research and analysis to try to "solve the problem". There was no way that I could continue that now with the daily onslaught of pain, hot flashes and the numerous other side effects I had to deal with. It had become so much a part of my daily life that the main Doug was the one with cancer and the other Doug was the one that showed up at work, looked healthy and who laughed at things that would make him want to cry about at home. Andrew cautioned me that it was going to be hard to keep this up and that I had to be really careful to manage the stress of this double life which, on top of everything else, could throw me into a serious state of depression. He promised to watch me closely for any signs of that.

The following Monday, I finally got to see a medical oncologist. Her name was Dr. Eastman and, although it was early for me to be looking into chemotherapy while I was still undergoing hormone therapy (the current approach to treating my situation), she understood that I wanted to know what was coming up and whether there was, if fact, something I could be thinking about now. For the most part, the clinical trials on new treatments were focused on hormone refractory disease however she mentioned a possible clinical trial that would compare the current, sequential approach with a combined hormone therapy and chemotherapy treatment approach. I told her that I would be very interested in hearing more about this and that, depending on the side effects, schedule commitments and other factors, might be something I would do. We didn't have enough time to discuss this that day so she booked me a future appointment to do that.

Dr. Eastman did, however, offer me something that I could immediately take advantage of. She mentioned a bisphosphonate drug called Zometa, or Zoledronic Acid, which I had discovered in my own research on bone metastases. This was a drug that could slow down the inevitable osteoporosis damage from the hormone therapy and slow the destruction of my bones by the cancer. In some cases, it could also provide a reduction in bone pain. All of this had great appeal to me so I told her I wanted to go ahead. She cautioned me on some of the potential side effects, such as osteonecrosis of the jaw (destruction of the jaw bone) and told me she would have to monitor my blood work, particularly my kidney function. On the way out, she sent me to the blood lab and included a PSA test to boot.

A few days later, I saw Dr. Maynard to follow up on my panicked email from Finland. She suggested that we wait another four to six weeks to see if the radiation would still work, although by that time I was convinced it hadn't worked at all. We did talk about where the pain was coming from, but it is something that is not really well understood and is apparently very unpredictable. Once again I was "unusual" given that my pain had initially spiked after the radiation, then decreased and then spiked again. I realized that, rather than try to understand it, I would just have to accept it. The doctor gave me the results of a bone density test that she had ordered to establish a base line for tracking my bone deterioration which indicated that it was a little low for my age, which further supported the use of Zometa. And on an extremely positive note, she advised me that my PSA was down to 0.37 which meant that the hormones were starting to do their job. This was another huge milestone for me because it eliminated yet another piece of uncertainty. Now it only remained to see how long they would work.

I had to wait another week or so for a follow up appointment at the Pain Clinic and for the start of my Zometa treatment. In the meantime, I continued to try to adapt and deal with the constancy of side effects and the continuing pain. I was travelling to Europe every week on business and it was taking its toll. On one trip to London, I collapsed from exhaustion in my hotel room and slept for the better part of a day. Part of this was the stress of travel and part was from the constant level of morphine in my body which had the additional effect of creating a serious constipation problem. In spite of the various drugs I was taking to combat this, my feces would build up in my intestines until I gathered up enough nerve to try to force it out. It was like shitting razor-sharp rocks, such that a session on the toilet left me bathed in sweat and with tears in my eyes. As if having cancer wasn't enough! I was becoming increasingly fearful of what the rest of my life was going to be like.

On my follow up appointment at the Pain Clinic, the doctor increased my slow-release morphine to three times a day and put me on a ten-day course of steroids. Steroids are not the best thing to be on, with their own Pandora's Box of side effects, but the doctor felt that they would help the pain while we waited for the Zometa to have some effect and I was all for that. She also gave me some pills to help reduce the frequency with which I had to get up to pee at night. Lack of sleep or broken sleep can apparently interfere seriously with pain control.

On the advice of a good friend, I had done some investigation into medical marijuana (which was legal in Canada for pain control) but decided that being stoned all the time would defeat the purpose. I decided to just keep this option in my back pocket for some time in the future when things would get worse for me. For the time being, I would stick with the injections and the pills. In one more step down the road of the sick, I had to buy a huge pill sorter box to keep track of all the medication I was taking for pain and side effects as well as my supplements. I was becoming my father. At Dianne's suggestion, I also ordered a Medic Alert medallion and wallet card in case I got into an accident or had a serious issue with all the drugs I was taking.

On October 6, I showed up at the Chemotherapy Day Care Unit in PMH for my Zometa injection. This was where so many cancer patients went for the regular chemo treatments that made them so sick and bald and it was sad to see this close up. I rationalized this a bit with the knowledge that some of them might actually be cured by their treatments while I was just there for a "palliative" injection. Dianne came with me, as she always did, and held my hand. While I was my usual stoic self through it all, I knew it was hard for her because it seemed so invasive and it brought back memories of the hours she had spent with Ruth when she was going through chemo many years ago. I felt very bad for her as she had seen far too much of this over the years. She told me I needed to stop worrying about her (as if that was ever going to happen) and worry about myself. A couple of days later , in spite of Dianne's warning to stay home, I lay by myself in a crummy hotel room in London, England burning up with a Zometa-induced fever. It seemed that there was no escape from this new reality.

In November, I went back to see Dr. Maynard for a follow up and to get my next injection of Lupron. The good news was that my PSA was now completely undetectable, which was a wonderful piece of news. I asked her specifically how long the hormones would work and she told me that it was very unpredictable. They could work for a month or for ten years, however, the median was only two years. This actually shocked the hell out of me. My own mind had obviously misremembered an earlier discussion I had with her when she had told me the median life expectancy was four to five years after metastasis. I had somehow transposed this in my mind to believe that the median effectiveness of hormone therapy was four to five years. I suppose it was a form of denial or some other kind of perverse coping mechanism, but it shocked me because it directly threatened my very strong belief and hope that I had five good years to look forward to. I might actually have this amount of time, but this "new" fact threatened that significantly. I told Dianne about it and she said that she remembered it correctly. And here I thought I was the knowledgeable one!

Dr. Maynard then asked me if I was pain free. I told her, happily, that my pain was under control with the drugs I was taking compliments of the Pain Clinic and the special chair I had bought for my living room (it hurt too much to sit in the softer living room chairs). But then she said, "So you're not really pain *free*." I was taken aback and said, "I guess not." It actually took me a few minutes to fully understand the implications of what she was saying and I realized that, no, I wasn't pain free. She was very concerned with this and told me that her objective was to get me to that point. The first thing she mentioned was a clinical trial that was using HIFU (high intensity focused ultrasound) to treat cancer pain from bone metastases. I was aware of HIFU being used as a primary treatment for Prostate Cancer (to burn out the cancer in much the same way as radiation therapy) and that it was very expensive. She told me that, as it was a clinical trial, it was totally free and that if I was willing, she would speak to the lead researcher and see if the trial was open. Other than that, she would speak to other specialists to see if there were any other alternatives. She had previously advised me that the Tumour Board had all agreed that my case was "unusual" and "unfortunate" (which was not what I wanted to hear), but that she would take it back once more for their opinion. I gave her permission to explore the HIFU option but told her that I wouldn't commit until I had all of the facts.

In due course, I was accepted into the clinical trial (the Tumour Board supported this option) and went through the lengthy process of further scans and tests (including a bone scan, CT scan and MRI) to clearly visualize the tumour/lesion on my sacrum to help guide the treatment. The researcher, Dr. Graham, told me that I would need only about seven or eight minutes of HIFU "sonations" which didn't sound too bad, and scheduled me for December 9, the day before I was to fly to Dallas on business for two days. I decided to go ahead with it because the side effects of the drugs (more on this shortly) were really beginning to destroy my quality of life.

Caralia came with me for the treatment (bless her) and waited with me for several hours while they calibrated the machinery and treated another patient with more extensive mets. When I was finally called in, I had to climb into an MRI machine (a claustrophobic experience at best) and sit in a puddle of water for what I was told would be about two hours! They even asked me if I could hold my bladder that long or if I wanted a catheter. As it turned out, the actual treatment was really only about seven or eight minutes, but I was stuck in the MRI for a full two hours, lying in water with one hand jammed down by my side and the other back above my head connected to an IV drip. It was like a medieval torture, only more advanced. Much of the time was spent using the MRI to clearly image the spot they wanted to treat. When the actual treatment occurred, I was giving a panic button (in addition to the normal panic button you get when you are stuffed in an MRI machine) and told to press it if the sonations became too painful. It would immediately shut off the sonation but they strongly encouraged me to grin and bear it if I could.

The treatment involved several sonations, before which I was given a shot of pain medication through the IV. After each one, I was asked to rate the pain on a scale of one to ten. After the first one, I told them it was a fourteen! While I was able to hold off pressing the panic button, it was unimaginably painful. Each time, the pain would start to rise to a near-unbearable crescendo and then level off ever so slightly such that I could actually stand it for the thirty seconds or so it lasted (at least if felt that long). I rated each one a ten from then on which they almost seemed to take positively. If the extra pain medication worked at all, I had no conception of it because the pain was incredible. But I was told I did very well and, when I was finally released, I ran to the bathroom to empty my bladder.

While it was a horrible experience, I believe it was ultimately worth it. The drugs I was on were keeping the pain at bay, but they were otherwise making my life miserable. At this point, I was up to about thirty pills a day (over and above my three month injections); not so bad except for the fact that they were all for treating symptoms and side effects rather than attacking the cancer itself. The morphine was making me so tired and fatigued that I was on the verge of falling asleep in business meetings. My friend Richard, at work, had told me several times that I looked like shit and should go home. I had been taking an ever-increasing dose of steroids to counteract this, but they had stopped working and had resulted in my putting on about eight to ten pounds and had puffed my cheeks out like a chipmunk! I got off them immediately and was given Dexedrine to help with my fatigue. To cap it all off, shortly after the treatment, I began to suffer from severe stomach cramps and diarrhea, in stark contrast to the ongoing constipation I was experiencing from the morphine. While I suffered tremendously from the constipation and was disgusted with having to practically dig the shit out of my ass (I know that sounds very crude, but that was effectively what I had to do), this new experience was worse, with each episode leaving me drained and drenched in sweat. I had had enough and was determined to do something about it.

In consultation with the Pain Clinic, I began to gradually lower the dose of the long-acting morphine, treating any increase in pain with the fast-acting ones. Slowly, over several weeks, I managed to get to a third of where I was before with limited pain, but also with a substantial reduction in the side effects (I did experience some withdrawal symptoms but they were very mild, much like a minor case of the flu). I stopped taking the extra acetaminophen and significantly reduced the stool softeners, and I eventually stopped feeling the same degree of fatigue I had been experiencing, getting by on the Dexedrine and the occasional can of Red Bull. For a while, I started to feel almost normal and was getting some quality of life back. The HIFU seemed to have worked, to some degree, and I began to entertain the dream that I could get off the drugs completely. But even with that in mind, I still realized that there was likely more pain to come when the hormones stopped working and the cancer began to spread further. I wondered if I could access HIFU again when it became necessary. I can only hope that my participation in the clinical trial would help to justify making this treatment available as a mainstream tool for cancer pain. In the meantime, I wanted to enjoy my new-found quality of life. Dianne and I were both thrilled.

Unfortunately, the thrill was short-lived. Shortly before Christmas, almost five months into the hormone therapy, I began to experience noticeable flu-like symptoms, including aching joints, chills and an overall feeling of malaise. At the time, I assumed that I had picked up a flu bug which was not unusual given that it was the middle of winter in Canada. But by mid-January, the symptoms were still there and were seemingly getting worse. As I visited each of my doctors, I would ask them if there was anything they were giving me or doing to me that would cause me to feel this way. They all suggested that it was probably the flu, but I was beginning to wonder if it was something else, particularly when I started to develop numbness in my hands and feet.

As usual, I dived into the Internet to research the side effects of all the drugs I was on and the treatments and tests I was undergoing. I had noticed that many of the symptoms I was experiencing were listed as potential side effects of the Lupron injections I was getting and for Androgen Deprivation Therapy (ADT) in general. On February 2, I met with Dr. Maynard for a PSA check and what would be my third hormone shot. I explained my symptoms (which were definitely getting worse) and my suspicions that it might be from the Lupron. She said that it was possible and suggested that I could go off the hormones for awhile. Although it was not considered fully proven as a treatment for Advanced Prostate Cancer, many men were going on and off their hormones periodically to give their bodies a "break" from the side effects. This was called Intermittent ADT, and there was some anecdotal support for it. I told her that I wasn't prepared to simply go off the hormones at that point (a scary thought), so she suggested I have a one-month dose instead of the three-month shot and we would see how things were in a month. I thought that was a pretty good compromise and readily agreed, making an appointment for March 2. In the meantime, she was going to arrange for me to see a neurologist to check on the numbness which she couldn't explain. I left feeling a bit nervous about the whole thing.

By the middle of February I was beginning to regret having even the one-month shot. My symptoms continued to worsen day-by-day and had advanced to the point where my right hand was permanently numb and literally every bone in my body ached. By the end of the day, I could barely pull myself up out of my chair and walking up the stairs was a nightmare of pain and exhaustion. I was becoming my dad! When he was ninety! To add insult to injury, I wasn't getting enough sleep as I would wake often with sharp jabs of pain in various bones and the numbness which turned into severe pain. It was practically unbearable. Unfortunately, I still had to work during the day (although, fortunately, I loved my job and was doing very well at it) but I cut back on travelling and worked from home as much as I could. And it became more than just physical as I found myself unable to juggle many things at once, often feeling (for the first time in my life) overwhelmed. One weekend, I couldn't even get out of bed. This was just not me and it was not normal.

I finally found a single document on one of the Prostate Cancer web sites that posited the existence of something called "Androgen Deprivation Syndrome" which suggested that some men (usually younger men or older men in really good shape) could develop acute or chronic side effects beyond the norm. In reading this, I saw myself and once again realized that I was "unusual". If there were a small percentage of men who could have a serious, adverse reaction to the treatment, why should I be surprised if I was in that minority? I was back in familiar territory. I realize how cynical that might sound, but even my doctors were beginning to comment on it. But this was very, very serious. If it were to continue getting worse day after day, I was toast. I would not be able to work or do much of anything. I had already reached a point where I had virtually no quality of life and I was deeply afraid that I was going to be bedridden a lot sooner than I expected. It scared me badly enough that I decided to discontinue my hormone therapy in March.

This was a big decision which I did not take lightly, talking it over with Dianne as I always did because it affected her as well. I was becoming useless to her and to myself and I was convinced that it would continue to worsen as long as I remained on the hormones. There was just no way that I could go on like that, so I would stop and see what happened. We went to the March 2 appointment with the decision made.

Dr. Mills met with us this time instead of Dr. Maynard. As I described my symptoms and the decision I had made, he kept shaking his head and saying that he had never seen this before ... ever. He suggested that I take some time off to reduce stress, but I explained that I had just taken three weeks off over Christmas and it was still getting worse. In the end, he agreed that it was okay to stop the treatment for awhile and see what happened, although I definitely felt that he thought it was all just stress-related. Later, when I had a chance to ask around, I found that some other doctors had seen these severe symptoms before, although there was nothing written up on the subject. In fact, some women treated with Lupron for ovarian tumours developed the same severe bone pain after four or five months. I was incredibly relieved to hear this and accepted it as one more stamp of validation for my uniqueness.

Within a couple of weeks of the decision to stop the Lupron, it became clear that these horrific symptoms were not getting any worse, a blessing in itself, but it would be months before I would notice any real improvement. During this time, I made an appointment with my family doctor and asked him to listen to my symptoms forgetting the fact that I had cancer and had been on hormone treatment. He said that they sounded very much like fibromyalgia, a relatively common affliction that can cause severe pain in bone, joints and muscle as well as significant fatigue. He called it a "pain amplifier" and explained that it can hit people in varying degrees. With what I was experiencing, this was clearly an extreme case if that's what it was. Naturally, I researched the hell out of it and came to the conclusion that this was what I probably had. Fibromyalgia can be triggered by a variety of things, including cancer, stress or traumatic injury. It can vary in intensity over time so some days will be manageable and on others, you may not be able to get out of bed. Unfortunately, there is no cure for this. Once you have it, you have it for life.

For the next several months, I was in a wait and see mode, watching closely to see what happened with my PSA and worrying about how fast the cancer might spread as my testosterone level returned to normal, feeding the cancer cells that had been held in check by the Lupron. Over this time, I began to notice an improvement in my overall levels of pain and fatigue (although I continued to have some very bad days) and began to wonder if there might be a connection between fibromyalgia and my level of testosterone. After all, testosterone is like a fuel for the male system and effects many bodily processes. This also seemed to make some sense given that fibromyalgia is much more predominant in women (around 95%). Through my research, I uncovered some work being done by a female doctor and researcher at Dartmouth College who suffered from fibromyalgia and was experimenting with testosterone gels to treat the symptoms with some success. In particular, she had found improvement in males with low testosterone levels. I was thrilled that I had found a possible explanation for what I was experiencing. I understood that it was just a theory, but none of my doctors had been able to put forth any alternatives. What does this do for me, then? Well, it doesn't point to any cure, but it provides a crucial working theory for me to help assess my ongoing symptoms and to make decisions about my treatment. For example, I had carpal tunnel surgery on my right wrist, which did nothing to address the pain and numbness. I was also experiencing severe bone pain in my right foot. Any of these types of pain could be related to the fibromyalgia rather than progression of my cancer. And while I prefer that, I had no interest in going back to the horrible state I was in when I was on Lupron. It gives me some basis to avoid testosterone-reducing drugs when the cancer does begin to spread.

At the time of writing, I seem to be "settling in" to a level of pain and discomfort that is bearable, even though I am unable to do many of the things that I could do before. The continuing effects of the fibromyalgia (if that's what it is) and the side effects of the drugs I must take for the pain in my sacrum (I'm back up to 90 mg of morphine a day) combine to make me feel crappy most of the time and, occasionally, debilitated. To be honest, I hate feeling this way. I hate never feeling well. I hate that I can't do things that used to be second nature to me. But Dianne has been, as always, very supportive of me. She watches me like a hawk and makes me lie down when she sees me in pain and then chastises me for not complaining more. I love her for this but I hate that she has to deal with it. But what else can I do?

All I can really do is to monitor my symptoms and keep track of my PSA and testosterone levels, while being nervously on the lookout for some progression of my cancer. So far, my PSA remains undetectable and a recent bone scan showed no new cancer sites and I am tremendously thankful for that. It gives me some hope that I can stretch this out longer. But when it does start to spread again, I will make a decision on what to do with the best information I have at that time – just like I always have. I'm not sure that I will go back on Lupron or similar drugs, terrified as I am of the side effects, but I know that will leave me with only experimental chemotherapy drugs that have not proven very successful. It is a tremendously scary time for me, for Dianne and for all of my family and friends. I am not treating the cancer, not even trying to slow it down, and that just doesn't feel right. It's just not me. And it terrifies me.

We had reached a new threshold. From that point on, there would be many more visits to the hospital - more tests, more drugs, and more side effects. There would be more results delivered with more "buts" to deal with. I would reach new milestones that simply began another countdown. I realized that I would have to try hard to live as well as I could - to "Live Strong" in the Lance Armstrong tradition (as it was tattooed on my arm). I knew that I could never say things such as "it's only pain" anymore now that I knew what chronic pain was really like. And I knew that I could never count on treatments working for me in the same way as they did for others. I was learning to live with a degree of pain and with chronic fatigue, searching for physical exercises that might help without making things worse, learning to lie down and rest when my body was screaming at me to slow down. I was getting used to being woken up frequently throughout the night with hot flashes, jabs of pain, or the need to pee. And while I would have to eventually come clean with the people I worked with, in the meantime, I would continue my double life. I had a great cover story, telling everyone that I had a bad back and that I couldn't drink because of the pain medication. It wasn't that far off the mark, but it worked well. Everyone has a bad-back story that they love to talk about, effectively deflecting attention away from me.

I realize that I am in the endgame, and it is a game that I am not likely to win. Where the game points I have are simply the days and months and years that I have left. Whenever I see older people I feel a new sense of respect for them, although it saddens me as I realize that I will not likely see those years for myself. Some days, my own death seems so close I can almost taste it. It makes me very sad ... for me, but especially for Dianne who will have to face those years without me. She tells me that she feels a profound sense of jealously, anger and sadness when she sees older couples together because it reminds her that she may not have that with me. It tears me up inside whenever I see her cry over what is happening, and on those rare occasions when Caralia's strong facade breaks down and she shows her genuine emotions, it's even worse. I fear that I may not be around to be at her wedding or at the birth of her first child. I hate what this is doing to all of us.

But I do have hope. Hope for a decent quality of life. Hope for a miraculous cure. Hope for the best years I can have with my dear, dear Dianne. Hope for a good legacy for my children. There is even, way in the back of my mind, the hope that this has all been a terrible mistake. So please join me in these hopes. If you believe in prayer, then pray for a cure, pray for my family, and pray for my mortal soul. But most of all, pray for an end to this horrible disease so that others can live the lives they deserve.

THE LEGACY OF MY CANCER

When I was a little boy,
So many years gone by,
I wished for a summer day;
I wished that I could fly.
Now that the days are short and the nights are blue,
I yearn for that little boy and all the dreams he knew would all come true.

Life was so much simpler then
When I was very small.
No complications,
I thought I knew it all.
Now that the days are short I lie awake at night.
I long for those simple times when everything was always black or white.

> *And as the years go by, I think about that little boy,*
> *And when I close my eyes, I see the way things might have been.*

The colours were much brighter then,
The sky was never grey.
My worries were much lighter then,
I lived from day to day.
Now that the days are short I need to tell myself
To be like that little boy when everything was always black or white.

Doug Gosling 2004

Cancer can take your life and, for about half of us that are diagnosed (including me), it will. But it can also change your life in many ways. If

214

you're lucky enough to survive, even for a short while, you need to realize that you have been given a precious gift; you have been given a chance to make your life better for however many years you have. Perhaps more accurately, you have been given a choice. It took me a while to realize this, overwhelmed as I was by the shock of having cancer and depressed as I was over the unfairness of it all. But as time distanced me from my initial diagnosis and treatment, I finally figured out that I had a choice to make. I could think of myself as a poor miserable bastard because I got cancer against all odds, or I could consider myself damn lucky to have discovered it, dealt with it (as best I could), learned from it and, from there, begin to move forward.

Yes, I got Prostate Cancer. Yes, it hit me at too young an age and with no family history. Yes, it was unfair. And yes, it put me through significant physical trauma and an emotional hell. But I was lucky that my doctors found it when they did. I had taken control and dealt with it as quickly and aggressively as I could and, as a result, I stopped it from killing me too soon. I was lucky in that respect at least. It was going to get me in the end – I wasn't going to win this battle - but I bought myself some valuable time that I could do something with. As long as I was fighting to prolong my life, I had an opportunity to make the most of the time I had and to perhaps make a difference.

So here I am now. I've been through a cancer diagnosis, a recurrence, metastases, and now I'm fighting for my life – for however many months or years I can possibly wrench away from the cold hands of this horrible disease. I face each day with an emotionally complex mixture of fear, fatalism, resignation and hope. Physically, I am always in pain in spite of all the treatments and the powerful drugs that I will be taking for the rest of my life. There are days when I find it hard to get out of bed in the morning and there are evenings when I can barely get out of a chair or climb the stairs. I understand that this is something that I will have to live with, so I continue to work hard but with a firm purpose and focus (to paddle hard and true) that helps me to achieve, on occasion, a semblance of balance in my life.

Dianne and I are closer now than we have ever been before. We are so intertwined with what is happening to us and so completely focused on making the most of the time we have together, that there is simply nothing more important. Our hearts and minds are completely open to one another. We have made some tough decisions and some very good decisions and, most importantly, we know ourselves better than we ever did before. My daughter Caralia has grown into a fine young woman, who constantly amazes me. I am so incredibly proud of her and what she has accomplished in her life already and I like to believe that her tremendous work ethic has been partly my influence. My son Sean calls often from wherever his restless feet take him and I am thrilled that he is back in our lives. He is a wanderer, a gypsy, and I cannot fault him for that. But he has a huge heart and I want to take some credit for helping to shape that. I talk often now with my brother and my sister, which fills a gap I am sad we let happen, and their unconditional love gives me added strength. My mother, who is getting on in years, continues to be my biggest supporter. She often says, "You are so much like your father," which is the greatest compliment I could ever receive. Dianne and I have also established a remarkable relationship with my nephew Craig, his lovely wife Dayna and their son Levi, which has redefined the meaning of family for us and has given us some needed strength. I have had a spiritual reckoning that has brought me a measure of peace.

In facing up to the reality of a shortened life, I have discarded a great many things that I simply do not have time for anymore; things that were less important or that would just fill time that I don't have. I have made a firm and conscious choice to focus on only four areas. Many people have asked me if I have a "Bucket List". Well.... this is mine.

The first area of focus is (of course) my health. Living with cancer is far more involved than I would ever have dreamed. Every minute of every day, I am dealing with the physical and emotional symptoms of the cancer itself and the side effects of the treatments and drugs that I must take to keep myself going. It is relentless and demands my constant attention.

The second area of focus is, of course, Dianne and our life together. Our relationship is the most important thing in my life and our time together is what I cherish most. I couldn't bear to be doing this alone and I am crushed by what my destiny will do to her. But she is strong and she will survive, and I have great hope that she can be happy. My children, Caralia and Sean, are also part of this. We raise our children to be happy, self-reliant adults and hope to hell that we have many years to enjoy with them and their families. For me, for now, I just want to embrace their love and respect - the same that I feel for them. I want to be there for them as best and as long as I can.

My job is the third area of focus, mainly because I have to work to bring in money to pay the bills and to make sure that Dianne is well cared for when I am no longer around. Although Dianne has suggested that we trade down to a smaller house and move out of the city to reduce the financial burden, I'm just not ready for that. I am incredibly blessed because I have a job right now that I love doing, which makes it so much easier. I couldn't imagine having to work at a job I hated while dealing with everything else. My job also gives me a sense of worth that can only have a positive impact on my overall happiness and well being. I truly don't know how much longer I will be able to keep up the pace of my work, but I will do it for as long as I can. I still find myself sitting in a business meeting or in a hotel somewhere in Europe wondering just what the hell I'm doing there. But I know the answer to that and I will continue to lead this double life for as long as it is giving me more than it is taking from me.

And finally (fourthly), I truly want to leave a legacy that has some benefit to the world. I'm not entirely sure where this comes from, but it is probably the same force or sense of duty that led me into volunteer work in the past. My focus this time is, not surprisingly, health care and cancer in particular. Telling my story in this book and on my blog site (talkingaboutcancer.com) are part of this, educating people on the true nature of cancer – that it is an emotional disease as well as a physical one. But I have also found a way to contribute that leverages the combination of my cancer experience and my information technology background. In fact, I am becoming somewhat of a recognized expert on this subject, increasingly in demand to speak or to participate in health-related activities. As I write this, I am working on proposals and projects that I hope will significantly improve access (for everyone, not just cancer patients) to the tremendous world of information and resources that are available on or through the Internet. So many people, diagnosed with cancer, just don't know how to do this or what to do with the information, and I want them to have all of the advantages that I have had by virtue of my own knowledge and skills. I think I can make a difference in this area and I will dedicate valuable time to it. Dianne understands how important this is to me and I love her for it.

But while I am doing all of this, I still have to live and I must remain continually vigilant to ensure that my remaining days don't pass me by. From time to time, when I'm down or when I begin to have doubts, I like to go back through my diary and reflect on the lessons that I had learned from my counsellor Andrew. He had helped me through so many rough times with his insight into the human psyche, and his advice has always struck a chord with me. Many of the lessons he taught me seem very obvious and straightforward but had tremendous meaning for me at various times. I would like to share a few of these with you, dear reader, who has struggled through this roller coaster of a story with me. Perhaps they can help you at some time in your own life. I consider them part of my "Life List".

- There is a natural ebb and flow to life and you must learn to take the lows with the highs.

- If you can handle cancer, you can easily handle a job change or any other major change in your life.

- Remember that what was meaningful to you in the past should also be meaningful to you in the future, regardless of what you have been through.

- You can get energy from helping others. Just caring is a powerful source of positive emotions.

- When you are depressed, everything seems distorted, negative or skewed. You should withdraw from thinking too much about the future when you're feeling like this. Stop trying to make life decisions when you're just not capable of it. Look at the broader picture and at the future when you are feeling "up".

- Consider the things that bring you enjoyment or that engage you. Take some time to smell the flowers, because they are there as well as the dark clouds, the wars and things like SARS.
- Focus on Dianne's smile when you get home.
- Plan specifically for the little things that bring you joy.
- Allow life to penetrate you!

Another great lesson of Andrew's was how life is a mosaic of "tiles", some black and some white, that form the pattern of your life. The black ones are the bad things in life, like war, illness, and just generally bad days. The white tiles are the good things in life. What we need to do every once in a while is to lay out all of these tiles and we would see that there are many more white ones than black ones. He encouraged me to think about what my white tiles were so that I could mentally picture the mosaic that was my life. Here are a few of mine:

- Having a BBQ in my back yard.
- Playing my guitar.
- Paddling in my kayak.
- Lying in a tent at night in a warm sleeping bag, breathing in the cool night air.
- Snuggling with Dianne.
- Lying down with one of my dogs beside me.
- Sitting outside on a nice day, feeling the breeze and the sun on my skin.
- Lying in bed, feeling the breeze and watching the full moon through an open window.
- Spending quiet time with my daughter Caralia.
- Joking with my son Sean on the phone.
- Driving in the car with all of the windows open and the music blaring.
- Watching a great movie at the theatre.
- Closing a business deal.

- Laughing with friends.
- Relaxing and talking with young people.
- Taking my daughter to her first day of university.
- Writing a book.
- Talking to others about cancer.

Andrew and I talked about many things in our hours together as I wrestled with the emotional impact of my cancer – the cancer in my mind. In particular, he truly helped me to discover the meaning of my life. Interestingly, he said that artistic people were much better at understanding the meaning of life because they could appreciate the beauty and meaning of the smaller things. In my own quest for meaning, I turned to the creative and artistic side of my own psyche, which I now know is the true reflection of who I really am. And I wonder sometimes, without something like cancer to force you to look at yourself, how you can know who you really are.

I now believe that the meaning of life is defined by how you choose to live it, and cancer has given me the freedom to make that choice. We are here on this planet because we are part of the greater Universe and are meant to interact with all facets of it, from the physical beauty that surrounds us to the people who share the mystery with us. It truly is a mystery and we are here to explore it, enjoy it and learn from it without necessarily ever fully understanding what it is all about. If we live our lives in this way, starting every morning with an open heart and an open mind, then we give meaning to our existence. And, as we touch other people, we give meaning to their lives as well.

As I agonized over the meaning of life during the bad times, I wrestled with the finite nature of life. We are only here for such a relatively few years and when we die, whether from cancer, accident or from our bodies wearing down with old age, it had seemed to me that it was all over, and that our existence on this planet was an inconsequential thing. But that narrow-minded view, in addition to being very sad, neglects our place in the Universe and the impact that our lives have on everyone around us. In a very profound way, we never really die. Each time we touch someone, it changes them and they carry that change with them.

And as they touch others, they change them too. In this way a part of us blends into the ever-flowing river of humanity and carries on. We are eternal. And we have meaning.

This understanding is the greatest gift of all.

I asked God, "How much time do I have before I die?"
God replied, *"Enough to make a difference."* (Anon.)

AFTERWORD

IT'S NOT ALL ABOUT YOU!

I believe I have been very open about how inwardly focused I became as a result of my initial cancer diagnosis. While it is critical to concentrate your efforts on battling the disease and on learning to live with the physical and emotional onslaught that accompanies it, it is incredibly important to understand that you are not alone. You never fight a disease like cancer all by yourself. You wade into battle surrounded by doctors, nurses, family and friends who are just as committed to the cause as you are and, without whom, you would just die - alone.

I will be forever grateful to Dr. Gates who found the lump on my prostate. To Dr. Bones who diagnosed my cancer. To Dr. Tracks for his human warmth and his exceptional surgical skills. To Dr. Goodman for his compassion at a critical time. To Dr. Andrew Matthew for his incredible insight and wisdom, and for his ongoing guidance and friendship. To all of the other doctors, nurses and technicians at PMH, particularly Dr. Maynard, who continues to work at helping me through the rest of my journey. To all my friends who came to see me in the hospital, who dropped by to visit at home, who drove me to my appointments and treatments, or who just gave me words of support and encouragement. To special friends like Steve, Gayla, Greg, Nancy, Eleanor, John, Sue, Russ, Randy, Pete, Elli, Janice and Steve M. To Ruth, my cancer buddy. And to my Mom and Dad, who couldn't be with me physically but who reached out to touch me every day on the telephone. And especially to my daughter, Caralia, who carried herself with strength through such a very rough time and who continues to do so.

But most importantly, I am grateful to my beautiful wife Dianne, who gave me life when I first met her, who has kept me going through more than thirty years of marriage, and who continues to give my life meaning. She, more than anyone else, has shared every horrible and every good moment throughout this ordeal. She is as much a victim of cancer as I am. And I was unforgivably neglectful of her in the beginning.

Dianne is such a good caregiver that it is easy to get used to her being there, and while I tried not to be a burden, I basked in her care and her kindness and I selfishly (though unintentionally) took her for granted. This is bad enough in itself but I compounded it by becoming totally immersed in the "cancer experience". Cancer became my primary focus and, after my surgery, my physical and psychological recovery dominated my thoughts. I allowed no room for "us" and, while Dianne is absolutely the most important thing in my life, it sure wasn't obvious during this time. Regrettably, we became distant and any sense of intimacy took a back seat to my struggles. And while it is not an excuse, my sexual difficulties made it much worse because I was unable to be physically intimate in ways that I could before.

We have come to terms with this and, with some admittedly hard work, we have managed to get "us" back. It was not easy, but we are both stronger than we were before and have a much better perspective on what is really important. And now we find ourselves having to continue to battle this horrible thing that has taken so much from us and that promises to take so much more. But through it all, I will never doubt the love of my wife and soul mate and I will never take her for granted. Without her, I would be lost.

ABOUT THE AUTHOR

Doug Gosling lives in Toronto with his wife Dianne, where he continues to battle advanced, metastatic cancer. Despite the physical and emotional toll of his disease, he continues to work full-time as a software company executive. He also volunteers extensively within the health care community to further his dream of providing everyone with better access to the information, resources and support they need to live meaningful lives. Doug is a frequent speaker at health and cancer conferences where he provides a unique patient viewpoint to discussions on key issues in health care. He blogs regularly about the emotional impact of cancer at talkingaboutcancer.com.

Doug loves kayaking, camping, reading, writing music (the lyrics of some of his original songs appear at the beginning of several chapters), and his two Beardies, Maggie and Izzy. Above all, he loves life and is determined to make the most of it.